The Plots Against the President

The Plots Against the President

FDR, A NATION IN CRISIS, AND THE RISE
OF THE AMERICAN RIGHT

Sally Denton

Bloomsbury Press
New York • Berlin • London • Sydney

Published by Bloomsbury Press, New York

All papers used by Bloomsbury Press are natural, recyclable
products made from wood grown in well-managed forests.
The manufacturing processes conform to the environmental
regulations of the country of origin.

LIBRARY OF CONGRESS CATALOGING-IN-PUBLICATION DATA

Denton, Sally.
The plots against the president : FDR, a nation in crisis, and the rise
of the American right / Sally Denton. — 1st U.S. ed.
p. cm.
Includes bibliographical references and index.
ISBN 978-1-60819-089-8 (alk. paper)
1. United States—Politics and government—1933–1945. 2. Roosevelt, Franklin D. (Franklin Delano), 1882–1945. 3. Roosevelt,
Franklin D. (Franklin Delano), 1882–1945—Adversaries.
4. Conservatism—United States—History—20th century.
5. New Deal, 1933–1939. 6. Depressions—1929—United States.
I. Title.

E806.D465 2012
973.917092—dc23
2011023857

First U.S. Edition 2012

1 3 5 7 9 10 8 6 4 2

Typeset by Westchester Book Group
Printed in the U.S.A. by Quad/Graphics, Fairfield, Pennsylvania

For my mother and father

In easy times history is more or less of an ornamental art, but in times of danger . . . we need to know what kind of firm ground other men . . . have found to stand on.

JOHN DOS PASSOS, *THE THEME IS FREEDOM*

Contents

Part Two: To Kill the New Deal

A Beleaguered Capital

WHEN DAWN BROKE IN WASHINGTON, D.C., on Saturday, March 4, 1933, the atmosphere was celebratory, if anxious. Slate gray and ominous, the sky suggested a calm before the storm. Even before the sun rose, more than a hundred thousand people had gathered on the east side of the Capitol. General Douglas MacArthur was in command of the inaugural parade, and he habitually expected the worst. By that morning, American depositors had transferred more than $1.3 billion in gold to foreign accounts, millions of people had been turned away from their banks, and rioting was expected in cities throughout the nation, prompting some state governors to predict a violent revolution.

Army machine guns and sharpshooters were placed at strategic locations along the route. Not since the Civil War had Washington been so fortified. Journalist Arthur Krock likened the climate to "that which might be found in a beleaguered capital in wartime." Armed police guarded federal buildings, and rumors swirled that Roosevelt was going to appropriate dictatorial powers and impose martial law. But if he had ever really entertained such a notion—as unused drafts of an inaugural address indicated—he abandoned it. Despite efforts made by William Randolph Hearst, Walter Lippmann, Bernard Baruch, and others to convince him of the necessity for a benevolent despot to seize control of the country, Franklin Delano Roosevelt was unswayed.

Hearst, the nation's most powerful publisher, went so far as to produce a Hollywood movie—*Gabriel Over the White House*, starring Walter Huston—to instruct both Roosevelt and the American public how to succumb to dictatorship. Even though Italy's Benito Mussolini and Fascism were enormously popular and highly regarded in America at the time, Roosevelt distrusted autocracy, did not believe that one could count on a benevolent dictator to remain so, and, especially, maintained an absolute commitment to the U.S. Constitution. "We could have had a dictator . . . and we would have had one but for the President himself, to whom the whole idea was hateful," a U.S. Army general later said in a speech at the Waldorf-Astoria Hotel in New York. Instead, Roosevelt determined to incite the public to action rather than to capture extra-constitutional authority for himself. He wanted not to assume enhanced powers, not to take advantage of a quavering nation to elevate his own stature, but rather to ignite the citizenry to banish apathy and recapture a spirit of confidence and achievement. He sought not to issue comforting bromides—as his predecessor, Herbert Hoover, had done incessantly—but to raise a battle cry, a call to arms for Americans to overcome their fear and march bravely into the unknown. His overarching message: If they had lost faith in themselves, he would restore it.

But he was not content to stop there. Even as he hoped to inspire and invigorate, he also intended to hold accountable those who had failed the nation and sent it plunging into its abyss. "When millions lived close to starvation, and some even had to scavenge for food, bankers . . . and corporation executives . . . drew astronomical salaries and bonuses," as one account described the disparity between the poor and the wealthy. In a profound departure from Hoover, Roosevelt promised not only to bring relief to the victims but also to punish the perpetrators of the catastrophe. He would make clear that the departure of Herbert Hoover signified the end of the old order.

PART ONE

Interregnum of Despair

I have never in my life seen anything more magnificent than Roosevelt's calm.

RAYMOND MOLEY, "BANK CRISIS, BULLET CRISIS,"
SATURDAY EVENING POST, JULY 29, 1939

CHAPTER ONE

Lofty Aspirations

BORN JANUARY 30, 1882—"a splendid large baby boy" weighing ten pounds—Franklin Delano Roosevelt was descended from gentility, if not American aristocracy, on both the maternal and paternal sides. He was the sole issue of the marriage between James Roosevelt and his second wife, Sara Delano, both members of New York's oldest and richest families.

James Roosevelt had practiced law with a distinguished Manhattan firm before becoming a financier invested in coal, railroads, and canals, and ultimately a gentleman farmer at Hyde Park, his Hudson River Valley estate. Like the rest of the Oyster Bay branch of his family, which included first cousin Theodore Roosevelt, he lived a life of sailing and fishing, horse breeding and fox hunting, skating and sledding, and a dabbling in politics—first with the Whig and then the Democratic Party. His wife Sara was twenty-six years his junior, the daughter of a neighbor and friend, who had been raised in the same rarefied world of the "River families." They were married four years after the death of his first wife, and he "brought his young bride back past the ivied stone columns and the broad lawns down the long drive through the magnificent trees to his comfortable country house at Hyde Park," as historian and biographer Arthur M. Schlesinger Jr. described the couple's return from their monthlong European honeymoon.

For her part, Sara was the offspring of the fabulously moneyed Delanos—a French Huguenot clan that had immigrated to America on the *Mayflower*. Her father, Warren Delano II, had made a fortune in the Chinese tea and opium trades, and she had been raised on an estate in Hong Kong and in a fashionable apartment in Paris. She had attended finishing school in Germany, had vacationed in England and France, and slipped seamlessly into the leisurely lifestyle provided by her new husband.

From the moment her beloved son Franklin was born, Sara Roosevelt defined herself through him. She breast-fed for a year or more, and then continued to bathe Franklin until he was eight years old. Dressing him in *Little Lord Fauntleroy* costumes and English sailor suits and coiffing his long curls, Sara carried the child all day long—in contrast with the parenting style of most women of her social class. There were the requisite governesses and tutors who had served America's nobility, but Sara took a primary role in educating and shaping the perfect being in her charge. Of keen mind and lively spirit, the good-natured little boy won the hearts of all who interacted with him. "Popsy," as he called his father, who had been fifty-four when Franklin was born, taught him to ride, hunt, fish, and sail. His mother read to him constantly and oversaw the exacting and regimented routine by which he would become a disciplined and learned man. Indulged as the only child of wealthy parents, Franklin Roosevelt amassed a valuable stamp collection by the age of nine, owned a pony and a sailboat, had traveled to Europe eight times while under the age of twelve, and spent his summers at the family's comfortable vacation home on Campobello Island, off the Canadian coast in New Brunswick. He was passionate about birds, first collecting their eggs and nests and eventually shooting, stuffing, and mounting them. His most avid interest, which he carried into manhood, was the sea—an enthusiasm inspired by his seafaring grandfather Delano, his father's yachting experiences, and the adventure stories his mother read to him. As a boy, he began collecting a naval history library, ship models, and photographs and prints of vessels.

He attended Reverend Endicott Peabody's Groton School—a predictable route for the adolescent boys of his social strata who eagerly entered the "little Greek democracy of the elite." Having been homeschooled, and two years older than the other students who had already formed friendships with each other, Roosevelt felt "left out" and found the "character building" academy a rude awakening. Modeled after the British upper-class boarding schools for boys, Groton was Spartan, stern, and intellectually exacting—

and his time there was a harsh contrast to his previous years. While the experience was challenging, he made the best of it and learned the fine art of ingratiating himself with both faculty and peers. He excelled in the classics, joined the debating and missionary societies, learned fluent French and German, became a manager of the baseball team and a dormitory prefect, and was a popular actor in the school drama club.

He then went to Harvard—another expected path for young men of his class—even though he desperately preferred to attend the Naval Academy at Annapolis. Both parents refused to allow it, fearing that a naval career would inevitably separate them from their son, and that their longing for him would be unbearable. He entered Harvard in September 1900 and was bereaved beyond expectation when his father died four months later. He found solace and diversion in college activity, throwing himself into the milieu. He joined several campus clubs, including the Republicans; acquired a bit of renown for his work on the campus newspaper, the *Crimson*; and attended lectures by such notables as Frederick Jackson Turner and Josiah Royce. He managed to receive his degree in only three years.

Blessed and charmed, the young man seemingly effortlessly glided into adulthood—"after all he had many advantages that other boys did not have," his mother remarked with understatement. If childhood friends, boarding school peers, and college professors harbored misgivings about Roosevelt's lofty aspirations, Sara Delano Roosevelt never faltered in her vision of her son's destiny. Now the unrivaled center of his widowed mother's world, Roosevelt stunned her when, shortly after entering Columbia Law School, he became engaged to a distant cousin, Anna Eleanor Roosevelt. Born October 11, 1884, "Eleanor" was the daughter of Elliott Roosevelt—former president Theodore Roosevelt's younger brother—and his stunningly beautiful wife, Anna Hall. Eleanor was not the wife that Sara had in mind for her perfect son, and since she could not openly disapprove, she urged Franklin to keep the engagement secret for a year to determine the certainty of his choice. Plain and shy, Eleanor was a stark contrast to her handsome, gregarious fiancé. The daughter of an unstable alcoholic and a domineering and mean-spirited mother who nicknamed her "Granny" for her toothiness, dowdiness, and gawkiness, the solemn Eleanor seemed no match for the charismatic and convivial Roosevelt. Still, she was the niece of a former president, a young woman with a fine mind and a compassionate spirit, statuesque and cultured, and, in any case, Roosevelt was unmistakably smitten with her, calling her "an angel" and "my darling" in his diary. Even Eleanor, in her self-deprecating and humble way, could not dampen his ardor. "I am plain. I have little to bring you," she responded to Roosevelt's marriage proposal. But he was undeterred, spurred by love and, perhaps, as some historians have suggested, a long-standing resolve to merge the Hyde Park and Oyster Bay branches of the Roosevelt family.

Bored with law school, Roosevelt failed two courses before dropping out altogether and focusing on his betrothal. Reverend Endicott Peabody officiated at the March 17, 1905, wedding, where two hundred guests watched as Theodore Roosevelt—one of the most revered men in America and the country's twenty-sixth president—walked Eleanor down the aisle. The couple moved into an apartment on West Forty-fifth Street in New York City, where Roosevelt began his quick, if conventional, political rise. He somehow managed to pass the bar examination and joined the Wall Street firm of Carter, Ledyard & Milburn, which represented such commercial clients as Standard Oil of New Jersey and the American Tobacco Company. Hudson River families were overwhelmingly Republican, but Roosevelt, like his father, became a reform-minded Democrat. Though an incorrigible snob, James Roosevelt had instilled in his son a sense of social justice. "In all countries and all ages there have been more workers than work," James Roosevelt once railed at a gathering in his Hyde Park church. "Help the helpless! Help the poor, the widow, the orphan; help the sick, the fallen man or woman, for the sake of our common humanity. Help all who are suffering . . . Work for humanity." Franklin recognized and admired in his new wife—Eleanor Roosevelt Roosevelt—this same responsibility of noblesse oblige inherent to their class.

The couple had their first three children in rapid succession—Anna born in 1906, James in 1907, and Franklin Jr. in 1909. Franklin's first foray into politics came in 1909, when he joined the New York Milk Committee mandated to fight infant mortality. Franklin Jr. had succumbed to influenza at seven months old, joining in death more than a thousand other infants in Manhattan during that summer. As would become a pattern in their long and historic marriage, it was Eleanor who served as Roosevelt's eyes and ears in the community, who first brought to his attention the tales of squalor that surrounded them. She volunteered in the slums on the Lower East Side, teaching calisthenics and "fancy dancing" to young girls. It was through this, and her work with the National Consumers' League, that she learned of the appalling conditions of women and children living in poverty. Eleanor was "deeply moved by the sight of a society undergoing fundamental transformations at every level," wrote one of her biographers, and, like her socially conscious uncle Teddy, was committed to economic and political change.

Roosevelt became a director of the First National Bank of Poughkeepsie, where he met several like-minded men who helped smooth the way for him to run for state senator in 1910. He became the first Democrat from that district elected to the New York State Legislature since 1856. Joining the progressives, he threw his support toward women's suffrage and other social legislation, and he set out to block the infamously corrupt Tammany Hall political machine that had controlled New York municipal and state politics since the late eighteenth century. "From the ruins of the political machines we will reconstruct something more nearly conforming to a democratic government," he promised, disenchanted equally with both crooked Democrats and fat-cat Republicans. In fact, it was Eleanor who had encouraged him to challenge the fraternal Tammany Society, which she saw as a "lair of predators" dating back to its 1888 effort to remove Grover Cleveland from the White House. Roosevelt's fight against them brought him his first national acclaim.

Conspicuous in the state capital for his upper-crust background and unabashed strivings—and bearing the fortunate surname of his wife's uncle—he used the opportunity to polish his oratory skills and deepen his thinking. It was during this time in the state legislature that he began to explore the role he thought government should play in the lives of Americans. Inspired by Teddy, whom he considered the greatest man alive, and whose promise of a "square deal" for every American he thought divinely guided, Roosevelt shaped his beliefs about what it meant to be a steward of nature's resources. He had always had an affinity for land, water, and wildlife, and now saw the conservation of natural resources as analogous to that of human reserves. "The conservation battle," according to Schlesinger, "thus helped shape in Roosevelt's mind a broad conception of the public welfare as something that had to be vigilantly protected against private greed."

At twenty-eight years of age, Roosevelt launched his national political life.

CHAPTER TWO

Rebuild His Broken Body

Louis McHenry Howe, a scrappy and diminutive newspaper correspondent, was an inveterate political junky who had knocked around Albany, New York, since 1906. Called a "gnomish cynic plying around in a miasma of whiskey and cigar smoke on behalf of the *New York Herald*," Howe had legendary political instincts. He immediately recognized Roosevelt's national potential upon first observing him as a freshman state senator. An Indiana native who was raised outside Albany in Saratoga Springs, Howe played a notable role in shaping Roosevelt, eleven years his junior, as a presidential candidate. Secretive and sarcastic, the chain-smoking, unkempt, and thoroughly unappealing little man alienated many in Roosevelt's cultivated circle. Even though Howe was not welcomed into the fold by Eleanor and others, his value as a strategist was irrefutable. Howe ran Roosevelt's 1912 reelection campaign, while Roosevelt simultaneously organized independent Democrats for Woodrow Wilson for president—a move both men hoped would launch Roosevelt into a showcase role in a Wilson administration.

Events proceeded as planned, and when Wilson won, he rewarded Roosevelt with an appointment as assistant secretary of the Navy under Josephus Daniels—a post Roosevelt wanted more than "any other position in public life." Thirty-one years old, with less than three years of political experience under his belt, Roosevelt was now following in his fifth cousin's footsteps. Teddy had used the same position as a springboard to the presidency. But even beyond the obvious parallels, Roosevelt was ecstatic, given his long-standing love of the sea and belief that naval power was essential to American supremacy. Roosevelt resigned from his second term as state legislator and, with Eleanor and Howe, moved to Washington, where he would serve the Navy for seven years. While Eleanor directed the family's social world in the nation's capital, Howe, acting as Roosevelt's secretary, began building a political organization for his protégé.

Roosevelt took his position seriously, working diligently to oversee the administrative affairs of the Navy and especially enjoying inspection tours of the Caribbean. In 1915, following a massive political massacre in Haiti, Wilson sent the U.S. Marines to occupy the island. In the winter of 1917, with great fanfare, Roosevelt and an entourage traveled by destroyer to Port-au-Prince to examine the U.S. Atlantic Fleet, composed of seventy-two ships. There he met Smedley Darlington Butler, the quintessential officer in the Marines-have-landed tradition that had stirred Roosevelt's armchair adventurousness. Donning a marine uniform, Roosevelt accompanied Butler, the commander of the Haitian gendarmerie, along with fifty American soldiers and 150 Haitian militiamen, on a 200-man horseback expedition through the country. Butler ran the Haitian customs, oversaw the country's finances, and administered a road-building program that forcibly recruited six thousand Haitians to build twenty-one miles of road in five weeks. It "would not do to ask too many questions as to how we accomplished this work," Butler later wrote to Roosevelt. Exactly the kind of soldier-of-fortune military man that Roosevelt admired, Butler would intersect Roosevelt's life in deep and mysterious ways in the coming years. So impressed was Roosevelt with Butler in the Haiti theater that he nominated him for a Medal of Honor.

In July 1918, Roosevelt traveled by destroyer to the European war zone, where for two months he immersed himself in the realities of war—visiting Great Britain, France, and Italy—and strengthened his stature as a dignitary. He returned to Europe the following year to oversee the postwar naval demobilization. By then his visibility had grown to such an extent that the Democrats—impressed with his name and energetic campaign style—nominated him for vice president on the ticket with Ohio governor James M. Cox. Though the ticket was doomed, Roosevelt was an impressive candidate, crisscrossing the country to give more than a thousand speeches. Still, Warren G. Harding, who took 61 percent of the vote, trounced them. The 1920 Republican landslide was seen as a rejection of the progressivism of the Wilson years and a severe curtailment of the thirty-eight-year-old Roosevelt's ambitions.

Presciently, Roosevelt sensed that the Republicans would fail miserably at governing, perhaps even usher in a national economic collapse. He felt that the Democrats would remain out of office until that happened, and he determined to wait in the wings while building a political organization and strengthening his résumé. Returned to private life and the prosaic law practice where he had remained a silent partner, he threw himself into the New York speaking circuit and myriad civic doings. He spent much of his first year out of public life fighting off partisan attempts to tarnish him with wartime Navy Department scandals. Beleaguered by congressional inquiries, he leaped at the opportunity to board a yacht for Campobello in the hot summer of 1921 to join Eleanor and the children. Arriving several days later with the hopes of enjoying a prolonged vacation, he engaged in the characteristically vigorous activities that he enjoyed with his family, which now included five children: Anna, James, Elliott, a second Franklin Delano Jr., and John.

On August 10, he steered the children through an action-packed day of swimming, running, and even fighting a brush fire on the other side of the island. That evening, Roosevelt was taken ill with what seemed to be a cold accompanied by a feverish chill. Suddenly overcome with exhaustion and loss of appetite—"I'd never felt quite that way before," he later recalled—Roosevelt was alarmed when first his left and then his right leg went numb. Two weeks later, a specialist diagnosed acute anterior poliomyelitis—or infantile paralysis—and soon the muscles in his hips and legs were fully atrophied. He was paralyzed from the waist down and confined to bed, and his political career seemed at an end. Indeed it might have been if not for the fierce determination and ambition of the triumvirate—Roosevelt, Eleanor, and Howe. While his mother predictably advocated that he resign himself to a life of genteel invalidism at the family's Hyde Park estate, his wife and mentor were united in their passion to force his rehabilitation. Though they had never been close, Eleanor and Howe now forged an alliance, the sole purpose of which was to steer Roosevelt's course to the White House. Their patient was a man of such resolve and perseverance that failure was not an option. Roosevelt felt tested by God, as if his path and its obstacles were preordained. Resolved to meet and conquer the challenge, he set out to "rebuild his broken body," as historian David M. Kennedy put it, in order to resume his political journey.

Though bedridden, Roosevelt maintained a demanding schedule of correspondence, study, and discussion, as well as a tenacious commitment to his physical therapy. By 1922, with his legs fortified with iron braces, he could walk on crutches. Upon discovering the therapeutic benefits of swimming and water exercises—especially in hot mineral springs—his upper-body strength soon compensated for his withering legs. Meanwhile, the ever-vigilant Howe had been carefully cultivating Roosevelt's public image and had a tacit agreement with the press to never photograph Roosevelt as a cripple. Though the polio had left him dependent on a cane, crutches, or a wheelchair, by 1924 he had made a political comeback and was conspicuously advising New York governor Alfred E. Smith, whom he would nominate for president at the Democratic National Convention. Perspiring and struggling, Roosevelt made his way on crutches to the podium at Madison Square Garden in New York City, where twenty thousand delegates and observers rose to applaud his miraculous victory over the debilitating disease. "No matter whether Governor Smith wins or loses," the *Evening World* said, "Franklin D. Roosevelt stands out as the real hero." Indeed, Smith lost the nomination, but Roosevelt won the hearts of the Democrats, foreshadowing his future.

Lore has it that Roosevelt never intended to run for president in 1932—as he ultimately would—but rather to run for governor of New York that year and then president in 1936. Such a game plan, scrupulously devised by him and the shrewd and ever-present Howe, provided time for Roosevelt to fully convalesce while also acquiring governing experience. But preemptive circumstances intervened, and the stars lined up to illuminate his ascension.

It began in 1928, when his political ally, four-term New York governor Smith, decided to run again for president and persuaded Roosevelt to seek the governorship he was vacating. What began as a manipulative power play by Smith turned into a masterful coup by Roosevelt. Smith begged a reticent Roosevelt to run for governor, promising that he would essentially be a puppet for Smith forces and could therefore spend his time recuperating his health. Smith implored Roosevelt to run as a personal favor—implying that if he refused, he would incur the wrath not only of Smith's powerful New York machine but also of the newly elected

Smith presidential administration. "The circumstances of Smith's importuning," as Roosevelt biographer Conrad Black put it, ". . . quickened Roosevelt's ever-active intuition that destiny might, at last, be knocking." Roosevelt finally agreed to run. Addressing the issue of Roosevelt's paralysis head-on, Smith famously noted that the candidate was running for governor, not "acrobat." But Smith had greatly underestimated the grit and intelligence of his hand-chosen successor, who won the gubernatorial campaign while Smith suffered a humiliating defeat to Herbert Hoover. "As 1928 drew to an end, Smith must have had an uneasy feeling that he had created a political Frankenstein's monster," wrote Black. "In barely six weeks, Al Smith had been eclipsed by Franklin D. Roosevelt, who had wanted to remain a while longer in the shadows. But he was now the unofficial leader of the opposition . . . the president in waiting."

To add insult to injury, Governor Roosevelt resisted all attempts by Smith to pull the strings in his administration, and Smith began to nurture what the *Baltimore Sun*'s H. L. Mencken described as a "fierce hatred of Roosevelt, the cuckoo who had seized his nest." The man Smith had misjudged as a malleable invalid proved to have the stamina of a superhero. Roosevelt's official day began at eight A.M. and often continued late into the night, as he rigorously fulfilled the duties of his office. Despite a hostile Republican legislature, he was able to extend a liberal program that provided Depression-era relief, including unemployment insurance, public works projects, and an old-age pension plan. Now his political views began to take shape in earnest, and as he set his sights on a national political career, he began to formulate possible solutions to America's burgeoning problems, focusing especially on government's obligation to its citizenry.

With Roosevelt's winning the gubernatorial campaign and his landslide reelection two years later (the terms were not yet four years), the momentum was clearly on his side. The 1932 presidential race was suddenly within reach, prompting Roosevelt and Howe to accelerate their schedule.

CHAPTER THREE

A New Deal for the
American People

THE COUNTRY HAD BECOME A NO-MAN'S LAND of poverty and unemployment, and the actions of the Hoover administration's economic stimulus
agency, the Reconstruction Finance Corporation (RFC), were not working.
Intended to finance up to $1.5 billion in self-liquidating public works proj-
ects and to advance $300 million to the states for unemployment relief, the
RFC was woefully inept, if not corrupt, and had been dubbed "a breadline
for big business." The wealthy began to genuinely fear the wrath of the hungry masses, and the economic catastrophe was becoming a national security
threat. Chicago mayor Anton Cermak voiced what many public officials
felt, warning Congress that if the government didn't send food to his city,
it would soon need to send troops. "There were miles of highways across
the country where people were walking, going nowhere, just walking to get
away from what lay behind," said a journalist who covered the Depression for the popular weekly magazine *Liberty*. "Sometimes they had a few
possessions on carts, like war refugees, and they called the carts Hoover-
wagons. On the edge of every town was the collection of tarpaper and
orange-crate shacks called Hooverville[s] . . . There were farmers with shot-
guns resisting foreclosure . . . Men shuffled along a few inches at a time to
get a bowl of gray gruel and a cup of coffee."

President Hoover was increasingly aloof and ineffectual and seemed completely out of touch with the reality of the nation at large. His hollowness was epitomized by his bizarre request to renowned author Christopher Morley. "What this country needs is a great poem," he told Morley after summoning him to the White House. "Something to lift people out of fear and selfishness. Every once in a while someone catches words out of the air and gives a nation an inspiration . . . I'd like to see something simple enough for a child to spout in school on Fridays." Incredulous, Morley reported the exchange to the national press, which saw it as confirmation that Hoover was deluded about the depth and breadth of the crisis. In yet another banal effort, Hoover asked the singer Rudy Vallee to write an upbeat song. Vallee's effort— "Brother, Can You Spare a Dime"—had the opposite effect and would become the sad anthem of the Depression.

Called a "wild-eyed Utopian capitalist" by historian Richard Hofstadter, Hoover had championed a consolidated, free-enterprise, monopolistic economy unfettered by government restraint. He had fully supported the merging of banks, railroads, manufacturers, and retailers into massive unregulated combines, and saw the resulting concentration of wealth as an embodiment of the American dream. But most of America was not sharing in this dream, instead traumatized—emotionally and materially—by the economy's continuing downward spiral and the ineffectiveness of Hoover's recovery initiatives. It was all the more traumatic because the decade leading up to the Depression was one of rollicking abundance, optimism, and prosperity. "During the 1920s business and political leaders spoke of the New Era," wrote David A. Shannon, a historian of the Great Depression. "The map to the New Eldorado had been found, they said with smug satisfaction. An ever-expanding economy, full employment, and the elimination of poverty were permanent features . . . Everyone could be rich. One had only to save his money and invest it in stocks of the industrial corporations that were transforming American society." But despite Hoover's reassuring public statements, the devastating reality could be seen in nearly all walks of life.

The 1929 stock market crash soon gave way to collective pessimism, followed by panic that the entire economic system would collapse. Within a few months of the crash, unemployment skyrocketed. Banks failed in record numbers. Farm prices hit rock bottom, and layoffs stymied manufacturing. City coffers were depleted, stalling relief efforts. It was a vicious cycle in which measures that should have brought about recovery had the opposite effect, resulting in what one witness told a congressional committee was "overproduction and underconsumption at the same time and in the same country." The most discouraging and depressing element of the situation was its seeming endlessness. Previous downturns in America had always reversed course, and the economy returned to normal. But by 1932, the nation had suffered intensely for a long three years, and there was no end in sight. Americans had become "a demoralized people," as Walter Lippmann wrote at the time, resulting in individual isolation, hopelessness, and deep distrust of government. The term "altruistic suicide" was coined, referring to the thousands of proud men throughout the land who killed themselves out of guilt and shame at their inability to provide for their families and who were determined not to become a burden to their communities.

President Hoover dug in his heels, resisting the pervasive appeals for the federal government to provide relief to a famished nation and reassure the country's business leaders that the state of the nation was fine. Known as the "Great Humanitarian," Hoover—who had coordinated aid to nine million starving Belgian war victims in 1914—had an entrenched stubbornness regarding his own countrymen, which stands as one of history's remarkable ironies. Ideologically opposed to what was called the "dole," Hoover thought government assistance to individuals would become addictive and undermine their work ethic. As unemployment swelled to nearly 25 percent, that attitude seemed not only uninformed and indifferent but also morally untenable.

Talk of political and social revolution became the norm, and many civic leaders anticipated armed rebellion. "Surely, thought thousands of people, the dispossessed and the hungry will revolt against the government and the economic system that had brought them to their desperate situation," Shannon wrote. "But no revolution came. At least, there was no revolution such as many anticipated, with rioting, blood in the gutters, and violent overthrow of government. Instead, a majority of the electorate switched its allegiance from the party of Herbert Hoover to the party of Franklin Delano Roosevelt."

An "anyone but Hoover" attitude swept the country, and the Democrats, who had retreated after Hoover defeated his Democratic opponent in the 1928 landslide, were now reenergized.

AN "AMIABLE BOY scout" was how Lippmann, the most prominent journalist of the day, described Roosevelt. In words that would come back to haunt him for the rest of his life, the powerful syndicated columnist Lippmann dismissed the then-governor of New York as a lightweight dilettante. In Lippmann's view, Roosevelt was charming and affable, but not substantive enough to lead the nation. Roosevelt was "a highly impressionable person without a firm grasp of public affairs and without very strong convictions . . . a pleasant man who, without any important qualifications for the office, would very much like to be President," according to Lippmann.

Lippmann defended this assessment to his "dying day," contending that in 1932, Roosevelt was in fact a political chameleon and an opportunist, devoid of a track record and guided by vague patrician populist notions. Lippmann was not the only journalist to so vastly underestimate the sheer will and tenacity of Roosevelt, who, after roundly—and disingenuously—denying his interest in the presidency, had suddenly announced his candidacy. Newspaper magnate William Randolph Hearst lambasted Roosevelt as a dangerous Wilsonian internationalist. Oswald Garrison Villard, publisher of the *Nation*, said that Roosevelt would lose the nomination if it were decided "on the grounds of great intellectual capacity, or proved boldness in grasping issues and problems, or courage and originality in finding solutions." The Washington correspondent for the *New York Times*, Arthur Krock, aligned himself with the stop-Roosevelt camp, and journalist Elmer Davis described Roosevelt as "a man who thinks that the shortest distance between two points is not a straight line but a corkscrew." *Vanity Fair* editor Clare Boothe Brokaw (later Mrs. Henry Luce) vowed that if Roosevelt were nominated, she would found a women's political party. "That they all lived to eat their words made them no less sure of their judgment at the time," wrote Lippmann biographer Ronald Steel.

But it was no fluke that in the summer of 1932 Roosevelt was the front-running Democratic presidential candidate. His rise was so stark and unexpected, his maneuvering so stealthy and deft, his strategy so brilliant and cunning, that he appeared suddenly and fully formed on the national stage as if by magic. In fact it was not smoke and mirrors, but the carefully planned machinations of a deeply ambitious and determined man—and his crony, Louis Howe. How he had usurped his political mentor, Al Smith, and leapfrogged into the limelight impressed even the most skillful strategists. His famous name, charisma, affability, and spectacular recovery from polio combined to create a viable candidate. Still, while well known in New York and Washington, D.C., he had little name recognition throughout the rest of the country. When he flew to Chicago on July 2, 1932, to accept his nomination from the Democratic National Convention, he was a virtual unknown to the delegates from the Western states. He was the first presidential contender in American history to appear in person before a nominating convention, setting the precedent for all future conventions.

Riding in an open car through the city's streets, Roosevelt waved his hat at the throngs of well-wishers and enthusiastic Democrats lining the route to the Chicago Stadium. Once he arrived, Roosevelt, dressed in a blue suit with a red rose in his lapel, thrust himself toward the podium, guided by the steady arm of his son. The crowd erupted in cheers. His distinguished bearing and famous smile lit the hall, and the electrified crowd could not be calmed. "I regret that I am late, but I have no control over the winds of Heaven," he said, referring to his turbulent nine-hour flight in a trimotor Ford airplane from Albany. His allusion to his unprecedented appearance before the assembly as a bold break from tradition was met with thunderous applause. "Let it be from now on the task of our Party to break foolish traditions," he said. "I warn those nominal Democrats who squint at the future with their faces turned toward the past, and who feel no responsibility to the demands of the new time that they are out of step with their Party. Ours must be a party of liberal thought, of planned action, of enlightened international outlook, and of the greatest good to the greatest number of our citizens."

Then, in what would go down as one of the more dramatic and memorable speeches in history, Roosevelt uttered for the first time the two words that would become indelibly embedded in political lexicon.

> I pledge you, I pledge myself, to a new deal for the American people. Let us all here assembled constitute ourselves prophets of a new order of competence and courage. This is more than a political campaign; it is a call to arms. Give me your help, not to win votes alone, but to win in this crusade to restore America to its own people.

The "New Deal" would become his campaign slogan and soon come to symbolize the economic recovery and social reform that Roosevelt envisioned for America. Men and women clambered onto their chairs, and the audience shouted their approval and excitement. Tears streamed down the faces of delegates overcome with emotion. Maybe, just maybe, they seemed to feel, America was not doomed after all.

CHAPTER FOUR

The Tombstone Bonus

JOSEPH T. ANGELO, A SCRAWNY AND PROUD veteran who, as a World War I enlisted private, had saved the life of George S. Patton on a French battlefield, walked more than a hundred miles—from Camden, New Jersey, to Washington, D.C.—to testify before Congress. "I done it all by my feet—shoe leather," he told the House Committee on Ways and Means on February 4, 1931. Impoverished, hungry, and unemployed, Angelo made an impassioned plea for the government to release bonuses promised eight years earlier to veterans who had served in the war. Representing 1,800 men from New Jersey, Angelo wore his medals, including the Distinguished Service Cross he was awarded after dragging a bleeding Patton into a shell hole. "They are just like myself—men out of work," he testified. "I have got a little home back there that I built with my own two hands after I came home from France. Now, I expect to lose that little place. Why? My taxes are not paid. I have not worked for two years and a half. Last week I went to our town committee and they gave me $4 for rations."

Vivid symbol of the ravages of the Great Depression, Angelo embodied the "forgotten man," as he and thousands like him would soon be dubbed. Penniless and often shoeless, the unsung heroes dressed in their threadbare uniforms and went door to door throughout America begging for food. Three weeks after Angelo's stirring testimony, on February 26,

1931, President Hoover vetoed the immediate-payment bill that emerged from the House and Senate Committees, claiming that the number of veterans in need of relief had been exaggerated, and that, in any case, local communities should shoulder the burden. The soldiers' "bonus," which had been authorized by the Adjusted Compensation Act of 1924, was not due until 1945. Early payment would have resulted in approximately $500 per soldier—cash desperately needed as the country entered its second year of economic stagnation. Given the dire situation, soldiers began calling it the "tombstone bonus," since it seemed likely that many of them would be dead by the time the government honored its commitment.

If Hoover underestimated the plight and doggedness of the soldiers, his apparent indifference served to galvanize them. Mobilizing from coast to coast, they called themselves the Bonus Expeditionary Force. Thousands of them responded to the clarion calls going forth from the Veterans of Foreign Wars, the American Legion, and smaller, locally based veterans' groups. By the end of the year, after petitions and resolutions had fallen on deaf ears in Washington, nearly three thousand "hunger marchers," as newspapers called them, descended on the capital, hoping for an audience with the president.

"Diamonds were the symbol of the depression. They glittered everywhere," investigative reporters Drew Pearson and Robert S. Allen wrote about the lavish White House dinners hosted by the Hoovers. For one such formal affair, the First Lady selected arrangements of pink chrysanthemums and snapdragons, said to be her favorite flowers in her favorite color, and she was praised throughout the evening for her exquisite hospitality. The sixty-eight well-heeled guests who came to honor the Hoover cabinet were serenaded by a celebrated tenor from the New York Metropolitan Opera. Political figures hobnobbed with heiresses and celebrities. Author Edna Ferber "regaled several Cabinet members with the story of how she got her nose Gentilized," Pearson and Allen wrote.

As the White House guests dined, the army of hunger marchers was rolling into Washington in a procession of jalopies and work trucks, the unemployed men wearing crude armbands identifying them as veterans from America's numerous foreign wars and skirmishes. Composed of many avowed Communists—the *Washington Star* reported that they sang the anthem of the Bolsheviks—the ragtag group alarmed many officials and legislators, who had heard rumors of the vets' plot to take over the government. The capital's police chief arranged for his officers to keep an eye on them and for the chef of the Mayflower Hotel to oversee the preparation of hot breakfasts, lunches, and dinners to appease the raucous protesters. "Despite all the Red rhetoric," said a history of the movement, "many marchers had been attracted to the event because they were legitimately hungry." At least one undercover government agent infiltrated the group and determined that half were non-Communists who had joined the cause because they were starving. He reported that the group was 35 percent Jewish, 35 percent Negro, and 30 percent "miscellaneous white," and that about a quarter of the protesters were women.

Their generalissimo, a Lithuanian immigrant and fervent Communist named Herbert Benjamin, tried to carry a petition to the president. But when White House guards blocked his entrance at the gate, Benjamin retreated to his "troops." A few days later, he led them noisily out of the city, all the while hurling epithets and threats that he would return with "a force superior to the thugs of the ruling class."

THE "CRUELEST YEAR," a time when America hit "rock bottom," as historian William Manchester described 1932, began and ended with despair. The crisis that had begun three years earlier with the stock market crash had only deepened and now seemed to be not a temporary downturn but a permanent condition. The indicators were staggering: Unemployment had tripled in three years and was at sixteen million and rising; farm foreclosures exceeded half a million; more than five thousand banks had failed and eighty-six thousand businesses had closed; industrial production had been cut by more than half; with the lack of purchasing power by the unemployed, consumption was at a trickle, compared with the prosperity of the previous decade; stocks were worth 11 percent of their 1929 value. Financial capitalists had bilked millions of customers and had been "permitted to rig the market and trick the public," said a *New Yorker* editor. As the *Nation* magazine put it: "If you steal $25, you're a thief. If you steal $250,000, you're an embezzler. If you steal $2,500,000 you're a financier."

The human toll was stark as panic swept the nation. Millions wandered the country in search of work. Suicide rates tripled. Soup kitchens could not accommodate the masses, and men often stood all night long in unemployment lines in order to be among the first applicants in the morning. Panhandlers crowded city street corners, and children suffering from

malnutrition sold pathetic scraps of food and clothes. People combed garbage dumps for usable items, often fighting over caches of kindling or
other materials of value. Boxcar hoboes and disheveled migrant children
haunted the newsreels. State and local governments were unable to pay
their teachers. The average weekly wage of those fortunate enough to
have a job was $16.21. One percent of the population possessed 59 percent
of the nation's wealth. A thousand homes per day were being foreclosed in
the nation's urban locales, where an estimated thirty-four million men,
women, and children were without any income—a figure that did not
even include the eleven million farm families who "were suffering in a
rural gethsemane of their own," wrote William Manchester. For the first
time in the country's history, Americans emigrating to foreign countries
exceeded foreigners immigrating to America, as skilled workers sought
jobs in the Soviet Union and elsewhere. Unable to sell their crops, farmers
burned their fields and killed their livestock to survive. "Babies go hungry
while farmers in Iowa dump their milk trying to get the price up to where
they can keep producing milk so babies won't go hungry," one report said,
capturing the inherent irony of the calamity. Hundreds of thousands of
families had been evicted from their homes.

At the heart of the disaster was a deep-seated uncertainty about the role
the federal government had played—and should play—in American life.
There were no safety nets in place: no unemployment insurance, minimum wage, social security, Medicare, or federal bank deposit insurance to
protect the life savings of millions of people.

"America was at a standstill," historian Blanche Wiesen Cook wrote.
"People spoke about gloom, despair, suicide, revolution." The Depression
reignited fears of Communism among many elements of American society and government, as unemployment and unrest swept the nation. Such
fear was not unfounded; economic despair of the magnitude found in the
United States was a natural breeding ground for class warfare. The "viability of the country's institutions and the stability of international relations" were at stake, according to one historian. Not surprisingly, the Red
Scare found its way into national politics, and, whether real or exaggerated, the fear was elevated to historic proportions.

The depth of the Depression stirred the most extreme impulses, even
paranoia, of those American conservatives who had long seen central government as a malign force. They promulgated conspiracy theories about the
international gold standard, the creation of the Federal Reserve, the gradu-

ated income tax, and the machinations of the world's financiers to control the global economy. As anxiety metastasized into widespread frustration and fury, a fearful populace sought villains to blame. The very nature of American political protest changed. Movements sprang up to appropriate the revolution that seemed imminent, if not already under way. Orators and flag-waving hate mongers used inflammatory rhetoric to shake the disaffected from their malaise, inciting first fear and then rage, and focusing on the Communist, Socialist, or Fascist threats *within* the country rather than abroad.

States trained militias to handle mass demonstrations staged by the unemployed. Even though there were no armed insurrections, scores died in riots throughout the country, and thousands more were wounded and arrested at the hands of aggressive police forces.

Throughout 1932, from New York to California, Oregon to Florida, Nebraska to Alabama, people wondered who would become the next president of the United States. A universal feeling persisted that the promised land of America was doomed, that its glory days were in the past, that the government was in the hands of wealthy men who had abandoned the citizenry, and that the crisis had moved beyond redemption.

It was a "precarious moment," historian David M. Kennedy said, "pregnant with danger and opportunity." Franklin Delano Roosevelt was poised to seize that opportunity.

CHAPTER FIVE

The Forgotten Man

By THE TIME ROOSEVELT WAS NOMINATED as the Democratic presidential candidate in the summer of 1932, there was a worldwide depression and U.S. and foreign currency were unstable. In America, the richest nation in the world, more than sixteen million men were looking for work.

Recruiting academics to join what would be known as his "brain trust," Roosevelt became a devotee of the Republican Wall Street lawyer Adolph Berle, who was an authority on corporations and had penned a progressive approach to the American economic system. Berle's bestselling book, *The Modern Corporation and Private Property*, helped set the stage "for the most fundamental realignment of power since abolition," according to a twenty-first century economist, and became Roosevelt's economic bible. Though Berle was committed to the corporate system, he warned of concentrating the market in a few hundred firms and examined how senior managers of Wall Street firms had seized control from the shareholders. According to Berle, the Depression was evidence that giant, unregulated corporate monopolies inevitably failed both the stockholders and the public. Berle and Raymond Moley, a Cleveland-born Columbia University political science professor, brainstormed with Roosevelt to devise a solution.

Roosevelt called for a new "economic constitutional order" in which government would intervene to break up the concentration of corporate wealth and power. Recalling the phrase "the forgotten man" from an essay written by a Yale philosopher in the 1880s, Moley inserted the expression into one of the candidate's most famous campaign speeches: If elected, Roosevelt would rely on methods "that build from the bottom up and not the top down, that put their faith once more in the forgotten man at the bottom of the economic pyramid."

Republicans and old-guard Democrats alike saw this concept—that government in a civilized society had an obligation to abolish poverty, reduce unemployment, and redistribute wealth—as dangerously radical. Roosevelt was now marked as a bald-faced progressive, and his advocacy of government-financed unemployment insurance and an old-age pension alarmed many members of his patrician class.

Meanwhile, Hoover's stuffy nature and inflexible devotion to laissez-faire economics gave way to a sudden passion for winning reelection. Stunned by what he gradually realized was a "hatred" of him in the country, the president "put on his high-button shoes and celluloid collar and went to the people" to incite fear of Roosevelt, as William Manchester described it. But what Hoover found on the campaign trail was a disdain and discontent so deep that he "was lucky to come back alive." He was hissed in Indianapolis, jeered in Cleveland, and booed in Detroit, where nearly a quarter-million people were unemployed. Hoover's jibes at Roosevelt's infirmity and implications that his rival was physically unfit for the office only solidified support for Roosevelt. That Hoover had kept Roosevelt standing for half an hour at a White House reception for the nation's governors underscored the president's insensitivity. "We've got to crack him every time he opens his mouth," said Hoover, who directed his aides to ramp up a smear campaign against his opponent with attacks focused on Roosevelt's infirmity, physical weakness, and crazy ideas. Gambling odds were running seven to one against Hoover, who "deliberately chose the low road," according to William Manchester, and confided to a cabinet member that the only way to win was to incite "a fear of what Roosevelt will do."

The Hoover administration was facing certain defeat at the hands of an invigorated Democratic Party and an agitated public. Then, in late July 1932, its calamitous handling of the forty-five thousand Bonus Army soldiers who marched on Washington was the final blow. A month earlier, on June 15, 1932, the U.S. House of Representatives had passed yet another bill authorizing immediate payment of the veterans' bonuses, a

$2.4 billion appropriation that had been ushered out of committee and to a floor vote by Speaker of the House John Garner. The vote of 211 to 176, with 40 abstaining, had come after a heated debate in which Democrats had overwhelmingly supported the bill and Hoover loyalists had opposed it. One Democratic congressman, Edward Eslick of Tennessee, had been so passionate in his support of the legislation that he had dropped dead of a heart attack in the midst of his speech: "Uncle Sam, the richest government in the world, gave sixty dollars and an IOU 'that I will pay you twenty-seven years after the armistice.'" While the House bill had been a victory for the Bonus Marchers, it faced stiff opposition in the Senate, prompting Walter W. Waters, an unemployed ex-sergeant from Portland, Oregon, to beseech every American veteran to hop a freight train for Washington and maintain a vigil on the U.S. Senate, which was scheduled to vote on the bill two days later on June 17. The Doughboys—as the World War I veterans were called—organized in companies and platoons and traveled by boxcar and flatcar, rattletrap and truck. Some walked or hitchhiked. "Every other interest has got lobbyists in Washington," author John Dos Passos quoted a veteran as saying in an article for the *New Republic*. "It's up to us to go to Washington and be our own lobbyists. Park benches can't be any harder in Washington than they are back home."

When a group of three hundred from Portland reached Council Bluffs, Iowa, they joined thousands more veterans who had gathered from burgs and cities throughout the land. As they made their way East, sympathizers provided them with money, food, and camaraderie. A dramatic new form of protest, the movement attracted the attention of the national media, which gave the march widespread radio and newspaper coverage. Unlike the American Expeditionary Force of World War I—a segregated army that excluded nearly half a million black soldiers from its military units—the Bonus Expeditionary Force, as they called themselves, was fully integrated. In the BEF, black and white men—along with their wives and children— marched and camped together, prompting at least one journalist to depict it as a model for an integrated society. Many wore empty bean cans strapped to their belts as improvised canteens for water and carried faded Stars and Stripes. They "made for America a picture of honest men in poverty," Waters wrote in 1933. "For Mr. Hoover had said there were no hungry men in America. Either he was wrong or these men imagined their hunger."

The "troops" marched up Pennsylvania Avenue—watched in silence by

nearly a hundred thousand Washingtonians who had lined the streets—
and set up camp on Anacostia Flats, an abandoned army base in the southeast corner of the city. They slept in lean-tos constructed out of cardboard
boxes and shipping crates—"every kind of cockeyed makeshift shelter
from the rain, scraped together out of the city dump." Led by a Medal of
Honor winner and several others who wore their Silver Stars, Croix de
Guerre, and Distinguished Service Crosses, they organized in divisions
and conducted military drills, sang war songs and listened to speeches by
their leaders and others hoping to persuade or dissuade them in their pursuit. At least two Catholic priests sought to influence them. Father James R.
Cox flew to Washington from Pittsburgh to implore the crowd to "stick it
out!" He told them, "You will never get what you're entitled to unless you
stick." Father Charles E. Coughlin—the highly controversial and nationally
famous "radio priest" whose program reached millions of listeners—sent
cash to help stave off starvation. "Cunning Communists are dicing for the
leadership of these World War Veterans," Coughlin wrote in a telegram,
"and tonight, both to cheer the hearts of the bonus army and to show that
Communism is not the way out, I am donating $5,000." Additional contri-
butions began to pour in from wealthy individuals, local merchants, and
various organizations sympathetic to the plight of the hungry Bonus
Marchers. Supporters throughout the country sent truckloads of food; one
baker sent a hundred loaves of bread a day; another sent a thousand pies.

Local Marines set up a clinic staffed by volunteer physicians and
dentists, which was immediately inundated by men, women, and children
suffering from bronchitis, rheumatism, blisters, pleurisy, the common
cold, toothaches, and "body vermin—American cousins of the 'cooties'
of French trenches." They bathed in the muddy Anacostia River and slept
in the open air. Mosquitoes and flies swarmed in the camp, spawned by
Washington's swampy, subtropical summer heat. Described by one newspaper as a "rag-and-tin-can city," Hooverville, D.C., was within sight of
the U.S. Capitol and was the largest shantytown in the country, its population swelling daily with new recruits.

On June 17, the day the Senate was scheduled to vote on the bonus, there
was a move to table the bill. Heated debate continued late into the evening,
when a vote of 44 to 26 tabled the bill until the Seventy-third Congress
convened in 1933. That night, the Hoover administration had genuinely
feared that the veterans might turn violent. Instead, the marchers sang
"America the Beautiful" and retreated quietly to their camps. While the

majority of the Bonus Marchers left the city and returned to their homes, more than eight thousand remained at what was becoming a permanent camp.

On July 19, retired Major General Smedley Darlington Butler, who had been Franklin Roosevelt's guide through Haiti fifteen years earlier, rode into the site to offer solidarity to the veterans, many of whom he had commanded in previous skirmishes in China and Latin America. Having won two Medals of Honor and been called the "ideal American soldier" by Teddy Roosevelt, the lean and controversial Butler was an outspoken critic of the military brass and a staunch advocate of the enlisted man. Butler had recently been threatened with court-martial for making accusatory remarks against the Italian Fascist leader Benito Mussolini. The charges were dropped when Butler retired as a Marine, but his tenacious support of the veterans continued. A heroic whistle-blower, Butler had run unsuccessfully for the U.S. Senate in Pennsylvania on a platform of exposing the grotesque war casualties being hidden in Veterans Administration hospitals. He had been slotted to become commandant of the Marine Corps for his long career dating back to the Boxer Rebellion, but President Hoover had passed him over after the offense to Mussolini.

Still, he was a soldier's soldier, and the veterans idolized him. A roar went up when he leaped onto a crude stage to address them. "I'm here because I've been a soldier for thirty-five years and I can't resist the temptation to be among soldiers," he announced to boisterous approval. "Hang together and stick it out till the gate bars of hell freeze over . . . Remember, by God, you . . . didn't win the war for a select class of a few financiers and high binders." When he finished his speech, throngs surrounded him. He seated himself on the ground and listened to the men's tales of woe until two thirty A.M. He repeatedly warned them not to "slip over into lawlessness," for if they did so, they would "lose the sympathy of 120 million people in this nation." The War Department had spies among the crowd, who reported to higher-ups that while Butler's speech had been demagogic and inflaming, at least he had "carefully advised the men to obey all the laws."

The veterans' leaders appealed to Hoover to receive a delegation from the camp. But the president declined, claiming he was too busy; he then proceeded to clear his schedule and isolate himself in the White House. In that "desperate summer of 1932," as Manchester described it, "Washington, D.C., resembled the besieged capital of an obscure European state . . .

[The] penniless World War veterans had been encamped with their wives and children in District parks, dumps, abandoned warehouses, and empty stores." Police erected barricades, chained the gates of the Executive Mansion, and patrolled its perimeter day and night. HOOVER LOCKS SELF IN WHITE HOUSE blared a newspaper headline. A veteran who had lost an arm in battle attempted to cross the line of guards at the White House, only to be brutally beaten and arrested. The incident portended the violence that was to come.

Though unarmed and generally passive during its two-month occupation of the city, the Bonus Army incurred the wrath of not only Hoover but also his most ill-tempered and militant Army adviser, General Douglas MacArthur. The only four-star general in the country, MacArthur had already established a reputation for hubris, dissembling, and grandiosity. Referring derogatorily to the veterans as "Boners," he took personal umbrage at their audacious defiance of authority. For two months he had been secretly training soldiers in riot control, and he had requisitioned three thousand gas grenades from the Aberdeen Proving Ground in nearby Maryland. Convinced that the army was mutinous, and repulsed by their ragtag appearance, MacArthur stirred Hoover to act precipitously and severely.

As it turned out, MacArthur, whom Franklin Roosevelt believed to be one of the "most dangerous men in America," delivered the death blow to Hoover's reelection campaign. MacArthur's determination to rout the tattered army and blustering brutality against America's forgotten heroes backfired with devastating consequences for Herbert Hoover and the Republican Party.

CHAPTER SIX

Warriors of the Depression

THE U.S. ARMY'S MILITARY INTELLIGENCE DIVISION repeatedly warned President Hoover that the Communist Party was controlling the Bonus Army and had its sights set on overthrowing the U.S. government. At the same time, a callow and ambitious law enforcement officer named J. Edgar Hoover saw in the veterans' movement a "public enemy" that would justify the expansion of his domestic spying apparatus. Director of the Bureau of Investigation, the thirty-seven-year-old Hoover was ever on the lookout for new menaces. Obsessed with the fear that Negro and Jewish Communists were plotting to take over America—a fixation that would ultimately lead to his founding of the FBI and its scandalous legacy— J. Edgar Hoover eagerly plied President Hoover with reports of treacherous homegrown terrorists. He portrayed the World War I veterans to the president as dangerous leftists and falsely warned that the group was made up of 473,000 "trained men" who had 116 airplanes and 123 machine guns at the ready.

Whether Herbert Hoover was convinced of the existence of a Communist conspiracy and believed General MacArthur's assertions that "incipient revolution was in the air," or was merely seeking an expedient solution, is unclear. Either way, MacArthur apparently persuaded Hoover that an armed insurrection was brewing at the Hooverville in Anacostia. In response, the president ordered the veterans' expulsion at the hands of three Army officers: MacArthur, George S. Patton, and Dwight D. Eisenhower— all destined to become famous American generals.

Dressed in full uniform—including the flamboyant regalia of his rank—MacArthur led the attack. Eisenhower, widely reported to have been a reluctant participant, strongly opposed donning military uniforms for a domestic clash. "This is political, political," he repeatedly argued, only to be rebuffed by MacArthur. "MacArthur has decided to go into active command in the field," the general barked, referring to himself in the third person, as he was wont to do. He ordered Eisenhower to dress for battle. Patton, who was more simpatico with MacArthur than with the measured and thoughtful Eisenhower, zealously took command of the troopers of the Third Cavalry.

At four thirty P.M. on July 28, 1932, MacArthur ordered the streets of the capital cleared. Brandishing drawn sabers, two hundred mounted cavalry pranced behind Patton from the Ellipse down Pennsylvania Avenue toward the Eleventh Street drawbridge and Anacostia. Next came a machine gun detachment and helmeted soldiers from the Twelfth Infantry, Thirteenth Engineers, and Thirty-fourth Infantry carrying fixed bayonets and loaded rifles and wearing gas masks. Five tanks followed the three hundred infantrymen. In what would go down in history as the worst-timed operation in MacArthur's long military career, he began the assault at the same moment that more than twenty thousand federal employees in the District of Columbia finished work and poured into the streets, mingling with the Bonus Army. "We thought it was a parade because of all the horses," a witness, who had been a small boy at the time, later recalled. The veterans initially thought it was a display that the U.S. Army was putting on in support of their cause, prompting them to let out a rousing cheer. But when the cavalry suddenly turned and charged the crowd of thousands, trampling the unarmed bystanders, beating them with the flat side of the sabers, prodding them with bayonets, and whooping as if in battle, mayhem ensued.

As the pedestrians and onlookers fled the scene, the Army lobbed hundreds of tear gas grenades at the crowd, sparking numerous fires. While the Arkansas native had a reputation as a ruthless military commander in foreign theaters, MacArthur's role in the assault against his fellow Americans is singular in the nation's history and marks the first time that tanks rolled through the capital, mowing down civilians. Women and children were coughing and crying while many of the veterans challenged the soldiers to dismount and fight fair and square. "Men and women were ridden down indiscriminately," reported the *Baltimore Sun*. "Nothing like this cavalry charge has ever been witnessed in Washington. The mad dash of these armed horsemen against twenty to thirty thousand people who were guilty of nothing more atrocious than standing on private property observing the scene." A U.S. senator from Connecticut watched as a tear gas grenade landed at his feet and fires from the explosions erupted all around him. "It was like a scene out of the 1918 no-man's land," reported the Associated Press.

By nine P.M., the troops were crossing the bridge to Anacostia, despite presidential orders forbidding entry to the veterans' camp. MacArthur ordered his troops to pause for nearly an hour at the north side of the drawbridge to assess the situation. He knew that there were approximately seven thousand people in the camp, and that at least six hundred were women and children. While waiting, he received duplicate orders from the president that the troops should not cross the bridge or force the evacuation of the camp. Characteristically, MacArthur "was very much annoyed in having his plans interfered with in any way," according to the messenger who carried the directive from the secretary of war to MacArthur. A belligerent MacArthur told Eisenhower that he "did not want either himself or his staff bothered by people coming down and pretending to bring orders."

"It would not be the last time that MacArthur would disregard a presidential directive," historians Paul Dickson and Thomas B. Allen noted in their account of the event in *Smithsonian* magazine, referring to the general's later defiance of future president Harry S. Truman. "I told that dumb son-of-a-bitch he had no business going down there," Eisenhower said of his exchange with MacArthur.

At ten P.M. the camp commander carried a white flag of truce to the Army and requested an hour's respite for the veterans and their families to evacuate. MacArthur agreed, and widespread panic ensued as parents awakened their sleeping children with shouts: "Come on! The soldiers are going to kill us!" Tanks blocked the roads and machine guns were mounted on the drawbridge, preventing the families' exodus by vehicle. Mothers and fathers carried babies and tattered suitcases, running in the opposite direction of the bridge. A gigantic searchlight scanned the camp, eerily illuminating the disorder. As MacArthur's forces entered just before eleven

P.M., hurling grenades into the shacks and tents and setting fire to anything in their path, the crowds booed, tears streaming down their faces. The tanks trampled the vegetable gardens the veterans had planted for food. Some threw rocks at the advancing U.S. Army in a pathetic gesture of defense. Within minutes the entire camp was burning, "a blaze so big that it lighted the whole sky . . . a nightmare come to life," wrote a reporter who had witnessed the flames that leaped fifty feet into the air. Watching the glow from a White House window, President Hoover demanded his aides determine what had gone wrong.

The cacophony resembled a war zone, with the blaring of ambulance and fire engine sirens and the thundering of galloping hoofs and rolling tanks. The wounded began pouring into Gallinger Municipal Hospital, located two miles away in southeast Washington, suffering from bleeding wounds and respiratory distress. There were more than a hundred casualties, including at least two infants who had been killed. The tales of brutality horrified Americans, who were outraged when photographs showed four troops of cavalry and a column of infantry with drawn sabers bearing down on the defenseless mass. When a seven-year-old boy attempted to rescue his pet rabbit from the family's tent, an infantryman rammed a bayonet through his leg. Universal Newspaper Newsreel called it "the most critical situation in the Federal District since the Civil War" and "the most cataclysmic domestic event of the decade."

At eleven fifteen P.M., Major Patton led his cavalry in the final destruction, routing out all who were left in the camp. Among them was Joseph Angelo—the man who had won a Distinguished Service Cross for saving Patton's life in the Argonnne Forest during World War I.

When it was over, the grandstanding MacArthur called a press conference shortly after midnight—despite Eisenhower's advice to evade reporters and leave details of the political operation to the politicians—and set out to rationalize the show of force, which included the use of two thousand tear gas grenades. "It is my opinion that had the President not acted today, had he permitted this thing to go on for twenty-four hours more, he would have been faced with a grave situation which would have caused a real battle . . . Had he let it go on another week, I believe the institutions of our Government would have been severely threatened." Although widely reported to be livid at MacArthur's insubordination, Hoover refused to reprimand the general, which only added to the perception that the president was weak.

In the predawn hours of July 29, 1932, MacArthur set out to impugn the validity of the Bonus Marchers and to set the stage for the Hoover administration's justification for the use of force, claiming that the men were not really veterans at all but rabble-rousing insurrectionists and Communists. "If there was one man in ten in that group who is a veteran it would surprise me," MacArthur proffered. No major news outlets bothered to obtain records from the Veterans Administration, which had recently completed a survey revealing that 94 percent of the Bonus Marchers had served in the U.S. military. A whopping 67 percent had served overseas, and 20 percent of those were disabled as a result of their Army or Navy tours of duty.

In any case, many saw MacArthur's rationale for the obfuscation that it was. Congressman Fiorello La Guardia of New York wired the president, expressing his great alarm at MacArthur's actions. "Soup is cheaper than tear gas bombs," the plainspoken fellow Republican wrote, "and bread is better than bullets in maintaining law and order in these times of Depression, unemployment and hunger."

The fallout was swift and decisive. "Hounding men who fought for their country was not a political master stroke," one historian wrote. "What a pitiful spectacle is that of the great American government, mightiest in the world, chasing unarmed men, women and children with army tanks," the *Washington News* admonished. Newsreel audiences throughout the country hissed as they watched the U.S. Army attack the Bonus Marchers.

At the governor's mansion in Albany, Franklin and Eleanor Roosevelt were appalled. Sitting up in bed in the master suite, on the morning of July 29, Roosevelt was surrounded by a sea of newspapers. Rexford Tugwell, a professor of agricultural economics and one of Roosevelt's advisers, later recalled that the governor felt deeply ashamed for his country. Embarrassed that he had once held Hoover in high regard, he revoked that opinion, telling Tugwell, "[There] is nothing left inside the man but jelly; maybe there never had been anything."

To Roosevelt, Hoover's overreaction underscored his own evolving mindfulness of how deeply divided America had become, how wide the swath was between the "haves" and the "have-nots"—as Depression-era novelist F. Scott Fitzgerald described America's divisions along lines of money and class. Hoover's actions highlighted to Roosevelt "the deep social cleavage in the nation and the possible difficulties posed by alarmists" such as MacArthur, whom he considered "a potential Mussolini."

In any case, Roosevelt knew better than anyone that the episode had sealed the president's fate, predicting, rightly, that Americans would be outraged by the events.

"Well, Felix," he said to his adviser Felix Frankfurter, "this will elect me."

CHAPTER SEVEN

Happy Days Are Here Again

THE BONUS ARMY FIASCO WAS the final blow to an ill-fated president. The 1929 stock market crash monopolized Hoover's first year in office; the spiraling American economy plagued his next three years. While the Depression obliterated Hoover's standing as a forceful American leader, his antisocial personality further undermined him. "But the rout of the bonus marchers shattered the remaining credibility of his administration," concluded one historian. "His personal reputation might have weathered some of the discontent engendered by the depression if federal troops had not attacked unarmed, hungry petitioners—victims of that depression."

Roosevelt was quick to capitalize on his rival's floundering, referring to him as "Humpty Dumpty" and never missing an opportunity to highlight his failures. In what would go down in history as a particularly bitter campaign, the Republicans' ad hominem attacks included spreading rumors that Roosevelt's paralysis was caused by a venereal disease, which had gone to his brain and was driving him "crazy." The Democrats held no punches either, accusing Hoover of colluding in the export of fifty thousand coolies as cheap labor to South African gold mines while he was a Chinese mining company executive.

In any case, Americans were uninterested in political squabbles and impatient for solutions to rescue them from the hardship that was growing harder. As the campaign headed into the general election, a journalist asked British economist John Maynard Keynes whether there was a historical comparison to the Great Depression. "Yes," Keynes replied. "It was called the Dark Ages, and it lasted four hundred years." Earlier, Keynes had warned a Chicago audience of the impending collapse. "We are today in the middle of the greatest catastrophe—the greatest catastrophe due almost to entirely [sic] economic causes—of the modern world. I am told that the view is held in Moscow that this is the last, the culminating crisis of capitalism, and that our existing order of society will not survive it."

It was this sense of fear and hopelessness that sent citizens in search of a messiah. Nearly fifty years old, the broad-shouldered and spirited Roosevelt had matured into a seasoned politician with governing experience and an eloquent speaker with an apparent grasp of the problems facing the nation. Still, the populace was fed up with Washington, with government, and with both parties, and while Roosevelt's charismatic personality enchanted many, others remained skeptical. "The way most people feel, they would like to vote against all of them if possible," social commentator and comedian Will Rogers quipped, though he would later become a friend of Roosevelt's. Third parties and "crank candidates" cropped up, spawned by the collective anxiety. Considered progressive, Roosevelt predictably aroused opposition from the Right, which alternately called him a Socialist, Fascist, or Communist—with no apparent comprehension of the contradictions. The fact that he was a die-hard capitalist and far more centrist than liberal was not lost on the Left, which saw him as an unreconstructed scion of America's elite. Walter Lippmann—"although subjected to massive doses of FDR's celebrated charm"—had not modified his assessment of the man, writing that "his mind is not very clear, his purposes are not simple, and his methods are not direct." *Time* magazine dismissed him as "a vigorous well-intentioned gentleman of good birth and breeding" who "lacked crusading convictions."

In the early stages of the 1932 presidential campaign, both the Right and Left were disaffected and disenchanted with the choice, seeing little difference between either Hoover and Roosevelt or the Republicans and the Democrats. Both candidates pledged to balance the budget and cut tariffs. Both promised to revitalize the economy. Both believed in the gold standard and unregulated corporate competition. Beyond platitudes, however, it was difficult to get a fix on Roosevelt's platform for the presidency. Though his speeches were generally ambiguous and noncontroversial, an outbreak of infectious optimism began to surround him. By early fall, audiences seemed less interested in shallow bromides than in the character of the man. Roosevelt's persistent smile and sparkling eyes, his indefatigable optimism and genteel manner, and his easygoing confidence and friendly nature implied that he could be the hero that all Americans subconsciously sought. "What they saw was a magnificent leader," William Manchester wrote. "His leonine head thrown back, his eyes flashing, his cigarette holder tilted at the sky, his navy boat cloak falling gracefully from his great shoulders. He was the image of zest, warmth, and dignity." Suddenly, the differences between the two candidates could not have been starker.

Roosevelt's speeches began to foreshadow the New Deal as he lashed out at Hoover's failed economic policy. He began to advocate for regulating banks and security firms and for reforming agriculture and private utilities—"to prevent extortion against the public." At the heart of his emerging ideology was the forging of a new partnership between the government and the citizenry—for "the development of an economic declaration of rights," as he told the Commonwealth Club in San Francisco on September 23, 1932. In one of his most powerful and revealing campaign speeches, Roosevelt spoke movingly of the birth of American democracy and its evolution to the modern day:

> A glance at the situation today only too clearly indicates that equality of opportunity as we have known it no longer exists. Our industrial plant is built; the problem just now is whether under existing conditions it is not overbuilt. Our last frontier has long since been reached, and there is practically no more free land. More than half of our people do not live on their own property. There is no safety valve in the form of a Western prairie to which those thrown out of work by the Eastern economic machines can go for a new start. We are not able to invite the immigration from Europe to share our endless plenty. We are now providing a drab living for our own people . . . The independent business man is running a losing race . . . If the process of concentration goes on at the same rate, at the end of another century we shall have all American industry controlled by a dozen corporations, and run by perhaps a hundred men. But plainly, we are steering a steady course toward economic oligarchy, if we are not there already.

Roosevelt made clear that it was time for a revolutionary reassessment of what democracy in America should look like in the twentieth century. "Every man has a right to live, and this means that he has also a right to make a comfortable living. He may . . . decline to exercise that right; but it may not be denied him." Hinting darkly of speculators, manipulators, and financiers, his words—written by Adolph Berle—left little doubt that he favored some kind of wealth redistribution. This concept of the sanctity of individualism, this championing of personal rights over property rights, this plea for relief to the masses, was a shot heard throughout the nation. That an American aristocrat had sounded the clarion call made it all the more poignant and uplifting—and, to members of Roosevelt's class, terrifying. "It was a real shocker for those who simply assumed that free competition was no more to be questioned than home and mother," recalled Rexford Guy Tugwell, who saw the speech as the turning point that launched Franklin Roosevelt into the realm of legend, which he would occupy into the next century.

Early returns on November 8, 1932, confirmed that the Roosevelt forces had accurately gauged the mood of the nation. No other Democrat had ever won such a large margin of the popular vote. Roosevelt had carried forty-two states, winning by 7 million popular votes and 472 electoral votes, compared with Hoover's 59. Democrats took over the Senate and the House as well, guaranteeing an opportunity for Roosevelt to manifest his vision for a New Deal. Listening to the results in a suite at New York City's Biltmore Hotel, surrounded by family and friends, the candidate was strangely somber.

Louis Howe refused to leave his own headquarters across the street, until victory was certain so as not to jinx the good luck. One of the guests described him as a "well of pessimism, overflowing now and then with dire predictions." Not until Hoover conceded shortly after midnight did Howe break out a twenty-year-old bottle of sherry he had been saving for the day his protégé was elected president.

Sitting in a corner of the suite, Eleanor broke into tears, lamenting her new role as First Lady. "Now I will have no identity," she said quietly to a cousin, unable to mask what she later described as the "turmoil" in her heart.

The couple returned to their town house at 49 East Sixty-fifth Street, where an exuberant Sara Delano Roosevelt was waiting. "This is the greatest moment of my life," she said, embracing her son.

For his part, Roosevelt was suddenly and uncharacteristically overcome with doubt and trepidation about the burden he was facing—a challenge equal to that of George Washington or Abraham Lincoln as the Great Depression entered its fourth year. Despite the Roosevelt theme song, "Happy Days Are Here Again," which was struck up throughout the country, "there was no excitement . . . no petty sense of impending personal triumph," Raymond Moley wrote years later of the election victory. The "gathering economic storm clouds—the tumbling prices, the mounting unemployment," he said, could not be shaken, even for a moment.

When his twenty-five-year-old son lifted him into his bed that night, Roosevelt uttered a heartfelt admission. "You know, Jimmy, all my life I have been afraid of only one thing—fire. Tonight, I think I'm afraid of something else."

"Afraid of what?" Jimmy asked, surprised.

"I'm just afraid that I may not have the strength to do this job," he said. "After you leave me tonight, Jimmy, I'm going to pray. I am going to pray that God will help me, that He will give me the strength and the guidance to do this job and to do it right. I hope you will pray for me too, Jimmy."

CHAPTER EIGHT

Brain Trust

ONE OF ROOSEVELT'S GREATEST GIFTS WAS the ability to recognize his own deficiencies and embrace the complementary genius in others. He harbored no delusions about his grasp of classical economics and knew that what he'd learned in a smattering of Harvard classes thirty years earlier was immaterial to the crisis at hand. Even before he had received the Democratic nomination, he had gathered a group of scholars and theorists—what he first called "my Privy Council"—to advise him on the entire range of issues confronting the nation. The economic emergency had reached such a magnitude that the stability of the country was at stake.

It was Samuel I. Rosenman, Roosevelt's chief counsel and speechwriter, who was credited with first suggesting that Roosevelt bring together a team of experts, to become the architects of his New Deal. Rosenman insisted that they "steer clear" of businessmen and politicians, who, after all, had coxswained the country into its present morass. Recommending that they seek some of the best academic minds in New York, he compiled a list of recruits from the departments of political science, law, and economics at prestigious Columbia University. Despite Rosenman's assertion that he "was the originator of this happy idea," as the prickly Raymond Moley put it, Moley claimed that *he* had first had the notion months earlier. But in fact, Roosevelt had been working closely with a small group of intellectuals—Moley, Tugwell, Frankfurter, and Berle—long before the group of advisers was formalized. While the provenance of the concept is disputed, it was Louis Howe who first used the phrase "Brains Trust," which he had seen in a dime store detective novel, and it was James Kieran of the *New York Times* who first published the term, which was later shortened to "Brain Trust."

By the time Roosevelt had been elected president, the group was solidified. Moley was a political scientist, Tugwell an agricultural economist, and Berle a specialist on public finance and credit. Basil "Doc" O'Connor, Roosevelt's law partner, was a legal expert with a singular knowledge of corporate structures. These young men, with often contradictory ideas—and called "notoriously impractical" by historian Elliot Rosen—shared a vision of economic recovery and industrial restructuring based on innovations that had never been tried before.

Other, nonacademic, creative thinkers were admitted into the circle. Brigadier General Hugh S. Johnson—on loan to Roosevelt from financier and supporter Bernard Baruch—brought extensive War Department experience, as well as a passion for fiscal stability and an aptitude for budget balancing. Honorary members included James F. Byrnes of South Carolina and Key Pittman of Nevada, who, as veteran Democratic senators, would be able to skillfully maneuver the Roosevelt program through Congress and keep other party leaders in line. Charles Taussig, a molasses tycoon, was another honorary member, though considered "an amusing hanger-on" by the others. James A. Farley, another adviser, was a political kingmaker who, as head of the Democratic Party in New York, had helped orchestrate Roosevelt's rise to the presidency.

While Roosevelt was magnanimous with them all, and each had his ear, rivalries and conflicts predictably erupted. Howe, who generally distrusted academics and "considered all policy an adjunct to electioneering," despised "Sammy the Rose" Rosenman, the Texas-born Jew who, Howe thought, monopolized Roosevelt's attention. O'Connor—"a shrewd salty Irishman" who had represented some of the most notorious of the utility holding companies—was seen as too sharp and pragmatic by the idealists. Tugwell, with his movie-star good looks and clear brilliance to match his blue eyes, was thought dangerously liberal by the realists, even if they couldn't help admiring his mind. "Rex was like a cocktail," Moley observed. "His conversation picked you up and made your brain race along." Though more intellectually pedestrian than the others, the stout, black-eyed, chain-smoking, ideology-averse Moley was the de facto leader of the group. Covetous and insecure, he relished his role as the cynical, unofficial quasher of his colleagues' pie-in-the-sky ideas. "I have not the slightest urge to be a reformer," Moley would say. "Social workers make me very weary . . . I am essentially a conservative fellow. I tilt at no windmills." The supercilious and aggressive Berle—a onetime prodigy who, at thirty-seven, remained the eternal man-child, according to those around him—managed to annoy or offend all the "president's men," even as he impressed them with his credentials. Berle had entered Harvard at fourteen, graduated with highest honors at eighteen, and in 1916, at the age of twenty-one, received his law degree from Harvard. He was soon attracting national attention for his research and writing on the modern corporation.

In his good-natured and amiable way, Roosevelt delighted in having thrown together such a disparate lot; he found that their varied passions and opinions fertilized his own mind. An inveterate optimist, his Pollyannaish outlook made him seem like "a grown-up Boy Scout" who believed that a happy ending could be found for every story, a solution for every crisis. Roosevelt's sanguinity annoyed his more hard-boiled advisers, but none doubted its genuineness. "He was a progressive vessel yet to be filled with content," Tugwell said of Roosevelt during those last days of 1932. Though his own philosophy and ideology may have seemed not yet formed, as many around him feared, and his intellectual processes too glib and shallow for the office he was about to assume, Roosevelt was, in fact, a far more intuitive and penetrating thinker than early appearances suggested.

Howe, Roosevelt's alter ego, who for two decades had been accustomed to having the candidate all to himself, now bristled at the encroaching influence of his upstart rivals—"men who rushed forward, all undeserving, to pluck fruits of triumph from a tree he himself had planted." The consummate insider now an outsider, Howe found an ally in Eleanor, who likewise felt shunned by her husband's new circle of intimates. Each knew that the other was Roosevelt's loyal ally and protector. So it was with a heavy dose of patience and restraint that the two took a backseat to the Brain Trust boys. Howe and Eleanor watched from the sidelines as Moley, Berle, Tugwell, and the others vied for Roosevelt's attention, for the president-elect to shine his favor on their individual policy proposals. The "new political landscape," according to one account of the tense situation, was "marked by intrigue and jealousy, stealth and duplicity."

The power plays occurred behind closed doors and not for public scrutiny. As far as the American populace was concerned, Roosevelt remained an unknown quantity—an opportunistic politician whose rhetoric and bearing inspired confidence. His ability to lead would remain a mystery until he assumed office four months later. The country continued its economic decline while he awaited his inauguration, scheduled for March 4, 1933—the date decreed by the U.S. Constitution. The 117-day interval between his election and inauguration was the most desperate stretch of the Depression, with two of every four heads-of-household out of work. All that Americans had left was hope: hope that the new president would be able to navigate the nation out of its darkness. The renowned Kansas newspaper editor William Allen White poignantly expressed such raw faith and expectation in Roosevelt's capacity to turn his weaknesses into strengths, his shortcomings into triumphs. "Your distant cousin is an X in the equation," White wrote to Theodore Roosevelt Jr. "He may develop his stubbornness into courage, his amiability into wisdom, his sense of superiority into statesmanship. Responsibility is a winepress that brings forth strange juices out of men."

CHAPTER NINE

Winter of Our Discontent

"I WISH FOR YOU A MOST successful administration," outgoing President Hoover wrote to Roosevelt the morning after the election. "In the common purpose of all of us I shall dedicate myself to every possible helpful effort." Whether Hoover's expressed sentiment was genuine or de rigueur, the two men feigned cooperation for a few weeks during the bleak winter of 1932. Given Hoover's ingrained belief that Roosevelt's election signaled the downfall of America, his congratulatory note was seen by Roosevelt's forces as disingenuous at best, calculating at worst, although Hoover allies vouched for his sincerity. Roosevelt's response to Hoover—revised and reworked numerous times with an eye toward ambiguity and legacy—indicated the delicate position in which the president-elect found himself. "On the subjects to which you refer, as in all matters relating to the welfare of the country, I am glad to cooperate in every appropriate way, subject, of course, to the requirements of my present duties as Governor."

Then, within a week of Roosevelt's election, Hoover sent a long telegram to the governor's mansion in Albany imploring—actually challenging—Roosevelt to embrace Hoover's economic recovery program for the good of the country. The unprecedented overture by a defeated president to his rival "rang alarm bells" in Roosevelt's instinctive mind. Hoover would forever claim that he was courteously and graciously including Roosevelt in the continuum of government. But Roosevelt saw the gesture as a cunning attempt, masked in altruism, to ensnare him in Hoover's failed policies, which, in Roosevelt's mind, went to the very heart of their political differences on economic relations. Hoover had consistently blamed the financial crisis on European developments and foreign instability, which Roosevelt had roundly mocked as utter nonsense during the campaign, calling it "the boldest alibi in history." In contrast, Roosevelt placed full responsibility on the American system. "The bubble burst first in the land of its origin—the United States," he contended. Roosevelt saw the domestic economic condition as the single gravest issue confronting the nation and saw the thrust of the recovery as putting America back to work—not to focus on events in foreign countries.

The core of Hoover's entreaties centered on the question of war debts— "the tar-baby of American politics," as historian David M. Kennedy described the money that the United States had loaned to Great Britain, France, and Italy during World War I. "To touch it was to glue oneself to a messy, intractable problem that had defied the genius of statesmen for a decade," Kennedy wrote. These notes were coming due, and Europe, never having fully recovered from the war, had fallen into a deep economic depression. The Allies were in varying stages of default on their loans, and Great Britain was threatening to suspend payment of its ninety-five-million-dollar installment, due December 15, 1932. While Congress and most Americans predictably favored holding the Europeans liable for their financial obligations, many intellectuals, financiers, and economists advocated forgiving the war debts in order to stimulate the international economy. Integrally tied to the debt issue was the question of whether every nation should return to the gold standard—in simplistic terms, a method requiring each monetary unit throughout the world to be backed by a fixed quantity of gold bullion, thereby stabilizing international currency exchange rates. Indeed, the system had worked for the last half of the nineteenth and early part of the twentieth century, but Great Britain had abandoned it in 1914 to finance World War I with treasury notes, which then forced several other countries off the standard.

Hoover strongly opposed cancellation of the debts and was so emotionally attached to gold that he once described it as a sacred substance "enshrined in human instincts for over 10,000 years." For his part, Roosevelt had not yet formulated a policy on the war debt issue. As for the gold standard, Roosevelt repeatedly joked that he didn't even know what it was—a remark that unhinged the humorless Hoover, whose biggest fear was that Roosevelt would abandon the gold standard and thereby destroy America.

If Hoover's gambit "had all the appearance of a magnificent gesture of statesmanship," as David M. Kennedy said in his magisterial *Freedom from Fear*, it "also contained sinister political implications." Ultimately, Roosevelt came to see Hoover's overture as a presumptuous power play and an effort to deflect blame away from himself, who, as president for four years and secretary of commerce for eight years before that, bore personal responsibility for the current disaster.

In any event, the pressure from Hoover had the unintended effect of prodding Roosevelt into deep analysis of the domestic and foreign policy issues that had only received perfunctory examination during the campaign. Ironically, Hoover's not-so-subtle scheming sparked Roosevelt's musings on what would become the New Deal. On December 22, 1932, Roosevelt diplomatically dismissed Hoover's advances—though not without implying that he did not appreciate the lame-duck president's "attempt to mousetrap him into agreement with the policies of a discredited and defeated administration"—and began in earnest his preparations for governing.

Cloistered with his advisers, Roosevelt began designing his program for recovery. "By March 4 next we may have anything on our hands from recovery to revolution," Adolph Berle told him. "The chance is about even either way. My impression is that the country wants and would gladly support a rather daring program." Even the habitually confident Eleanor wondered whether anyone could "do anything to save America now."

As the nation slipped deeper into distress, Roosevelt was powerless to act until he was sworn in on March 4, 1933. The Twentieth Amendment to the Constitution had been ratified two months earlier, moving the presidential inauguration from March to January 20 of the year following the election. But since that amendment would not take effect until 1937, the old rules currently applied.

Some observers—contemporaneous journalists and later historians—found it cruel and calculating for Roosevelt to sit on the sidelines as the economy sank and the misery widened. Roosevelt "used Hoover as a foil," wrote author Jonathan Alter, seeing the situation in the most Machiavellian terms. "He let the outgoing president hang himself—and the American economy—so that he could enter stage left as a hero . . . He understood that the lower Hoover and the country slid, the better he would look upon assuming office." Even Moley, one of his closest advisers, ultimately took a similarly cynical view, later commenting that Roosevelt "either did not realize how serious the situation was or . . . preferred to have conditions deteriorate and gain for himself the entire credit for the rescue operation."

But most of Roosevelt's supporters thought his position unavoidable. Aside from that during the run-up to the Civil War, it was the most dangerous interregnum in the history of America. Roosevelt was convinced that Hoover was setting a trap for him—a suspicion confirmed when he learned that a Hoover cabinet member had said of Roosevelt, "We now have the fellow in a hole that he is not going to be able to get out of." It seemed that Hoover, like Al Smith before, had grossly underestimated his adversary. As it was, Roosevelt decided to keep his own counsel and wait until he could grab the helm of a country rocking dangerously on turbulent seas.

In the short span of 150 years—from the American Revolution through the Civil War to the twentieth century—the democracy envisioned by the founding fathers was an evolving work-in-progress. As in the "Jeffersonian Era" and the "Age of Jackson," the stakes were astronomical, the threats were both internal and external, and the perils were potentially fatal. The nation's financial order had collapsed. Powerless, Roosevelt was relegated to the dugout while Hoover presided over the nation's wallowing. Roosevelt could do nothing but watch as unemployment rose to seventeen million and thousands of banks and businesses failed. And that was just on the home front.

The global economy was disintegrating. Events in Europe and Asia signaled the inevitability of another world war. In India, Mahatma Gandhi was at the peak of his civil disobedience against the British occupation. Blood was flowing in the streets of Havana, where a dictator had suspended the Cuban constitution. People throughout the world, it seemed, were in varying states of unrest.

The impulse that had swept America to overwhelmingly elect Franklin Roosevelt, the upheaval that was shuffling the world order, and the global reassessment of philosophies and ideologies were all colliding as 1933 began. The year was a gateway to the modern half of the twentieth century, a turning point in America's direction—in the powers of the presidency, in the relationship between the government and the people, and in the expansion of a new mass media.

It was a decisive moment in American history, one when the country, born fifteen decades earlier out of hope and idealism might have toppled.

CHAPTER TEN

Year of Fear

"THE SITUATION IS CRITICAL, FRANKLIN," Walter Lippmann told the president-elect in early 1933. "You may have no alternative but to assume dictatorial powers."

The columnist was not alone in his anxiety that the revolutionary climate could spawn a demagogue. Many had a deep premonition that American democracy as it had existed was coming to an end. For his part, Lippmann—a "reluctant convert" to Roosevelt—now believed that the state of emergency demanded measures that transcended the routine methods of government. Congress should not be allowed "to obstruct, to delay, to mutilate, and to confuse," he wrote, recommending that it suspend debate for a year, giving Roosevelt free rein to rescue the country from its deathbed. "The danger we have to fear is not that Congress will give Franklin D. Roosevelt too much power, but that it will deny him the powers he needs. A democracy which fails to concentrate authority in an emergency inevitably falls into such confusion that the ground is prepared for the rise of a dictator."

The fears were not unfounded. In New York City, thirty-five thousand men and women crowded into Union Square to listen to Communist Party agitators. A mass march on the Columbus statehouse by the Ohio Unemployed League threatened to "take control of the government." Five thousand teachers in Chicago stormed the city's banks. Dozens of American cities and towns were broke, their streets filling with garbage and protesters, their coffers empty of funds for sanitation or law enforcement. Anton Cermak, mayor of Chicago, where six hundred thousand men were out of work, told the Illinois State Legislature: "Call out the troops before you close the relief stations." Leading citizens of Dayton, Ohio, organized a committee to plan the city's survival if the power lines were cut and the railroads stopped running. Governors and mayors throughout the land worried about the spark that might ignite mob violence among the have-nots, while the haves became increasingly nervous and began to arm themselves. The wealthy—and even the simply comfortable—began stockpiling guns, ammunition, and canned goods and hoarding their money in case of a nationwide revolt. Farmers in Iowa, armed with clubs and pitchforks, were engaged in an "organized refusal" to market products for which they were being underpaid. Iowa dairy farmers went on strike, refusing to deliver milk to national distributors.

The War Department concentrated its armed units near the country's larger cities in case of a takeover by the "Reds," as the Communists were called. The very "glue that holds societies together"—to use Senator Daniel Patrick Moynihan's description of institutions and authority—was disintegrating. "Capitalism is on trial," the dean of the Harvard Business School pronounced, in what would have been a remarkably radical statement at any other time in American history. "And on the issue of this trial may depend the whole future of Western civilization."

"The farmers will rise up. So will labor," a Los Angeles banker predicted. "The Reds will run the country—or maybe the Fascists. Unless, of course, Roosevelt does something." Leaders of both major parties watched helplessly as the situation worsened, prompting Democrats and Republicans alike to call for Hoover to step down and let Roosevelt assume command.

"They weren't paranoid," William Manchester wrote years later of the vociferous alarmists who had cropped up. "The evidence strongly suggests that had Roosevelt in fact been another Hoover, the United States would have followed seven Latin American countries whose governments had been overthrown by Depression victims."

On January 30, 1933, Roosevelt's fifty-first birthday, Adolf Hitler became chancellor of Germany. "I want," Hitler said upon his ascendance, "precisely the same power as Mussolini exercised after the March on

Rome." The sudden explosion of the Nazi revolution frightened the other European nations, which heard horror stories of gangs of young Nazis terrorizing Jewish-owned businesses, beating the merchants and raiding the stores. With alarming swiftness, Hitler added sixty thousand storm troopers to the hundred-thousand-man German army, suspended civil liberties, and removed non-Nazis from official posts.

In contrast to Italian Fascist dictator Benito Mussolini, who had been in power since 1922 and who was considered the most prestigious political figure in the world, Hitler seemed a belligerent and unpredictable leader. Indeed, many thought a Mussolini-like leader a perfect counterweight to a dangerous radical like Hitler. "I do not often envy other countries their governments, but I saw that if this country ever needed a Mussolini, it needs one now," proclaimed one of President Hoover's closest Republican allies in the U.S. Senate. Mussolini had revived the Italian economy, and his Black Shirts—the military arm of his organization, made up of two hundred thousand disgruntled soldiers, and analogous to America's Bonus Army— were highly regarded. Even the term *Fascism* implied a strength and unity desperately needed in America: "The word itself derived from the Latin for a bundle of sticks bound together and thus unbreakable."

Indeed, Italy in the time of Mussolini, who had legendarily made the trains run on time, seemed a viable model for what America could and should become, and talk of dictatorship was rampant during the interregnum of despair. The nation's scholarly and trade journals analyzed the political atmosphere, some predicting revolution and others espousing new forms of government. There was no consensus of opinion, as authors, politicians, journalists, academics, and laymen explored the gamut, from Communism to Fascism to Socialism. If any uniformity existed, it was the conclusion that capitalism was dead in its present iteration. Nicholas Murray Butler, the president of Columbia University, the recipient of a Nobel Peace Prize, and an arbiter of the academic establishment, encouraged college students to embrace totalitarianism, which produced "men of far greater intelligence, far stronger character and far more courage than the system of elections."

Renowned writers such as John Dos Passos, Erskine Caldwell, Malcolm Cowley, Lincoln Steffens, and Upton Sinclair were champions of Communism. "Those rascals in Russia . . . have got mighty good ideas . . . Just think of everybody in a country going to work," Will Rogers opined about Joseph Stalin's regime. It was a fertile and confusing intellectual environment. "Communist Party members were venomous to socialists, old-guard socialists were battling new-guard socialists, mutant strains of Marxists were battling one another," wrote political journalist Myra MacPherson in her biography of I. F. Stone. "Working-class ideologues were joined by middle- and upper-class Ivy League graduates who played at being radically chic Marxists."

While Communism was much feared in America, Fascism was not only venerated but also avant-garde. Mussolini was wildly popular among the country's intellectual elite, who believed that democracy, and its belief in the common man, had run its course. Italy's thriving economy and corporatist discipline held great sway with those seeking a solution to the fiscal, social, cultural, and political crisis facing the country. "Even the iron hand of a national dictator is in preference to a paralytic stroke," declared Governor Alf Landon of Kansas. Al Smith, Roosevelt's mentor turned vicious critic, proposed—only somewhat facetiously—taking the Constitution and putting it "on the shelf" until the crisis had passed. "What does a democracy do in a war?" Smith asked. "It becomes a tyrant, a despot, a real monarch."

As dictators "swaggered across Europe and Asia," and countries reneged on their war debt, Roosevelt decided he needed to find out for himself what "people like Hitler and Stalin, Mussolini, Chiang Kai-shek, and Hirohito" were up to. He decided to send newspaperman Cornelius Vanderbilt Jr., his friend and adviser, as a secret presidential envoy. Under the auspices of *Liberty* magazine, Vanderbilt would interview Hitler and Mussolini. Meeting with Roosevelt at Hyde Park before embarking on the cruise liner *Empress of Britain*, Vanderbilt got his instructions. Roosevelt "told me that what he wanted me to do in Germany was find out if the German people were really behind Hitler and, if so, why," Vanderbilt said. "Facing the reality of Hitler's accession, he also wanted to know whether there was anything within reason we could do to make for a better relationship with Germany."

The obsessive anti-Semitism of Hitler stunned Vanderbilt. After interviewing the führer twice, Vanderbilt became convinced that an improved relationship with Germany would be impossible. "He told me that the only thing he wanted from us was to end all trade with the Jews! He said I should be grateful for his anti-Semitic campaign, as the Jews were 'selling out the world to the Communists.'"

His meeting with Mussolini was underwhelming, almost banal. Il

Duce's great pearl of wisdom was that "you seize power with one group and govern with another."

Ultimately, Roosevelt and his advisers would conclude that the potential for a homegrown demagogue posed a far larger threat to their political agenda, and the country's stability, than the current martinets of foreign lands.

CHAPTER ELEVEN

American Mussolini and the Radio Priest

"WHO IS THAT *AWFUL* MAN SITTING on my son's right?" Roosevelt's mother, Sara, exclaimed sotto voce, directing her attention to the preposterously flamboyant governor of Louisiana. Huey Long, the "pudgy pixie" whose shock of auburn hair fell messily onto his forehead, was wearing a purple shirt and loud pink necktie—a sartorial statement intended to shock the aristocracy. The occasion, a formal luncheon at Hyde Park, was Roosevelt's overture to the man most threatening to him from the Left. Dubbed the "Incredible Kingfish" by *Time* magazine, the populist Long was widely considered a rising political star who might challenge Roosevelt in the 1936 election. Indeed, Roosevelt considered Long "one of the two most dangerous men in the United States today." (The second, in Roosevelt's opinion, was General MacArthur.)

Pressing the liberal agenda, Long was considered symbol and icon for the progressive wing of the Democratic Party, his radicalism descended from the William Jennings Bryan tradition of the late nineteenth and early twentieth century. Long's "Share Our Wealth Society," with its slogan "Every Man a King" and motto "Soak the Rich," was in its nascent phase. But his vision for the decentralization of wealth in America was already molded. He saw himself as the spokesman for the Far Right and Far Left of both national parties—an "American Mussolini" whose passionate anti-elitist rhetoric could lead to the creation of a new third party that would elevate him to the presidency. None of this was lost on the insightful and pragmatic Roosevelt. At the luncheon, as Long badgered Roosevelt about the need for enlightened economic reform in America, the president-elect listened intently.

"Frankie, you're not going to let Huey Long tell you what to do, are you?" Sara reportedly cried out. Long appeared unfazed by Sara's rude remarks, but they had not gone unnoticed. "I like him," Long would later say of Roosevelt in relating the peculiar encounter. "He's not a strong man, but he means well. But by God, I feel sorry for him. He's got even more sonsofbitches in his family than I got in mine."

During the interregnum, both conservative and liberal Democrats concentrated on moving the president-elect into their court. They made their way to his homes at Hyde Park, Albany, Manhattan, or Warm Springs, Georgia—the retreat he frequented for his unending physical therapy. Roosevelt listened to them all and ravenously inhaled their ideas, suggestions, observations, theories, predictions, prophesies, revelations, and concepts. It was as if he could not get enough, devouring facts and considering solutions with the exhilaration of a curious and precocious student. "The countless visitors who trooped to see FDR between election and inauguration ranged from congressional barons to local farmers, from haughty industrialists to mendicant job-seekers," said one account of the period. Propositions ranged from government intervention to wealth distribution to laissez-faire to job creation to trust busting to budget balancing, and from them, Roosevelt drew the framework of his New Deal policies.

Meanwhile, Huey Long and his counterpart on the Right, the rabidly anti-Communist Father Charles E. Coughlin—whom one journalist called his "twin terror"—increasingly saw Roosevelt as an equivocating, bourgeois politician rather than a man with a plan. Long began to believe that Roosevelt was placating all sides, playing them off against each other without any real conviction or strategy for ending the Great Depression or redistributing the nation's wealth. "When I talk to him, he says 'Fine! Fine! Fine! Maybe he says 'Fine!' to everybody," Long complained of Roosevelt's propensity for trying to please everyone.

Though partisan opposites—Huey Long was "secretly contemptuous of the priest"—Coughlin and Long inspired protest movements that defined the nation's response to the Great Depression in the weeks and months leading up to Roosevelt's inauguration. What they had in common was a

great distrust of Roosevelt—a skepticism Roosevelt felt tenfold toward both
of them—and an alliance to catapult Long to the presidency. Coughlin
"capitulated" to Long, according to Long biographer T. Harry Williams.
"Huey was a political man and was going to work toward his goal with
political methods. Coughlin was a theorist, a voice, an instrument that the
political man could use but would never completely trust."

Coughlin, called the "father of hate radio" by his biographer Donald
Warren, broadcast to nearly forty million people from his Church of the
Little Flower, in Royal Oak, Michigan. Denouncing Wall Street financiers as "shylocks" and "money changers," his anti-establishment populism struck a deep chord with the millions of unemployed and destitute
throughout the land. Like Long, the Roman Catholic priest had been an
early supporter of Roosevelt, but even before the president-elect was inaugurated, Coughlin had become disillusioned, suspecting that he was a
tool of Wall Street. Long and Coughlin—mirrored extremes of the populist movement in America—both sought to break the concentration of
power in the hands of the government. Both hinted at financial conspiracies. Both used rhetoric that was "laden with appeals to the idea of the traditional, rooted community and the special virtues of the common people,"
as historian Alan Brinkley described it, and that "warned constantly of the
dangers posed by distant, hidden forces. It emphasized with special urgency the issue of money—of unstable or scarce currency, of tyrannical
bankers, of usurious interest."

With the swagger and showmanship of a Southern evangelical preacher,
Long was one of the first American politicians to master the new medium
of commercial radio in the early 1920s. Broadcasting from WCAG in New
Orleans to eight thousand radio sets in the city, Long grasped the significance of a system of communication in which each radio reached an
approximate five listeners as families huddled together to hear the
transmissions. The audience, he realized, was exponential. One broadcast
speech could be heard by as many as forty thousand people in the relatively
unpopulated state of Louisiana, providing historic access to his all-white
voting constituency. With vitriol and ever-mounting oratory skills, he
lambasted the exploitative rich and the venal corporations. Initially, the
Roosevelt forces and the mainstream print media ridiculed Long, calling
him the "Messiah of the Rednecks" and "Whooey the 14th." Roosevelt,
however, saw in him an aspiring demagogue and thought it no laughing
matter.

For his part, Long was brazenly disrespectful of the blue-blooded Roosevelt, calling him "Frank," refusing to remove his hat upon entering Roosevelt's suite at the Mayflower Hotel in Washington, and denigrating him as "all wool and a yard wide." Long thought that Roosevelt's refusal to distance himself from the Wall Street power brokers signaled a personal corruption and portentous disinclination to break from his class.

Like Long in Louisiana, Father Coughlin in Michigan was at the vanguard of mass politics and also recognized the power of radio. In 1926, seeing radio as a potential fundraising vehicle for the little church he had built in a Detroit suburb, Coughlin asked a local station to broadcast his Sunday sermons. Those weekly one-hour speeches—"once pleasant discourses on the life of Christ and the lessons of the Bible," as Brinkley described them, soon evolved into political diatribes. At first his programs were relatively benign, as he responded to the anti-Catholic Ku Klux Klan cross burnings on the grounds of his church and railed against birth control. But in 1930, in response to the stock market crash and the sudden unemployment in Detroit of nearly two hundred thousand people, Coughlin took a different tack, shifting away from religion and toward politics and the economy. His sermons became rabidly anti-Communist and highly incendiary, and were but a precursor for the right-wing venom to come.

By 1933, Coughlin was drawing crowds of thousands into auditoriums in Cincinnati, Chicago, Boston, Baltimore, New York, and St. Louis, his invective carried over loudspeakers to thousands more in the streets who gathered to listen. He was described as "a priest who was more famous at the microphone than at the Mass," one "who could woo more men to a convention hall than to a communion rail, and who spent more time in politics than in parish halls . . ." He had four personal secretaries and more than a hundred clerks to answer the eighty thousand letters he received every week, and his annual contributions reached nearly half a million dollars. As his popularity soared—and his ego swelled—his rants grew ever more angry. What had started as an outgrowth of the European Catholic social movement, and a personal attempt to minister to the recent immigrants to Michigan from Germany, Italy, Ireland, and Poland, who were facing harsh anti-immigrant, anti-Catholic abuse, had evolved into an equally hate-filled response. He too had his eyes on the creation of a third party and supported the founding of the Christian Front—a pro-Fascist political movement designed to counteract Marxism and secularism. He was inspired by the teachings of Pope Leo XIII, who, in 1891, issued his *Rerum Novarum* warning that Socialist efforts to redistribute the wealth were pernicious to all nations as well as to the Vatican. Simply put, Coughlin sought to be the guardian of America, uniting Christians to fight the "Christless" Communism that was threatening to destroy it. "Choose to-day!" he appealed to his audience. "It is either Christ or the Red Fog of Communism." Wrapping himself figuratively in the Stars and Stripes, he oozed patriotism from his lips as he spoke reverentially about George Washington and Abraham Lincoln.

In February 1933, Coughlin's focus changed yet again with a sudden tirade about the "spirit of gold trading in the heart of the international Jew." Suggesting that Jewish control of international finance had wreaked havoc with the gold standard, Coughlin was entering a new phase of anti-Semitism, which would lace his future sermons. For the first time, his "money changer" enemies had a face: They were Jews, and Franklin Roosevelt was their puppet. In his mind, democracy was coming to an end, and America's only choice was to become either Fascist or Communist—"I take the road to Fascism," he would declare unabashedly.

The two ideologues, Long and Coughlin, along with their bitter defections from the Roosevelt camp and the movements they germinated, revealed an American-bred anti-Semitism and an anti-European isolationism that would have enduring national and global consequences. Roosevelt watched their feverish antics closely, once writing to a colleague that "in normal times the radio and other appeals by them would not be effective. However these are not normal times; people run after strange gods." Still, he concluded a viable partnership could never exist between the two men. "There is no question that it is all a dangerous situation but when it comes to a showdown these fellows cannot all lie in the same bed and will fight among themselves with almost absolute certainty."

CHAPTER TWELVE

The *Nourmahal* Gang

By THE END OF JANUARY 1933, conditions in the United States and around the world were menacing. Japan was escalating its movements into China, having already invaded Shanghai. Forebodings of America's possible embroilment in a war in the Far East were palpable, especially given Roosevelt's strong commitment to an independent China. His sympathy with China against Japanese imperialism was borne out of familial affection for the country that had made his maternal grandfather wealthy. With Hitler's rise to power in Germany through the brutal intrigues of the Nazi Party that so far had left hundreds dead, Europe was in political upheaval in addition to economic collapse. Roosevelt had an immediate and visceral dislike of Hitler and saw him as a dangerous threat to global stability, telling Rexford Tugwell that he anticipated a German-Japanese alliance that could conceivably lead to war with the United States. (That Roosevelt and Hitler came to office within weeks of each other—and would die in office within weeks of each other—is one of history's great parallels, as the pair symbolized the stark distinction between democracy and totalitarianism.) At the same time, Mussolini's Italy was arming Fascists in Austria.

The domestic situation was also in a nosedive, with the Depression hitting its lowest point. Personal incomes had dropped by more than half. National exports were essentially stalled as production and distribution came to a standstill. The country was broke and the U.S. Treasury didn't have enough cash to meet the federal payroll. The national banking system was beginning the final stage of its collapse, with banks closed or closing in twenty-one states, unable to meet the demands of depositors trying to withdraw their money. Stock prices had dropped by 75 percent since the crash of 1929, and most Americans blamed Wall Street and crony capitalism for the entire catastrophe. "Wall Street was not merely accountable for the country's dilemma," historian Steve Fraser said of the widespread perception, "it was its perpetrator, the principal villain in a national saga of guilt, revenge, and redemption." Joseph P. Kennedy, himself a businessman and Wall Street speculator, wrote of the pervasive loss of confidence in the system: "The belief that those in control of the corporate life of America were motivated by honesty and ideals of honorable conduct was completely shattered."

Despite his landslide election just three months earlier, Roosevelt—"waiting affably but without authority in the wings"—was now perceived as yet another fat-cat politician and upper-crust playboy. America's ruling elite was under fire, and Roosevelt seemed utterly evocative of that despised, exploiting class. This image of a gallivanting dabbler was not dispelled when movie theater newsreels showed him relaxing in the swimming pool at Warm Springs while the rest of the country was falling apart. Then, following his two-week vacation in Georgia, Roosevelt headed to the Caribbean for yet another twelve days of leisure and sportfishing.

On the evening of February 3, he boarded a special overnight train from Warm Springs to Jacksonville, Florida, to embark on a cruise to the Bahamas on one of the largest private yachts in the world. The German-built *Nourmahal*—flagship of the New York Yacht Club—belonged to his longtime friend, neighbor, and relative through marriage, Vincent Astor, one of America's richest men. The 263-foot vessel was the fastest ocean-going yacht ever built and was appointed with teak paneling and mahogany furnishings. Astor, a multimillionaire philanthropist whose father had died on the *Titanic*, was hosting the president-elect and five other wealthy men: Theodore Roosevelt's alcoholic son, Kermit; Justice Frederic Kernochan; William Rhinelander Stewart, a prominent New York and Florida landowner who was a major fixture on the Manhattan nightclub scene; George St. George of Tuxedo Park, New York; and Dr. Leslie Heiter of Mobile, Alabama.

Raymond Moley and another close aide, the veteran Bronx political boss Edward J. Flynn, rode with Roosevelt on the private train from Georgia to Florida. They were both appalled by the ostentation of such a holiday, and especially that Roosevelt's host was the "scion of a family whose huge income derived in good part from Harlem slum property," as one account put it. Still, they found Roosevelt to be mentally engaged in addressing the colossal problems of the nation, and whatever doubts they harbored about the seriousness of the man were completely allayed. He was attentive, determined, and thoughtful, and he had settled on a clear path of action to bring remedy to the nation. Roosevelt asked Moley to draft the inaugural address while he was at sea, and the two men discussed the ideas to be included, with Moley taking notes.

> Moley wrote in his notebook: "1. World is sick. 2. America is sick. Because failure to recognize Eco[nomics]. Changes in time, vast development of machine age in 20 years from point of view of replacing manpower [have] moved faster than in 100 years [before] producer capacity in agri[culture]—capacity in industry outrun consumption . . . Time to face the facts and get away from idea we can return to conditions of 29-30 . . . What is needed is action along . . . new lines . . . Action . . . Action . . . [If necessary] I shall ask Cong[ress] for . . . broad executive powers to conduct a war against the world emergency just as great as the powers that would be given if we were invaded by a foreign foe."

Nearly twenty-five thousand people gathered in Jacksonville to cheer Roosevelt, including the city's mayor and the governor of Florida. The local American Legion drum and bugle corps joined a police band to play the Roosevelt theme song, "Happy Days Are Here Again." Touched by the enthusiastic turnout, he gave an impromptu speech praising the city. If Americans were disappointed with the incoming president—as was the conventional wisdom—South Florida was an apparent exception.

In any event, both Moley and Flynn retained their qualms about the wisdom of Roosevelt's grand cruise on the luminous white luxury liner. In addition to the logistical and security complications it posed—Roosevelt's advisers would by necessity communicate in code by ship-to-shore radio—the excursion was a public relations nightmare. Watching them depart from the Jacksonville dock at Commodore Point, Flynn remarked sarcastically to

Moley: "The Hasty Pudding Club puts out to sea," referring to the Harvard theatrical society. Donning bright sports clothes and boyish grins, the men were more suggestive of boisterous fraternity brothers than a head of state and his councillors. Even his own son James was forever "fascinated by the mystery" of how Roosevelt could enjoy the companionship of "the *Nourmahal* Gang" at a moment when "he was doing so much to change the sort of world of which the *Nourmahal* was a symbol."

Indeed, both the Left and the Right made hay of the event. Liberal journalists decried Roosevelt for going on such a highbrow extravaganza at a moment of such desolation in the land, and conservatives lambasted his populist facade. The famously right-wing *New York Sun* lampooned the president in a poem, "At Sea with Franklin D.," which included the lines:

> *On the splendid yacht in a climate hot*
> *To tropical seas they ran*
> *Among those behind they dismissed from mind*
> *Was the well-known Forgotten Man.*

Among those disgusted by the jaunt were Huey Long and Father Coughlin, who saw it as confirmation of Roosevelt's hollowness. Likewise, President Hoover—stuck in Washington overseeing the demise of the nation's banking industry—was apoplectic at Roosevelt's seeming frivolity. In fact, he had come to believe that Roosevelt was responsible for the current emergency by refusing to cooperate with him and thereby sabotaging the recovery the Hoover administration had under way. The building crisis reached a climax on February 14, when the governor of Michigan ordered a bank moratorium, closing all 550 banks in the state for eight days. It became clear on that day that the bottom had fallen out of the economy and that the Michigan panic "could be neither stemmed nor localized," Moley would later write. Those bank failures set off a chain reaction, as anxiety spread, and six days later the governor of Maryland followed suit, closing that state's 200 banks. Rumors swept the land that the money held in banks was no longer safe, and depositors rushed to retrieve their savings. Ordinary Americans stashed their money under their mattresses or the floorboards of their Model T Fords, or placed it in tins and buried it in their backyards. The wealthy shipped their gold fortunes to Europe; nearly every vessel traveling across the Atlantic was carrying a treasure.

The president-elect was blissfully uninvolved with the spiraling events on shore, basking in what he rightly sensed would be "the last holiday for many months." He penned a letter to his mother from aboard the *Nourmahal*, stating that he was "getting a marvelous rest—lots of air and sun" and looking forward to returning "full of health and vigor."

CHAPTER THIRTEEN

Magic City

MIAMI WAS A NOTORIOUS TROUBLE SPOT with a long-standing history of political violence and searing racism, anti-Catholicism, and anti-Semitism. The least populous of its Confederate counterparts, Florida had been controlled since Reconstruction by a Democratic machine that governed with an iron fist. (The only Republican presidential candidate to carry the state had been Herbert Hoover, who walloped Catholic Al Smith in 1928.) Nearly 40 percent of the state's inhabitants were African Americans, who, along with the large population of poor whites, were systematically disenfranchised through poll taxes and literacy exams, along with the more manifest brutality of lynching.

A hotbed of race-based conservatism, South Florida had been hit hard by the Depression, which had slammed the area several years earlier than it had the rest of the country. Flying high during the economic prosperity of the 1920s, Miami was the epicenter of the modern real estate boom, with thousands of middle-class Americans moving into what was nicknamed "Magic City" for its supernatural growth. In a five-year period, Miami's population had doubled. New York speculators invested in hotels and retirement communities, luring Northerners to the tropical paradise on Biscayne Bay. Creating a classic bubble, thriving commercial banks loaned easy money collateralized with inflated property values. By 1925, potential investors were already starting to steer clear of what seemed to be a shady land grab, and federal revenue agents were inspecting the "orgy of speculation." Then, in 1926, the Category 4 "Great Miami Hurricane"—at the time, the most destructive hurricane to ever hit the United States—was dubbed "the blow that broke the boom." By the time of the 1929 stock market crash, Miami was already on the skids.

What followed during the next four years of the Depression was a level of insolvency, unemployment, and foreclosures to rival the country's poorest locales. There were few Jews or Hispanics in Miami; "Gentiles Only" signs were ubiquitous at the resort city's many hotels, and the large black population was relegated to second-class citizenry. The Ku Klux Klan—with thirty thousand members throughout Florida—was a visible and powerful presence in Miami and openly colluded with local police against Catholics, immigrants, and labor leaders, and intimidated Jews and African Americans. They were especially on the lookout for "radicals"—the all-inclusive word that captured Socialists, Communists, and anarchists.

"Columns of hooded, robed Klansmen marched for blocks during parades, funerals and other public displays in the city," wrote a former Florida prosecutor. In the winter of 1933, the Klan was very much in evidence in Miami, with local and state government officials and prominent figures in the community among its members.

It was into this atmosphere of xenophobia and hatred, fear and want, that the gleaming *Nourmahal* and its happy-go-lucky passengers glided gracefully into Biscayne Bay on the evening of February 15. Roosevelt had initially intended to disembark from the yacht and travel immediately by train to New York to prepare for his swearing-in on March 4. But his grand reception in Jacksonville two weeks earlier, where thousands of well-wishers had turned out to see him, gave Miami's boosters an idea for a "welcome home" celebration in their benighted city.

While the *Nourmahal* had been idly skirting the coastline, Robert H. Gore, the publisher of the *Fort Lauderdale Daily News*, was promoting a massive rally. Gore conceived of the plan with the goal of raising the morale of a dejected populace while also providing local political leaders and influential Miami businessmen an opportunity to meet and greet the president-elect. He had contacted the ship by radio and proposed the event, which Roosevelt embraced. Louis Howe had insisted that Moley's negotiations with prospective cabinet appointees were too delicate to be set forth in a letter to Roosevelt, transmitted by radio to the ship, or delivered by an intermediary. The rally would provide Moley with the opportunity to meet Roosevelt in Miami, report his findings personally, and accompany him on the train back to New York, and Roosevelt could simultaneously use the event to gin up support for his new administration.

Gore and his cohorts lost no time in planning the historic event—an official visit by a U.S. president-elect. The local newspapers promoted the upcoming rally, explicitly detailing plans for the presidential motorcade route and a parade with several bands, honor guards, and drum and bugle corps, culminating with Roosevelt's speech from the bandstand at Bayfront Park. Roosevelt would ride in an open car from the pier to the park, snaking through streets lined with people, to the amphitheater, where he would make a few remarks and then proceed several blocks west to the train station for his departure. A parade would follow him to the station, and from the platform of his railway car he would wave to the crowd as his train pulled away.

Upon learning of the celebration, several local and national notables decided to attend. Anton Cermak, Chicago's mayor and the Democratic Party boss of Illinois, who was hoping to mend fences with Roosevelt after opposing his nomination, owned a vacation home in Miami Beach. He decided to travel to Miami on a "begging expedition" for patronage for friends and financial aid for his city, which owed its teachers twenty million dollars in back pay, according to Alex Gottfried, author of *Boss Cermak of Chicago*. Along with national political figures and presidential advisers, according to the newspapers, mayors and judges from nearby communities and the governor of Florida would also appear.

As the yacht docked at seven P.M., the men on board were relishing a lavish farewell dinner. Roosevelt's vacation with what his wife, Eleanor, called "those people" was apparently beneficial. He looked tan, fit, and well rested. "I didn't even open the briefcase," he boasted to the newsmen who rushed on board to interview him, hoping to glean the identities of the incoming cabinet. "We fished and swam . . . We went to a different place each day. Usually we fished in the morning and came back to the yacht for lunch. One day we had an all-day trip to the middle bight of Andros Island after bone-fish. The only difficulty is that you can't talk and fish for bone-fish. It's silent fishing and that put an awful crimp in it." He refused to discuss presidential business—doggedly speaking only of the laid-back days at sea filled with swimming and fishing and more swimming and fishing—and the frustrated reporters left him alone with Moley.

Moley, by now his chief economic adviser, quickly summarized the confidential cabinet negotiations, and the group left the yacht for three automobiles that were lined up on the pier. They were running ten minutes late for the nine P.M. gathering, and thousands had congregated in the streets, at the park, and at the train station to see him. Roosevelt, wearing a gray suit selected by his appointments secretary, Marvin H. McIntyre, ten-pound leg braces, and no hat, was helped down the gangplank and into the backseat of the lead car—a green Buick convertible. Seated next to him was his official host, Miami mayor Redmond Gautier. McIntyre, Augustus "Gus" Gennerich, his personal bodyguard and aide, and Robert Clark, a Secret Service agent, got into the front seat. Fitzhugh Lee, a Miami policeman, drove the convertible.

The second automobile, also with its top down, carried five more Secret Service operatives. In the third convertible were Moley, Vincent Astor, Kermit Roosevelt, and William Rhinelander Stewart.

Ever since the assassination by an anarchist of President William McKinley in 1901, the Secret Service—a division of the U.S. Treasury— had become the full-time security detail for American presidents. Traditionally, the Secret Service relied heavily on assistance from local law enforcement officers, and Miami was no exception. Close to two hundred police officers had been pooled from nearby communities—one hundred patrolled Bayfront Park, sixty were stationed along the route, and twenty motorcycle police escorted Roosevelt's car.

The caravan crawled through the throngs of people—the largest crowd ever assembled in Miami history. Estimated at over twenty-five thousand, the mass cheered and applauded, yelled out and thrust toward Roosevelt's car. The police tried to maintain control, but the unexpected swarm created chaos that was exacerbated by the murky darkness. The bands were blaring, cheers filled the warm air, and red, white, and blue floodlights bathed the stage. Rows of palm trees presented a path, their fronds waving gently in the breeze. Thousands lined the roads, and the seven thousand seats in front of the brightly lit stage were filled. On the garish, ocher-colored three-story bandstand were the dignitaries, including Cermak. Several in the motorcade found the situation unnerving.

"It would be easy," Astor said to Moley and the others in his car, "for an assassin to do his work and escape." Night was falling, and an assassin could slip into the darkness. Astor was so edgy that he made a second remark about how risky it was to subject Roosevelt to such a crowd. Moley would later remember Astor's comments as "one of those improbable coincidences that never seem believable after." Moley assured him that they had passed through many such crowds before on the campaign trail when they had only one personal bodyguard and were forced to rely solely on the assistance of the local police. At least now they had the Secret Service.

Roosevelt's vice president–elect, John Nance Garner, had recently warned him of the danger of assassination, especially in times of such national anxiety. Roosevelt had dismissed the concern. "I remember T.R. [Teddy Roosevelt] saying to me 'The only real danger from an assassin is from one who does not care whether he loses his own life in the act or not. Most of the crazy ones can be spotted first.'" Naturally, Roosevelt understood that the presidency carried inherent danger. "Sono gli incerti del mestiere"—"These are the risks of the job," King Umberto of Italy famously remarked in 1897 after escaping the knife of a would-be assassin. Indeed, it was a newspaper clipping of that attack that had inspired McKinley's assassin.

For his part, Roosevelt was buoyed by the turnout, smiling and waving exuberantly with no apprehension. In just seventeen days, he would *finally* become president.

Twenty minutes after disembarking from the *Nourmahal*, the lead car arrived at a paved area in front of the bandstand. The crowd erupted with cheers and then became respectfully silent as Gennerich stealthily hoisted Roosevelt onto the top of the Buick's backseat.

"We welcome him to Miami," Mayor Gautier spoke into the microphone. "We wish him success and are promising him cooperation and support, and we bid him Godspeed. Ladies and gentlemen, the president-elect of the United States of America."

CHAPTER FOURTEEN

I'm All Right

A SCRAGGY MAN WEARING CASUAL WHITE trousers and a long-sleeve print shirt pushed his way to the front of the crowd, shoving two women aside.

"Where do you think you're going?" an annoyed tourist snapped at him.

H. L. Edmunds, a visitor from Ottumwa, Iowa, had been waiting for more than two hours to see Roosevelt, and he wasn't going to let some little punk elbow his way through.

"I go right down to front."

"I'm sorry, but you can't go down there. It's full," Edmunds replied.

"It no look to me like it full," the slight, dark-skinned man said.

"There are many people sitting on the ground, ladies and children sitting on the ground, and it isn't proper, it isn't right for you to go and stand out and push yourself in front of someone else," Edmunds continued.

The man, barely five feet tall, accepted Edmunds's explanation and seemed satisfied with his current positioning. He had made his way to the second row and was now about twenty-five feet from Roosevelt. In his pocket was a five-shot, .32 caliber, pearl-handed, nickel-plated revolver that he had bought at a downtown pawnshop for eight dollars a few days earlier. Folded next to the gun was a newspaper clipping with the headline

ROOSEVELT TO SPEAK BRIEFLY IN PARK HERE, a story about the McKinley assassination, and five more bullets.

Just before he began speaking, Roosevelt noticed "Tony" Cermak, the Chicago mayor, on the stage and motioned for him to come down to the car. "After the speech, Mr. President," Cermak responded. Then, in perhaps the most trite presentation of his life, Roosevelt merrily entertained the crowd with anecdotes of his cruise, perched on the back of his car and bathed in floodlights. "I have had a very wonderful twelve days fishing in these Florida and Bahama waters. It has been a wonderful rest and we have caught a great many fish."

He spoke for a mere two minutes—162 words—and just as he uttered his last word, a man clambered onto the back of his car, somehow eluding the Secret Service. One of "the talking picture people," as Roosevelt later described him, the man presumptuously told him to turn around and repeat for the camera the remarks that he had just made. When Roosevelt refused, the man rudely accosted him: "But you've *got* to. We've come one thousand miles."

"I'm sorry, it's impossible," Roosevelt responded icily, and as he glided back into his seat, he saw Cermak advancing with his arm outstretched.

It was nine thirty-five P.M. when Cermak and Roosevelt shook hands. They spoke briefly and agreed to meet in Roosevelt's railroad car for a private conversation. Then Cermak moved to the back of the car, where he stood next to Secret Service Agent Robert Clark. A man carrying a six-foot-long welcoming telegram containing the names of 2,800 residents of Miami approached Roosevelt. Before he could receive it, five shots rang out in rapid succession.

Screams and shouts filled the air, and pandemonium ensued. Roosevelt, immobilized by his paralysis, and after some initial confusion in which he thought the "pops" were firecrackers, was eerily calm. He saw someone grab the man with the telegram, and at the same moment, his driver, Fitzhugh Lee, started the car and shifted it into drive. He turned to the back and saw blood on one of Clark's hands. Then he saw Cermak, white-faced, doubled over, and bleeding from the chest, being held upright by Clark. "The President: get him out!" Cermak instinctively shouted. A woman next to Cermak collapsed. Gennerich leaped from the front of the car, pushed Roosevelt down onto the seat, and sat on him.

Lee gunned the car for a getaway and was moving forward when Roosevelt ordered him to stop and have Cermak loaded onto the seat next to him. The chief Secret Service agent, George Broadnax, yelled at Lee to "get him the hell out of here," and Roosevelt ordered him once again to stop. "It was providential" that the car had moved thirty feet beyond where he had spoken, Roosevelt later said, for "it would have been difficult to . . . get out" since the agitated crowd was filling the empty space.

"I saw Mayor Cermak being carried. I motioned to have him put in the back of the car, which would be the first out," Roosevelt told reporters the next day. "He was alive, but I didn't think he was going to last." With the decisiveness of a commander in chief, he barked out orders to the chauffeur to depart for the hospital. As the convertible finally began to pull away, escorted by the motorcycle policemen with sirens blaring, Roosevelt raised his right arm to the crowd and yelled, "I'm all right. Tell them I'm all right."

As the car sped off, Roosevelt put his left arm around his onetime political rival and felt for a pulse. Cermak slumped forward and Roosevelt thought he was dead. Sitting on the rear mudguard of the car was Miami's chief detective, who said, "I don't think he is going to last."

After they had driven another block, Cermak suddenly sat up and Roosevelt felt a pulse. "It was surprising," Roosevelt recalled to the *New York Times*. "For three blocks I believed his heart had stopped. I held him all the way to the hospital and his pulse constantly improved." He talked continually to Cermak, trying to reassure him and keep him conscious. "Tony, keep quiet—don't move," he said repeatedly. "It won't hurt you if you keep quiet." He told him that they were on the way to the hospital and that he would be fine: Cermak's surgeons would later say that Roosevelt had saved his life by preventing him from going into shock. When they arrived at Jackson Memorial Hospital, Cermak was rushed into the emergency room. An X-ray showed that a bullet had entered his right side just below the ninth rib, collapsing the right lung, clipping the diaphragm and liver, and lodging against the spine. His doctors determined that the injury was not life-threatening—listing him in "serious" rather than "critical" condition—and decided to leave the bullet embedded until he recovered from the trauma.

Meanwhile, back at the waterfront park, four others had been shot and several more had been wounded by glances and in ensuing struggles. Three policemen and two beefy Legionnaires had subdued the gunman. Astor, Moley, Kernochan, and Kermit Roosevelt were crammed in their sedan, along with a young man who had a superficial head wound, whom

Astor held in his lap. But the crowd prevented them from moving forward. Once two police officers slammed the assassin onto the luggage rack, hand-cuffed him to the trunk, and then sat on him, the crowd dispersed to let the car leave. His clothes had been ripped off during the melee, and he had been beaten with a blackjack and almost strangled, prompting a spectator to intervene, lest the angry mob crush him to death. When they placed him on the rear of the car, he was silent. Two more cops hopped onto the running board, and Moley held one of them by the belt as the car edged through the hysterical mass of people yelling, "Kill him, kill him!" and "Lynch him!" Finally the car cleared the crowd and sped to the hospital in what seemed to Moley an interminable time period, especially since he assumed that Roosevelt had been shot. When they careened around a sharp corner, one of the officers on the running board lost his balance and flew onto the pavement. The driver stopped briefly to retrieve the uninjured man, and the vehicle—carrying at least ten people, possibly eleven—raced on to the small community hospital.

The third car in the madcap convoy was driven by a Miami police officer and carried forty-six-year-old William Sinnott, a former New York City policeman who had once guarded Roosevelt as governor and came to Bayfront Park to pay his respects. Sinnott had been shot in the head. Also in the third car was Margaret Kruis, a twenty-three-year-old tourist from New Jersey who had been shot in the hand and whose head was grazed by a bullet. Mabel Gill, the wife of the president of the Florida Light and Power Company, was critically wounded, having been shot in the abdomen. Russell Caldwell, a twenty-two-year-old chauffeur from Coconut Grove, lay across the backseat with a bullet embedded in his forehead.

The night resident at sleepy Jackson Memorial was reading a "girlie" magazine when suddenly someone banged on the door to the emergency room. "Open the door for the president of the United States!" a voice boomed. With that, a Secret Service agent wheeled in Roosevelt. The two other cars arrived shortly afterward, and the hospital was swarming with the wounded victims and dozens of police officers. Moley was beyond relieved to see Roosevelt standing, with the help of Gennerich, obviously uninjured and exhibiting remarkable equanimity. One reason for Roosevelt's peculiar composure under the circumstances was his initial assumption that the assassin's intended target was Cermak—not him.

"F.D.R. had talked to me once or twice during the campaign about the possibility that someone would try to assassinate him," Moley later wrote in the *Saturday Evening Post*. "To that extent, I knew, he was prepared . . . But it is one thing to talk philosophically about assassination, and another to face it."

The battered and bleeding gunman was transferred to a squad car and whisked away to the jail at the Dade County Courthouse, accompanied by Moley, in his capacity as an academic criminologist. Meanwhile, Roosevelt and his entourage of friends, bodyguards, and law enforcement officers began piecing together what had happened. When word came that the assassin had been identified as an Italian immigrant named Giuseppe Zangara, Roosevelt assumed that Zangara was a Mafia hit man whose intended target was the mayor of Chicago. Otherwise, Roosevelt reasoned, the assassin would have shot him while he was vulnerably seated atop the car. Indeed, a gangland war was occurring in Chicago, and Cermak was widely known to be cracking down on the organized crime syndicate headed by Al Capone. Cermak's support of the repeal of Prohibition stood to decimate Capone's bootlegging empire. Just weeks earlier, Capone's enforcer had been shot by a member of Cermak's personal police detail. Cermak had received retaliatory threats and ordered a bulletproof vest to be ready upon his return to Chicago. He had traveled to Miami with a retinue of Chicago detectives serving as personal bodyguards. At the time, Miami was crawling with Chicago gangsters who were hanging around the Hialeah Racetrack. Ironically, a horse named "Roosevelt" won the second race that day, a winning ticket paying $3.35.

Still assuming that the gunfire had not been meant for him, Roosevelt called his wife. It was ten forty P.M., and Eleanor had just arrived at their East Sixty-fifth Street town house after giving a speech at the Warner Club. "These things are to be expected," she had said calmly, upon hearing the news from a distraught butler. Franklin and Eleanor spoke for a few minutes. Learning that her husband had held Cermak in his arms prompted her to write that the ride "must have been awfully hard on Franklin. He hates the sight of blood."

Roosevelt spent four hours at the hospital, visiting the victims and awaiting word of their condition. He was able to see them all except for Mrs. Gill, who was undergoing surgery. At two A.M. he was driven back to the *Nourmahal*, where he spent the night, having postponed his return to New York until the next day.

There, in the well-appointed saloon of the luxury yacht, Roosevelt downed a tumbler of whiskey while Moley reported the results of his interview with Zangara: Roosevelt, not Cermak, had indeed been the target. The assassin's shots went awry when he lost his balance on the chair on which he was standing.

Moley had observed Roosevelt closely over the many hours and was astonished by his self-possession and compassion for the victims. He recalled the moment:

> Roosevelt's nerve had held absolutely throughout the evening. But the real test in such cases comes afterward, when the crowds, to whom nothing but courage can be shown, are gone. The time for the letdown among his intimates was at hand. All of us were prepared, sympathetically, understandingly, for any reaction that might come, now that the tension was over and he was alone with us. For anything, that is except what happened.
>
> There was nothing—not so much as the twitching of a muscle, the mopping of a brow or even the hint of a false gaiety—to indicate that it wasn't any other evening in any other place. Roosevelt was simply himself—easy, confident, poised, to all appearances unmoved.
>
> . . . And I confess that I have never in my life seen anything more magnificent than Roosevelt's calm that night on the Nourmahal.

Word of the shooting spread quickly, as newspapers and newsreels reported the dramatic events. Extra editions and bulletin announcements blanketed the country. The attempt on his life, and his courage in the face of crisis, brought Roosevelt a surge of public support. If he had disembarked from the *Nourmahal* a wealthy dilettante, he returned to it a hero. "The President-elect, feeling the bullets were intended for him, straightened up, set his jaw and sat unflinchingly with calm courage in the face of danger which would be expected from one of his family," the *New York Times* said of his heroism.

The next morning, February 16, Roosevelt returned to Jackson Memorial Hospital to visit Cermak and the other victims. On the ride from the pier to downtown, his car was encircled by a phalanx of motorcycle police, and Secret Service agents stood on its running boards. As on the day before, unprecedented crowds lined the route. When he was wheeled down the hospital corridors to Cermak's room, all the staff lined up in awe of the paralyzed man who had acted with such heroism.

"Tony, I hope you'll be up and around soon. We'll need you at the inauguration."

"I'm glad it was me instead of you," Cermak reportedly answered, though later accounts disputed this exchange. Whether apocryphal or real, the sentiment was a poignant reflection of how the two men would be bound to each other throughout history.

CHAPTER FIFTEEN

Too Many People Are Starving to Death

Investigators, including Moley, who was the first to interrogate Zangara at the Dade County Jail, worked quickly to determine the motive, intent, and background of the Italian-born itinerant laborer—and, especially, whether he had acted alone. Zangara had railed against capitalists from the moment he began shooting, indicating an obvious political motivation for the assault. "I have the gun in my hand. I kill kings and presidents first and next all capitalists." Roosevelt—the quintessential capitalist from one of America's wealthiest families—was his target and had his aim not been thwarted, Zangara would have radically changed the course of history. What had transpired in Miami's Bayfront Park—the identity of the hero or heroine who saved Roosevelt's life and whether Zangara had an accomplice, as several witnesses claimed—was intensely scrutinized as Florida police and prosecutors scurried to build a criminal case.

J. Edgar Hoover, the director of the U.S. Bureau of Investigation in Washington, set out to determine the broader implications, assigning a special agent in Miami to assist in the local investigation and sending out a bulletin to all his agents throughout the country requesting information on Zangara. Since the Secret Service was the lead agency, Hoover's agency "conducted only minor, collateral investigations," as he put it. He coordinated his efforts with both the U.S. attorney general and the

Secret Service, as the agencies pursued possible co-conspirators and followed Zangara's elusive trail from Italy to New Jersey, Philadelphia, New Orleans, Panama, Los Angeles, and ultimately Miami. An operative from the U.S. Army's Military Intelligence Department reported to Hoover that Zangara had been identified as "among the bonus diehards who were still on the streets of Washington" in August 1932.

On February 16, Hoover received an urgent telegram from one of his officers informing him that Zangara was a suspected member of "an Italian anarchistic terrorizing group with headquarters at a farm near Newark, New Jersey," where the explosives detonated in a recent post office bombing had been manufactured. Other intelligence information received in the proximate days following the shooting indicated that Zangara "was the representative of a certain group of Communists or Anarchists in Cuba," according to U.S. Justice Department files, and that the plot against Roosevelt had been formulated the previous December in Galveston, Texas. A longtime Russian informant of Hoover's sent him a confidential letter stating that he had seen Zangara at a *vetcherinka*—"dances conducted by the Russian Anarchist groups." One particularly intriguing communiqué from a British intelligence agent stated that Zangara had ties to an international seditionist organization that had carried out the assassination of French president Paul Doumer the previous year. That organization, according to the informant, had been thwarted in an attempt to kill President Hoover in Palo Alto, California, when he went to vote in the November election.

Hoover was inundated with letters from witnesses insisting that another small Italian man had accompanied Zangara and from informants claiming direct knowledge that Zangara had not acted alone. A municipal worker in Miami reported that while replacing the old flag at the bandstand with a newer one more befitting of the president, he saw Zangara sitting on a park bench between two women a full five hours before Roosevelt was scheduled to arrive. All three were speaking a foreign language, and the two women were carrying oversize handbags.

Zangara himself was cooperative and boastful, and even wrote a jailhouse "autobiography" detailing his actions.

> When I fired the first shot, the chair I was standing on moved and the result was that it caused me to spoil my aim, and at the distance of at least thirty feet to miss by one foot. I then tried to get my aim again but after I had fired the first shot the people crowded

around the car and I could hardly see Roosevelt's head. I saw two heads in front of the President's and figured on firing another shot between those two heads but the bullet struck them both in the head. And this is what saved his life. This was also the reason for me shooting six people with a five shot gun.

Investigators reconstructed the events of February 15 that began when the thirty-two-year-old Zangara left his boardinghouse early in the morning and went to the Bostick Hotel. "Someone sent me here and I am looking for a room," he told the hotel manager. Carrying a small black package under one arm, he said that he needed a place "to be quiet" until six P.M. He paid $1.50 for the room, where he spent several hours pacing and chain-smoking, while wracked with his chronic stomach pain. In the early evening, he loaded his gun and began walking toward Bayfront Park. Surprised by the size of the crowd even hours before Roosevelt was expected, Zangara became anxious and pressed his way toward the elevated bandstand in the forty-acre park.

What happened next is mired in controversy and contradiction. At least two eyewitnesses—a forty-six-year-old carpenter named Thomas Armour and a woman named Mrs. Willis McCrary—claimed they saw Zangara and another man move to the front of the bandstand at approximately eight P.M., an hour and a half before the shooting. Mrs. McCrary described Zangara's companion as dark, of the same diminutive stature as Zangara, and wearing a blue coat, white striped trousers, and a pair of white and tan sport shoes. Seated behind Mrs. McCrary in the second row of stadium seats—folding chairs made of wood and metal that were fastened to each other and bolted to the ground—was her friend Lillian Cross. Cross, the forty-eight-year-old wife of a Miami physician, told police that she had climbed onto her seat to get a better view of Roosevelt. From that vantage point, the five-foot-tall Cross had an unobstructed line of sight to the rear of the presidential car, twenty-five feet away.

Suddenly, she said, Zangara hopped onto the small chair with her, causing her to lose her balance and nearly collapsing the folding seat. "Don't do that please. You're going to knock me off," she told him, her seat tottering. As she turned to him, Cross saw that he was her same height while standing on tiptoe. At the same moment, he reached his right arm over her right shoulder, and she saw that he was holding a pistol. Her immediate thought was, "He is going to kill the president!" In a split second she pushed his arm up, she later claimed, deflecting his straight shot at Roosevelt. His arm, according to numerous witnesses, was raised above the heads of those in front of him, with his hand pointed down toward the presidential vehicle. The revolver was so close to Cross that the gunpowder of the first shot burned her cheek. Zangara continued shooting until he emptied all five rounds and "two Legionnaires and three Miami policemen" crashed into him "like a ton of bricks," according to several accounts.

Robert Gore, the newspaper publisher who had come up with the idea for a Roosevelt rally in Miami, was standing next to Margaret Kruis, who had been shot in the hand and whose hat was grazed by a bullet later found in Cermak's shirt collar, with a piece of her hat fabric still attached to it. Gore carried the young woman away from the scene, placed her in the care of another spectator, and rushed back to the pile of people who had tackled Zangara and were pummeling him. Gore told police that Cross was on top of the suspect, trying to strangle him, and that Zangara was yelling, "I want to kill the president! I kill the president. Too many people are starving to death. I'm glad I got Cermak." Gore's account, though strongly challenged by Cross, who claimed that Zangara didn't speak at all, and by numerous other witnesses, gave rise to the early and continuing theories that Cermak was the intended target.

Armour, the carpenter who was standing behind Zangara when he fired the first shot, dismissed Cross's testimony as hogwash. Armour discounted Cross's claims that she had saved Roosevelt's life by knocking Zangara's arm. Armour reported that Zangara's first shot was unimpeded and poorly aimed, and that it was he, Armour, who had grabbed Zangara's forearm and forced it downward as Zangara continued his shooting rampage. "I sprang but before I could get him he fired the first shot. I grabbed his right arm, which held the gun, between the wrist and the elbow with my right hand before the second shot exploded," Armour wrote in an affidavit. "I then pushed the arm which held the gun up in the air. An officer jumped over the benches from the front and knocked Zangara off the bench."

For months, and then years, Cross and Armour would dispute each other's testimony, each calling the other a liar. Initial press accounts credited Armour with the heroism. But after Florida Democratic congresswoman Ruth Bryan Owen—daughter of William Jennings Bryan—suggested that Cross be awarded a Congressional Medal of Honor, Roosevelt invited Cross to attend the upcoming inauguration, and her legacy as the woman who saved Roosevelt's life was sealed. When she sold her story to a true-crime magazine, it became nationally sensational. That did not stop the controversy in Miami, however, where Armour supporters, irked by her fame and fortune, carried on a long-standing campaign to convince Roosevelt that Cross had lied. Nor did her story waver when Zangara himself contended, "Nobody take my arm, sure, one lady over there on my side when I try to shoot president on a little iron chair and when I try to shoot him the chair move because the lady, she move, and I missed the first shot and the lady try to get away. She no try to touch me because she was scared." But Zangara's confessions and jailhouse memoir would vacillate. Publicly he would blame Cross's interference for the shooting of the other victims when he had intended to kill only Roosevelt. Privately, though, he told his attorneys that he went along with her account because he didn't want to "deprive Mrs. Cross her glory."

Miami police reportedly doubted Cross's story, but, perhaps like Zangara, they were reluctant to spoil the inspirational tale of the petite housewife who saved the president's life. In the end, the "little lecture on manners" from H. L. Edmunds, the tourist from Iowa, "possibly had a far greater effect," a *Los Angeles Times* reporter wrote. "It halted Zangara in his tracks . . . From that time on he stayed back where he was, walled in by spectators at an inconvenient distance from his ultimate target."

Whatever the truth about the heroics, Zangara was performing in less-than-optimal conditions. As Robert J. Donovan, author of *The Assassins*, wrote, "The fact remains that Zangara was a poor marksman firing at a difficult target from an unstable perch under trying conditions and at a considerable range and an unfavorable angle."

"I'm such a little fellow I didn't have a chance," Zangara concluded.

CHAPTER SIXTEEN

Typical of His Breed

THE FIRST NEWSPAPER ACCOUNTS OF GUISEPPE Zangara emphasized his foreign origins: "The little Italian, defiant at first, sat quiet and almost courteous as they questioned him. . . . His bulging eyes dilate in the dim light as he speaks. His hair, dark and curly, is awry. He sits on a narrow bench, nude after the officers have removed his clothing to search for other messengers of death . . . His bone-like arms are taut, his fingers are clasped around two slender, brown knees. His face is dark, the heavy growth of beard common to his race showing prominently."

The short, 105-pound Zangara—"a swarthy Italian, typical of his breed," said the *Miami Herald*—was immediately portrayed as an unhinged anarchist with a perverse obsession with regicide. Indeed, Joe—as his few friends called him—had tried to assassinate King Victor Emmanuel III of Italy eleven years earlier, but the Royal Guards and an impenetrable crowd thwarted him. He, like droves of anti-Fascist Italians, had emigrated to the United States in 1923 after the king handed over power to Mussolini's National Fascist Party. Once he'd arrived, he'd contemplated shooting President Calvin Coolidge but never had the opportunity, and before he knew it, Herbert Hoover had become president. He apparently cooled to the idea of assassination for a decade, manifesting his anti-capitalist, anti-Fascist proclivities by joining groups of Italo-American radicals in the labor movement bent on keeping Fascism from gaining a foothold in the United States.

Then, while living in Miami in the winter of 1933 he decided to assassinate President Hoover and made plans to travel to Washington to do the deed. He blamed Hoover for the Depression and had absorbed the anti-Hoover rhetoric permeating the nation. "I was figuring to go to Washington—straight to Washington—to kill Hoover before Hoover go out," he said. He kept delaying his trip because he preferred the balmy weather in Miami to the freezing temperatures farther north. Sitting on a pier one morning, he heard a newsboy shout that President-elect Roosevelt was going to make an appearance at Bayfront Park on February 15, and he decided Roosevelt would be a more convenient target. Zangara drew no distinction between Hoover and Roosevelt. In his mind, Roosevelt was just another exploitative bourgeois politician who, like Hoover, was a rich man simpatico with the oppressive Mussolini regime. "I want to keel all presidents," he said in one of his many rants. "I see Mr. Hoover, I kill him first. Make no difference. President just the same bunch. All same. Run by big money," he testified.

Born September 7, 1900, to Rose and Salvatore Zangara in Ferruzzano—a farming village in the dirt-poor hill country of Calabria— Zangara had an inauspicious beginning. As an infant, he required surgery for an inner-ear defect, which convinced his mother that he brought bad luck to the family. When she died in childbirth two years later, the tragedy was attributed to his curse. His father quickly married a widow who had six daughters, and Zangara's status changed overnight from only child to the only boy in a brood of girls. He habitually fell as a toddler, once breaking his wrist when he tumbled down a flight of stairs and another time becoming burned when he fell into a fire.

His father was a brutal abuser who refused to let him attend school, forcing him to work in the fields instead. "You don't need no school. You need work," Zangara recalled his father telling him. He instilled in the young boy a deep-seated resentment of authority and an absolute loathing of the wealthy "capitalists." Zangara began to "hate very violently" while he was just "a little boy," he said. At the age of seven, he worked with his father's livestock, and when he once lost a cow, his father beat and kicked him "like a dog." "From that day on," he said, "he worked me so hard I became sick. I was beaten and starved and overworked when I should have been going to school, and eat and sleep like other children. That was when my stomach trouble started."

He yearned to escape from his father's tyranny and developed fantasies about traveling the world. He became an apprentice bricklayer and mason, and at the age of eighteen, near the end of World War I, he joined the Italian army as a laborer. He was dispatched to the Austrian front to build trenches. When the war ended, he left the army, but after a minor brush with the law in 1921, he was drafted as a soldier and referred to the Seventieth Infantry Regiment. Zangara hated military life, and while at basic training in Tuscany, he began suffering from what he called "the stomachache"—chronic pain he ascribed to his forced labor as a child. He attended the Italian Military College in Rome and was assigned to be an orderly for a captain and his wife, who were members of the privileged class he had learned to despise.

After an uncomfortable period during which he was expected to attend to the couple's every need—and received severe punishment when he failed to meet their expectations—Zangara repeatedly requested a transfer. Eventually he was appointed as a gardener at the college, and then as a guard for the paymaster's office, where he plotted to steal the payroll. "I needed it," he wrote in his memoir, "for my suffering." It was during this stint that he took a pistol to a railroad depot with the intention of killing the king. But, as in his ill-fated attempt on Roosevelt, his short stature and inability to navigate a crowd deterred him. "The guards got in front of me and I could not get a shot at him because the guards are over six foot tall and I could not even see the king."

Once discharged, Zangara applied for a visa at the U.S. consulate in Sicily, and on August 16, 1923, he embarked on the S.S. *Martha Washington*, sailing from Naples to Philadelphia. There he met up with his maternal uncle, thirty-five-year-old Vincent Carfaro. The two men moved to New Jersey, where Zangara quickly found work as a bricklayer during Bayonne's building boom. When it became clear that the most lucrative jobs were controlled by the Bricklayers, Masons, and Plasterers trade union—an American Federation of Labor affiliate that required its members to be U.S. citizens—Zangara underwent the rigorous examinations in English and American history then required to obtain citizenship. Motivated solely by the union prerequisite, and not out of any desire to become an American, Zangara was finally naturalized on September 11, 1929. He swiftly joined the union and the Republican Party.

As it turned out, the long citizenship process did him little good. A month after his naturalization came the market crash and then the Great Depression, which stymied the New Jersey construction industry. But his previous six years of solid employment—including stints as an independent contractor of small houses and as a laborer on commercial projects like the Alexander Hamilton Hotel and Fabian Theater in Paterson, New Jersey—during which he earned an average of twelve dollars a day, enabled him to buy fine clothes, drive a new Chevrolet, and maintain as much as three thousand dollars in a savings account. He had once checked himself into a hospital in Paterson complaining of sharp pains and no appetite. Doctors were unable to diagnose the problem, but they removed his appendix for good measure. In a short period of time, the pain returned, further fueling his distrust of authority figures.

Most of his neighbors and acquaintances thought him quiet, subdued, unremarkable, passive, and nonthreatening. He was described as a loner who had little or no interest in women and whose only pastime was an occasional game of checkers. He hated cold weather, never went outside after dark, and compulsively sought out remedies for his ongoing abdominal pain and flatulence.

Some, however, said his benign demeanor belied a virulent radicalism and violent underpinnings. A Hackensack contractor who had hired Zangara for numerous jobs over a nine-year period called him "an anarchist, socialist and Communist . . . an inflammatory character" and "lunch-hour orator" who would animatedly denounce "governments and men in power, preach radical doctrines and advocate the killing of government leaders." Likewise, Los Angeles police captain William F. Hynes, an infamous subversive-hunter, claimed that Zangara "fostered and founded" a group of bomb-making anarchists who operated throughout the country and that he was planning to assassinate Mussolini. Hynes told the *Los Angeles Times* that his agency's Red Squad had conducted a lengthy undercover investigation of the group and that Zangara had fled California when he got wind of the probe. Hynes's account was undermined when he told the Associated Press that he had no information in his files on Zangara. That did not prevent Hynes from later contending that he had evidence that Zangara was an organizer for L'Era Nuova (the New Age), an Italian anarchist organization that had recruited operatives planning to kill Herbert Hoover when he attended the opening ceremonies of the 1932 Olympics in Los Angeles. (That attempt was ostensibly spoiled when Hoover dispatched his vice president instead, according to Hynes.)

The day after the shooting, W. H. Moran, the director of the Secret Service, announced that his agency had concluded that Zangara was "not a maniac, but a member of a recognized anarchist group making its headquarters in Paterson, New Jersey." But only twenty-four hours later, that agency was backpedaling, downplaying any political motivation and depicting him instead as "a lonesome, morose character, sorely beset by a chronic stomach ailment since 1923, but with no particular grudge against the government."

The most substantive allegations tying Zangara to a violent anti-Fascist organization headquartered in Germantown, Pennsylvania, and Newark, New Jersey, were the FBI reports relating to a 1931 bombing of a post office in Easton, Pennsylvania, and 1932 bombings in Chicago, Detroit, Cleveland, and Youngstown and at the Vatican in Rome. This same group was responsible for the bombing of the Philadelphia home of John Di Silvestro, a prominent attorney and banker and the pro-Mussolini head of the Sons of Italy. Occurring just two weeks before the assault on Roosevelt, the prodigious explosion, in which more than ten sticks of dynamite were used, captured national headlines. Di Silvestro was not home at the time, but his wife, Elizabeth, died instantly. Four of his children and their governess fell from the third story to the first, and were all wounded, as were eleven neighbors. A close friend of Mussolini's and active supporter of promoting Fascism in America, Di Silvestro was a lightning rod for American anti-Fascists.

The day after the assassination attempt on Roosevelt, Di Silvestro told the Bureau of Investigation that not only was Zangara a primary suspect in the bombing of his home but that he also possessed information indicating Zangara had "associates" in his attempt on the life of Roosevelt. Di Silvestro had also made sufficient inquiries in Italy to become convinced that the name "Zangara" was an alias.

On February 17, five unemployed New Jersey bricklayers were arrested in connection with plots "against the lives of President-elect Roosevelt, President Hoover and other high government officials." The arrests came after a letter written by one of the suspects was found lying randomly in a Newark street gutter. "With my most sincere regrets," the letter read, "am forced to tell you of my brother bricklayer's unsuccessful attempt on the life of our President-elect, and am also forced to say that everything here is in order. If I were the one who had the honor of shooting at our present President, I assure you that I would take a week to practice and make a good job of it. It seems a shame that we have in our midst a man with such poor aim. I do believe we should have a place where we could all go and practice up on our shooting, as it looks like an open season on Presidents and politicians."

That same day, a fifteen-year-old American-born son of Italian parents sent a crude bomb made of a gun shell to Roosevelt's New York address. "I am friend of Zangara," said the letter accompanying the explosive, which was defused. "I want to take up work that he fail to do. I kill all Presidents, Governors, and millionaires. I am calabrian same as Zan. I hate police-men and kill all your officers who I see on street at midnight. I am one who killed Kansas City millionaire so I kill police." It was signed, "Paul Antonelli of Italy." Two weeks later, postal authorities intercepted another letter bomb addressed to Roosevelt.

Meanwhile, C. James Todaro, a federal prosecutor in Philadelphia, believed that Zangara was a member of a "wide-spread group of Anar-chistic and Anti-social individuals who are responsible for a long series of bombings in this state." In a February 21, 1933, letter to the U.S. Attor-ney in Pennsylvania, Todaro wrote that "Zangara must have had associ-ates and the attempt upon the President-elect was an effort on the part of these Anarchists to throw the country into turmoil as a prelude to a pos-sible revolt." Todaro also claimed to have information tying Zangara to famous Trotskyite Carlo Tresca. Hero to thousands of anti-Fascist Ital-ian immigrants, notorious radical to J. Edgar Hoover, outspoken adver-sary of Mussolini, and mentor to American intellectuals and labor leaders, Tresca was rumored to be living in Los Angeles "under the protection of a high-ranking Sicilian Mafia chief."

In 1933, Mussolini was considered to be an über-capitalist by Leftists who saw Fascism as the "natural political mode of class rule if the class is too weak to maintain its profits and position through democracy," as the scholar Nancy Bancroft wrote. "The ruling class in a modern capitalist country consists of owners of the largest banks, corporations and real estate, along with closely allied public officials and intellectuals." That Calvin Coolidge's administration had granted Italy a lenient debt settle-ment, and that J. P. Morgan had secured a hundred-million-dollar loan to the Fascist Italian government, convinced American anti-Fascists that there was an alliance between Italy and America that undermined democracy. Most of the anti-Mussolini sentiment in America was fostered by the labor movement, which saw Fascism as an attempt to sabotage the union movement and which was ever watchful of Fascist organizations cropping up in the United States. Because of Zangara's long-standing ties to the bricklayers' union, federal investigators scrutinized his political activities, including allegations that he had planned to assassinate Mussolini.

Zangara consistently denied that he was part of any organization or that he was accompanied to Bayfront Park by anyone. "I do not belong to any society. I am not an anarchist. Sometime I get big pain in my stomach too, then I want to kill these presidents who oppress the working men."

Even before a background investigation of Zangara had been conducted, government officials immediately assumed that he was an anarchist like President McKinley's assassin—the Polish immigrant Leon Czolgosz. In such a moment of incipient revolution throughout the world, the possibility of a conspiracy, from either the Right or the Left, was both real and alarming. "This is the United States, not Russia," U.S. Senate Majority Leader Joseph Robinson remarked. "No fanatic, crank or revolutionist, or any number of them will be permitted to prevent the orderly transfer of power in the government of the United States."

Moley played a crucial role in the containment of conspiracy theories; he was concerned that the violent act would incite further political instability at a moment of already heightened tension. With the economy struggling for survival, democracy under attack, a long and leaderless interregnum, and the very fabric of American society frayed, it was in the interest of Roosevelt, Herbert Hoover, J. Edgar Hoover, and Congress to rapidly paint Zangara's act as an isolated eruption by a deranged man. Moley thought it imperative to downplay Zangara's political connections, telling the *New York Times* that Zangara was neither "socialistic" nor "anarchistic" but that he had a "fixed idea of opposition to all heads of government." Privately, Moley admitted that he believed Zangara to be sane and a man of considerable intelligence and that he "felt it was desirable to avoid, so far as possible, any hysteria on the subject of radicalism."

When police officers went to Zangara's austere Miami boardinghouse they found all of his belongings, including expensive clothing, packed in a cheap suitcase. Three books were placed carefully in the luggage: *Wehman Bros.' Easy Method for Learning Spanish Quickly*, *Italian Self-Taught*, and an Italian-English grammar. On top of those were newspaper clippings about

Roosevelt's visit to Miami, about Roosevelt's half-million-dollar life insurance policy, which named the Warm Springs rehabilitation retreat in Georgia as the beneficiary, and about the assassination of Abraham Lincoln.

Zangara and his intended victim were polar opposites: Zangara was the clichéd immigrant and Roosevelt the blue-blooded American. Zangara impoverished and Roosevelt a millionaire several times over. Zangara tiny and insecure, Roosevelt larger-than-life and brimming with confidence. Zangara uneducated and barely articulate, Roosevelt a product of America's best academies and an eloquent speaker. Zangara a zealous anti-capitalist and Roosevelt an avid defender of capitalism. Above all, Zangara was one of life's losers, while Roosevelt had triumphed over polio and won the nation's highest office.

Whether he was part of a larger conspiracy or a crackpot loner, Giuseppe Zangara's brief appearance on the national stage revealed the country's fragility, the breadth of the Depression, and the perilous limbo of the long interregnum. He did not act in a vacuum, but rather in an atmosphere of class resentment, want, hatred, and fear. "For even if he had remained passive in his misery upon a park bench, utterly alone in the crowd," historian Kenneth S. Davis wrote, "this unemployed little man with a bellyache would have been both symbolic and representative of the depression's human waste."

CHAPTER SEVENTEEN

The Bony Hand of Death

THE EVENTS IN MIAMI SHOOK the nation and ushered in a groundswell of enthusiasm for the president-elect. Roosevelt had literally dodged a bullet and exhibited the kind of courage that Americans were desperately seeking. His own life had been spared, and he had valiantly saved a dying man. Maybe he could save the country itself from its terminal illness. The press reported his every utterance to an engrossed audience, and when he attributed his good fortune to "Divine Providence," Americans believed their prayers for a leader had been answered. In those dark days of the Depression, as banks were teetering and people were terrified of what the future might hold, Roosevelt had become the embodiment of hope and courage.

Paralyzed and immobile, Roosevelt had sat fixed atop his car, more defenseless than any other president had ever been. Yet, through a series of chance occurrences—a shaky chair, a cheap gun, an alert witness, a rude reporter, a stunted assailant—destiny took a sharp turn. "To a man, his country rose to applaud his cool courage in the face of death," wrote *Time* magazine. "He is a martyr president at the start of his term."

The attack on Roosevelt was a stark reminder of the violence of American society, and though few journalists or observers noted it, the statistics were shocking. Since Abraham Lincoln's assassination in 1865, one out of every ten presidents had been shot and killed, and one out of every five had been fired upon. In fact, from 1865 to 1901, the United States was the world front-runner in "killing its elected leaders," according to the Secret Service. "The average was one killing every twelve years and all three of the targets died from bullets fired at point-blank range." Given the indicators and the recent episode, the federal bodyguards were on high alert. Roosevelt's paralysis, coupled with his gregariousness, made the task of protecting him all the more challenging. "Guarding any President is difficult," wrote his chief Secret Service agent, Michael F. Reilly. "Guarding Franklin D. Roosevelt, a crippled man who refused to allow his infirmities or their pain to keep him from traveling whenever and wherever he felt he should, was considerably more difficult."

Roosevelt's train left Miami at ten fifteen A.M. on Thursday, February 16, and arrived in Jersey City at four ten P.M. the following day. There, he was met by what the *New York Times* called "one of the most elaborate police guards ever accorded an individual." More than a thousand police officers and Secret Service agents surrounded him at the train station and accompanied his motorcade to his East Sixty-fifth Street residence. It was the first and last time that he allowed such an ostentatious security detail. But on the heels of the Miami crisis, the show of force underscored Roosevelt's—and the government's—need to appear inviolable.

On Saturday, February 19, Roosevelt was the guest of honor at the Inner Circle Club dinner at Manhattan's Hotel Astor. Hosted by political reporters, the event attracted several hundred guests and included numerous sharp-edged skits comparable to the roasts of Washington's famous Gridiron Club. Roosevelt was greatly enjoying the levity when, shortly before midnight, he was approached by a Secret Service agent bearing an envelope with the presidential seal. Inside it he found another envelope, addressed to "President-elect Roosevelt." Roosevelt thought the misspelling, penned by Hoover himself, an intentional affront. He skimmed the ten-page handwritten letter as inconspicuously as possible and then handed it under the table to Moley. "Circumstances made it impossible for me to read carefully," Moley recalled, "but a glance was enough to tell me the news it brought. The bank crisis was getting out of hand." Once again Roosevelt's cool demeanor under pressure enthralled Moley, for Hoover's missive about the nation's state of emergency was both alarming and insulting and would have agitated a less self-possessed man.

"A most critical situation has arisen in the country of which I feel it is my duty to advise you confidentially," the letter began. It then set forth Hoover's hackneyed appeal to Roosevelt to cooperate with him and abandon the New Deal for the sake of the country. Hoover contended that the economy was so dire that the only thing that could save the nation from collapse was Roosevelt's endorsement of the policies of the Hoover administration.

When Roosevelt and his entourage returned to his East Sixty-fifth Street home after midnight, "the letter from Hoover was passed around and then discussed," Moley said. Hoover announced, "That the breaking point had come somehow made the awful picture take on life for the first time . . . Capital was fleeing the country. Hoarding was reaching unbearably high levels. The dollar was wobbling on the foreign exchanges as gold poured out. The bony hand of death was stretched out over the banks and insurance companies."

Indeed, the run on the banks was unprecedented. Nearly every bank in the country was closed, and it was impossible for the existing banking structure to survive the onslaught. "It would have been inconceivable—if one had not seen it happening right under one's eyes—that one hundred and twenty million odd of people should, apparently, at one and the same time fall into terror, and rush to withdraw their deposits from the banks," a J. P. Morgan partner wrote to a friend. What had begun with withdrawals by millions of depositors who had hit hard times, causing the depletion of the banks' resources, mushroomed into a full-blown mistrust of the nation's banks and an overall disgust with government. The more severe the crisis became, the more Hoover blamed Roosevelt and his refusal to cooperate with the outgoing administration. "Fundamentally, the millions of small depositors were not worried about the credit of the federal government or the gold standard, which seemed far-off abstractions, but about the soundness of their banks," historian Frank Freidel wrote.

Although Hoover's sense of urgency was genuine and well founded, Moley thought the timing of the letter—three days after Roosevelt's narrow brush with death and two weeks before his inauguration—was disgracefully inappropriate. Not only had Roosevelt's life been threatened, but now Hoover was telling him the nation's banking system was "mortally stricken" and that it was Roosevelt's fault. Beyond that, Moley was especially outraged by the antagonistic and condescending tone of the letter, which blamed the "steadily degenerating confidence" of Americans on their "fear of Roosevelt's policies" and "assumed that Roosevelt would succeed—where Hoover had failed—in hornswoggling the country with optimistic statements which everyone knew weren't justified." A few days later, Hoover confided in a private memorandum to Republican senator David A. Reed of Pennsylvania that he realized he was asking the incoming president to abandon "90 percent of the so-called new deal." But Hoover grandiosely believed that only his policies could save the republic. Roosevelt agreed with Hoover that fear was driving the run on the banks, but he thought it was a fear of the insolvency of the banks and the inadequacy of Hoover's strategies, not of the incoming administration.

If Hoover truly believed that such an overture would sway Roosevelt, he had deeply misjudged his rival yet again. Roosevelt had successfully ignored Hoover's demands since the previous November's election, his advisers considering them offensive and self-serving, and he now dismissed this last-ditch effort as "cheeky." Roosevelt decided not to answer the letter immediately, which had the predictable result of further upsetting Hoover. When Hoover had not received an answer after five days, he told his secretary of state that Roosevelt's refusal to follow Hoover's designs was the act of a "madman." Roosevelt finally responded to Hoover, but only after he had received yet another urgent letter, delivered by a Secret Service agent to Hyde Park on March 1—just three days before the inauguration. "It is my duty to inform you that the financial situation has become even more grave and the lack of confidence extended further than when I wrote to you on February 17," Hoover wrote, once again placing the blame on Roosevelt. Roosevelt responded immediately, this time disingenuously apologizing that an earlier letter he had dictated had been misplaced—a ruse the Hoover camp never believed, convinced that Roosevelt had been biding his time so that the economy would collapse and he could rush in as its savior.

"I am equally concerned with you in regard to the gravity of the present banking situation," Roosevelt wrote, perhaps as much for posterity as for Hoover. "But my thought is that it is so very deep-seated that the fire is bound to spread in spite of anything that is done by way of mere statements. The real trouble is that . . . very few financial institutions anywhere in the country are actually able to pay off their deposits . . . and the knowledge of this fact is widely held."

Hoover was livid. Roosevelt had outmaneuvered him, consigning Hoover's legacy to the wreckage of the economy while elevating himself as its rescuer. Hoover would take the hatred to his grave, convinced that

Roosevelt was attempting "revolution and not reform." While Hoover wallowed in powerlessness, Roosevelt worked tirelessly to build his team of advisers, write his inauguration speech, and prepare the recovery legislation that he intended to implement as soon as he took office.

By Thursday, March 2, more than half the states had closed their banks. The Federal Reserve Bank of New York, the most important financial institution in the country, was, according to author Liaquat Ahamed, the "center of the storm," having fallen below its minimum gold reserve ratio. The New York Stock Exchange and the Chicago Board of Trade were shuttered. Panicked bankers and governors beseeched Hoover to declare a national banking holiday, but the outgoing president refused, stating that he "did not want his last official act in office to be the closing of the banks." At the same time, powerful businessmen and legislators were imploring Roosevelt to seize power and declare a bank holiday. Late that afternoon, Roosevelt's cavalcade proceeded down Fifth Avenue in New York toward the Hudson River ferry, his car surrounded by motorcycles with earsplitting sirens. The French Line steamer *Paris* was docked in the river awaiting the president-elect, her cargo space reserved for "nine million dollars in fleeing gold," though no one in his party knew that at the time. Once across the icy Hudson, he boarded the special Baltimore & Ohio train waiting to carry him to Washington. A freezing rain enveloped the nation's capital, yet tens of thousands of supporters greeted him at Union Station. By the time he checked into the presidential suite of the Mayflower Hotel later that evening, a cluster of telegrams were waiting to inform him of more bank closures and of Federal Reserve figures showing the week's gold withdrawals to be a staggering $226 million.

By noon on March 3, New Yorkers were forming long lines in front of Bowery Savings Bank—the largest private savings bank in the world—demanding cash withdrawals. At three P.M. the bank closed with hundreds of angry customers still waiting. In just two days, more than $500 million had been emptied from the nation's banking system. Once again Hoover begged Roosevelt to join him in bipartisan action, asking that he approve a proclamation for a temporary banking holiday until Monday, March 6, at which time Roosevelt would commit to calling Congress into a special session. Once again, Roosevelt declined. The next day, he would become president, and he intended to take action then—without Hoover.

An incensed Hoover refused to host the inauguration eve dinner with the president-elect, a long-standing social ceremony that symbolized

continuity and civility. He reluctantly sent word to the Mayflower invit-
ing Roosevelt to tea at four o'clock in lieu of the dinner. Roosevelt accepted and, accompanied by Eleanor and their son Jimmy, went to the
White House. Hoover kept the Roosevelt family waiting for more than
thirty minutes, and although Roosevelt was "imperturbable and betrayed
no irritation," Jimmy knew that his father was seething inside. But Roosevelt instantly stiffened when he saw that Hoover was using the occasion
to blindside him at the eleventh hour with more demands and arguments,
in what Jonathan Alter described as "another game of chicken between
two proud men."

"I decided to cut it short," Roosevelt later recalled. He made a gesture
to leave and said to Hoover, "Mr. President, as you know it is rather difficult for me to move in a hurry. It takes me a little while to get up and I
know how busy you must be."

For the first time that day, Hoover looked Roosevelt squarely in the eye.
"Mr. Roosevelt," Hoover said, "after you have been President for a while,
you will learn that the President of the United States waits for no one."
With that, Hoover left the room. "That was that," Roosevelt recalled. "I
hustled my family out of the room. I was sure Jimmy wanted to punch him
in the eye." Indeed, Jimmy was furious at the treatment his father received.
"It would be putting it mildly to state that Mr. Hoover was not happy with
Father," he wrote of the occasion. "It was obvious that he had taken his defeat as even more of a personal humiliation than it should have been." Roosevelt thought the occasion would be politely social and was unprepared to
be "treated like a schoolboy or to have his own integrity thrown into question by Hoover," his secretary said. After they left the White House, Roosevelt told his son that the meeting "was one of the damndest bits of
presumption he ever had witnessed in politics." Decades later, Jimmy said
that it was one of his "earliest lessons in how to avoid political booby traps"
and that he thought his father had been more appalled than angry.

Back at the Mayflower, Eleanor told a group of women reporters of a
heated exchange between Hoover and Roosevelt that she had overheard.
Only years later was it revealed that the reporters had all pledged to keep
the details secret, reasoning that in the midst of a national emergency, it
would be unbecoming to portray the two men "squabbling like children."

CHAPTER EIGHTEEN

Fear Itself

EARLY ON THE MORNING OF MARCH 4, 1933, Roosevelt's valet, Irvin McDuffie, and bodyguard, Gus Gennerich, helped him with his steel leg braces and dressed him in the formal morning attire of striped trousers, black astrakhan-collared coat, and silk top hat. At ten fifteen, accompanied by his wife, mother, and oldest son Jimmy, he rode by open car to a religious ceremony at St. John's Episcopal Church across Lafayette Square from the White House. He had requested that the seventy-six-year-old Reverend Endicott Peabody conduct the service—apparently unaware that his one-time spiritual mentor had voted for Hoover—and invited nearly a hundred friends, family members, secretaries, cabinet officers, and advisers to attend. Throughout the twenty-minute service, he held his head in his hands, and remained in that position for several minutes after the final blessing: "Oh Lord . . . most heartily we beseech Thee, with Thy favor to behold and bless Thy servant, Franklin, chosen to be President of the United States."

After church, he returned to the Mayflower Hotel, where he conferred quickly with Moley, who briefed him on the current tally of more than ten thousand bank closures. He made final edits to his speech and decided on new measures to address the financial emergency immediately after taking the oath of office, though he kept what Tugwell called an "almost impenetrable concealment of intention."

He and Eleanor arrived at the north entrance of the White House a few minutes before eleven A.M., where they waited in their open touring car until a hostile President Hoover and his amiable wife, Lou, appeared. Roosevelt flashed his trademark smile at Hoover, who remained silent, unmoved, and surly as he slid into the seat on Roosevelt's right. The two wives followed in a second car, and five vehicles carrying Secret Service agents shadowed the motorcade. Roosevelt had refused to allow his bodyguards to construct a glass barrier to protect him from the crowd, so a trotting cavalry surrounded the car, forming a solid rectangle. "Here was a president who would not barricade himself at Rapidan," one historian said. "He was right there with them in this time of crisis. The pilgrims could not believe their luck."

As they made their way up Pennsylvania Avenue toward the Capitol, onlookers cheered and clapped, pushing against the ropes for a closer look. At first Roosevelt maintained the decorum—and fiction—that the crowds were there to honor the outgoing president. But when Hoover sat there "grim as death, looking stonily forward" and refusing to acknowledge them, Roosevelt finally began waving his hat and beaming to the enormous crowd. "Protocol or no protocol, someone has to do something," Roosevelt said of his thoughts at the moment. "The two of us simply couldn't sit there on our hands, ignoring each other and everyone else. So I began to wave my own response with my top hat and I kept waving it until I got to the Inauguration stand and was sworn in." More than half the population of Washington—over four hundred thousand people—had turned out, and while the crowd was more somber than usual, the excitement was palpable.

Once they arrived at the Capitol, Roosevelt was wheeled into a Senate chamber, where he watched as Vice President John Garner and several new senators were sworn in. He continued rewriting his inaugural address until the presidential procession began at one o'clock. He remained in his wheelchair until he arrived at the entrance to the canopied stand. A lone bugle cried out, and when the Marine Band began playing "Hail to the Chief," Roosevelt stood with the help of his son, Jimmy, and began his laborious "walk" to the rostrum. Before he reached the platform, the hundreds of thousands of spectators, spread out over forty acres of Capitol grounds, erupted in applause. Placing his hand on the three-hundred-year-old Roosevelt family Bible, open at the thirteenth chapter of Paul's First Epistle to the Corinthians, he repeated the oath after the chief justice of the U.S. Supreme Court: "I, Franklin Delano Roosevelt, do solemnly swear that I will faithfully execute the office of the President of the United States and will, to the best of my ability, preserve, protect and defend the Constitution of the United States. So help me God."

Without pausing to absorb the wild ovation, he turned to the crowd—one of the largest audiences to ever attend an inauguration—unfolded the longhand manuscript he had been writing for weeks, and immediately began his address. "This," he began slowly for effect, "is a day of *national* consecration." He had added the opening sentence just moments earlier, determined to set a religious tone to the somber state of affairs. The audience listened in silence.

> This is preeminently the time to speak the truth, the whole truth, frankly and boldly. Nor need we shrink from honestly facing conditions in our country today. This great Nation will endure as it has endured, will revive and will prosper.
>
> So, first of all, let me assert my firm belief that the only thing we have to fear is fear itself—nameless, unreasoning, unjustified terror, which paralyzes needed efforts to reconvert retreat into advance.

Uncharacteristically intense and unsmiling—his shoulders thrown back, his posture regal, his voice strong—he castigated the bankers and emboldened the masses.

> We are stricken by no plague of locusts . . . Plenty is at our doorstep, but a generous use of it languishes in the very sight of the supply. Primarily this is because rulers of the exchange of mankind's goods have failed through their own stubbornness and their own incompetence, have admitted their failure, and have abdicated . . . The money changers have fled from their high seats in the temple of our civilization. We may now restore that temple to the ancient truths.

His words struck a deep chord, not only with the hundreds of thousands in the capital but also with the many millions throughout America gathered around radios to hear their new president. "The radio networks carried his ringing voice out across the suffering land, over the sweatshops and flophouses, the Hoovervilles and hobo jungles, the rocky soil tilled by tenant farmers, the ragged men shivering in the iron cold outside factory gates," William Manchester wrote in *The Glory and the Dream.*

Restoration and recovery would come only when Americans banded together, Roosevelt said, "as a trained and loyal army willing to sacrifice for the good of a common discipline." He vowed to go immediately to Congress with a course of action for a national program to put Americans back to work, to prevent foreclosures and regulate banks, to enact a "good neighbor" foreign policy that respected the rights of others, and to ensure a "sound currency." Above all, Roosevelt called for "action and action now."

> We do not distrust the future of essential democracy. The people of the United States have not failed. In their need they have registered a mandate that they want direct, vigorous action. They have asked for discipline and direction under leadership. They have made me the present instrument of their wishes. In the spirit of the gift I take it.

Then, to underscore his sincerity, he pledged to take unprecedented steps if Congress or any other force sabotaged his efforts.

> I shall not evade the clear course of duty that will then confront me. I shall ask the Congress for the one remaining instrument to meet the crisis—broad Executive power to wage a war against the emergency, as great as the power that would be given to me if we were in fact invaded by a foreign foe.

He ended the speech at one thirty-four P.M., and as he gave a broad smile and final wave, the sun broke through the clouds.

Conservative and liberal newspapers alike praised the speech for its courage and confidence. Even Roosevelt thought it divinely inspired and would eventually consider it "sacred ground," according to his secretary of labor, Frances Perkins. Italy's *Il Giornale d'Italia* praised it as a Mussolini-like edict. "President Roosevelt's words are clear and need no comment to make even the deaf hear that not only Europe but the whole world feels the need of executive authority capable of acting with full powers of cutting short the purposeless chatter of legislative assemblies. This method of government may well be defined as Fascist." The *New York Herald Tribune* seized on his proclamation that he intended to ask Congress for "broad executive power," publishing the banner headline: FOR DICTATORSHIP IF NECESSARY. The *New York Daily News*—America's largest-circulation newspaper—took the unprecedented step of announcing a yearlong moratorium from criticizing the new president. "A lot of us have been asking for a dictator," the *News* editorialized. "Now we have one. His name is not Mussolini or Stalin or Hitler. It is Roosevelt . . . Dictatorship in crises was ancient Rome's best idea . . . The impression we get from various quarters is that practically everyone feels better already. Confidence seems to be coming back with a rush, along with courage."

The "fear itself" phrase did not elicit applause when Roosevelt spoke it, though it would go down in history as one of the greatest presidential quotes of all time. Several would take credit for it, but in fact it had been Eleanor who had given Roosevelt a book of Henry David Thoreau's writings with the line "Nothing is so much to be feared as fear." He had the book with him at the Mayflower Hotel that morning while finalizing his speech.

People around the world, listening on shortwave radio, welcomed the speech almost as much as Americans did. Congratulatory telegrams poured into the White House from England, France, Italy, Australia, and New Zealand.

Among the tens of millions who listened on America's 180 radio stations was Anton Cermak—now on his deathbed in a Miami hospital room. In the two and a half weeks since he had told Roosevelt "I'm glad it was me instead of you," Cermak had declined steadily. First he had developed colitis, then he had contracted pneumonia, and finally gangrene had settled in his punctured lung. As it turned out, surgeons should have removed the bullet embedded in his spine.

CHAPTER NINETEEN

Bank Holiday

IN KEEPING WITH HIS INAUGURAL VOW to "act, and act quickly," Roosevelt went to work even before the inaugural ball had commenced. While nearly two thousand guests mingled at a White House reception hosted by Eleanor, Roosevelt sent his cabinet nominations to the Senate and obtained unprecedentedly rapid confirmation. Then he gathered them all in the Oval Office and had a Supreme Court justice swear them in as a group. After a brief pep talk, in which he urged them to work together to solve the nation's many crises, Roosevelt directed Secretary of the Treasury William Woodin to draft an emergency banking bill that could be submitted to Congress when it convened the following Thursday. As fireworks filled the sky near the Washington Monument and the formal ball began, Roosevelt closeted himself with Louis McHenry Howe in the Lincoln Study until he retired for the night.

The next morning, Sunday, March 5, he awoke for the first time in the White House. After breakfast in bed, he rode in his new presidential limousine to St. Thomas's Parish, an Episcopal church off Connecticut Avenue. Returning to the White House, he summoned his cabinet. "The President outlined more coherently than I had heard it outlined before, just what this banking crisis was and what the legal problems involved were," recalled Secretary of Labor Perkins, the first female cabinet secretary ever appointed. Woodin reported on myriad conversations he had had with the bankers who had arrived in the capital from around the country to meet with the new president. The bankers themselves were panicking and clueless about how to rescue the industry, he told the president. Many banks had been invested heavily in the stock market and had "leant recklessly to speculative investors," according to one account, finding "themselves without sufficient capital and in many cases without reserves."

Before taking office, Roosevelt had already settled on his primary course of action. He had written two presidential proclamations, which he now showed to his cabinet. One called for a special session of Congress to begin Thursday, March 9. The other declared a bank holiday until Congress convened, which would close every bank in America. Then, relying on a little-known provision of a World War I act designed to prevent gold shipments to foreign foes, he stopped the export and private hoarding of all gold and gold bullion in the United States. The order also prohibited any foreign exchange transactions. His new attorney general, Homer Cummings, quickly provided him with the constitutional authority to invoke the 1917 Trading with the Enemy Act, and Roosevelt's bold proclamations were issued within hours.

Next he spoke with congressional leaders, including Senator Carter Glass and Representative Henry B. Steagal of the respective banking committees, and informed them of his call for a special session to address three emergencies: the banking crisis, unemployment, and the federal budget.

That evening, his press secretary invited four newspaper correspondents to meet with Roosevelt in the Red Room. Roosevelt was in top form— *Washington Daily News* reporter Raymond Clapper portrayed him as a genuinely sanguine and an optimistic new leader. "Behind the plain desk . . . looking across under the shaded desk lamp," Clapper wrote, "sat the President, in a blue serge business suit. Sturdy-shouldered, smiling, calm, talking pleasantly, with an occasional humorous sally, he was a picture of ease and confidence. As he talked, he deliberately inserted a fresh cigarette in an ivory holder. It was as if he was considering whether to sign a bill for a bridge in some far away rural county." All he asked of the journalists, whom he stroked by giving them the big news scoop about his proclamations, was that they refer to the bank closures as a "holiday"—in stark contrast to Hoover's depressing term, "moratorium."

At eleven thirty P.M. eastern standard time, Roosevelt gave the first radio address of his thirty-four-hour-old presidency. Directed to the American Legion, the short speech was carried live across the nation by all radio networks and may have been a calculated attempt by Roosevelt to rally the million-member veterans' organization in the event of civil unrest. "With so many banks involved, the U.S. Army—including National Guard and Reserve units—might not be large enough to respond," Jonathan Alter wrote in *The Defining Moment*. "This raised the question of whether the new president should establish a makeshift force of veterans to enforce some kind of martial law." Alter, in researching his book on Roosevelt's first one hundred days in office, located a never-before-published draft of this speech, which included this "eye-popping sentence":

> As new commander-in-chief under the oath to which you are still bound I reserve to myself the right to command you in any phase of the situation which now confronts us.

While it is not known who in Roosevelt's inner circle wrote the phrase and inserted it into his text—and can only be guessed why Roosevelt chose not to utter it—the nature of it was, as Alter described it, "dictator talk—an explicit power grab." Instead, Roosevelt delivered a five-minute speech about the merits of peace but calling upon "all men and women who love their country" to provide the same "sacrifice and devotion" that would be expected of them in wartime.

Then, at one A.M. on Monday, March 6, he signed the proclamation. With the flourish of a pen, and the assumption of wartime powers, he had seized control by the government of all the banks in the land and all the gold in the Federal Reserve. "For the first time since the Civil War, the dollar had been cut adrift from the gold standard," according to a history of America's finance capitalism. Finally, he retired for the night. When he awakened in the morning, his first full working day as president, he asked Irwin McDuffie to take him down the newly installed wheelchair ramp to the Oval Office. There, left alone, he was startled by the emptiness. "Hoover had taken everything movable except the flag and the great seal," said one account. "There was no pad, no pencil, no telephone, not even a buzzer to summon help." The walls were bare, the desktop cleared. He saw it as symbolic of the plight of the nation—that its heart center had come to an absolute standstill. It also brought him a moment of sheer terror, in which he was reminded of his utter helplessness and forced to shout for help. When his secretary rushed in, his equilibrium returned. It would be the only moment in the Roosevelt presidency in which the office was not pulsating with activity.

To the surprise of many in the administration, government, and industry, the overall reaction to the bank holiday was joyous, ushering in "almost a springtime mood" that raised Americans' spirits and elicited nationwide cooperation. It was as if the closures signified that the economy had hit rock bottom and had nowhere to go but up. Merchants readily extended credit to their customers, and dozens of municipalities issued more local scrip to keep things running. Americans suddenly found comfort in the fact that they were all in the same boat, and a camaraderie was born. Nearly half a million jubilant telegrams and letters poured in to the White House during the first few days after the inauguration. The fear had miraculously evolved into hope, and if in fact Roosevelt did not know precisely what the outcome would be, at least *someone* had finally done *something.* "If he had burned down the Capitol, we would cheer and say 'Well, at least we got a fire started anyhow,'" Will Rogers wrote of the national mood in his Monday morning syndicated column. "We have had years of 'don't rock the boat.' Go ahead and sink it, Franklin, if you want to. We might just as well be swimming as floundering around the way we are."

Roosevelt saw the role of president as equivalent to that of school principal. The chief executive of the nation, like the strong predecessors in his party—Thomas Jefferson, Andrew Jackson, Grover Cleveland, and Woodrow Wilson—should essentially be a preacher and lecturer. His job, as he articulated it, was to use the office for "persuading, leading, sacrificing, teaching always, because the greatest duty of a statesman is to educate."

Closing the nation's banks was a far-reaching experiment with unknown consequences, prompting one of Roosevelt's friends to tell him that if he succeeded, he would go down in history as the greatest American president; and if he failed, he would be known as the worst. "If I fail I shall be the last one," he responded, fully comprehending the precipice on which America tottered.

While a sense of excitement and euphoria filled the White House during those first few days of Roosevelt's presidency, Eleanor was apprehensive. She thought her husband's inaugural address "very, very solemn and a little terrifying," she said during her exclusive first-ever interview of a First Lady, which she gave to her closest friend, Associated Press reporter Lorena Hickok. The audience was "so tremendous and you felt that they would do *anything*—if only someone would tell them what to do." She had been particularly alarmed by the crowd's exuberant response to Roosevelt's vow to assume wartime powers. What went unsaid between the two women, as Hickok later recalled, was the precariousness of democracy and its vulnerability to the ascendance of a demagogue such as Huey Long or some other charismatic firebrand. "One had the feeling of going it blindly because we're in a tremendous stream and none of us know where we're going to land," Eleanor said, her thoughts turning inevitably toward Adolf Hitler, who had risen to power just a month earlier and vowed to replace the German republic with a dictatorship. Eleanor "feared the kind of desperation that had upended Germany," her biographer Blanche Wiesen Cook wrote, "and she feared the random acts of violence and assassination aimed at her husband."

Indeed, hourly bulletins over the inaugural weekend brought reports from Miami of Mayor Cermak's sudden and rapid deterioration. On Inauguration Day, his physicians gave him twenty-four to forty-eight hours to live and issued a statement:

> Mayor Cermak, last evening, developed pain in the right shoulder, together with tenderness over the right lower chest and liver. This together with his general septic appearance, caused us to suspect the presence of either a subphrenic abscess or pleural empyrema.
>
> For this reason the space between the liver and the diaphragm was aspirated with negative results. The pleural cavity yielded old bloody serous fluid.
>
> The lung itself, on aspiration, yielded a very foul, fetid air, but no pus, giving evidence that a gangrenous process was occurring in the lung.

CHAPTER TWENTY

I Want to Keel
All Presidents

On the night of February 15, 1933, having been disarmed and transferred to the Dade County Jail, Zangara said repeatedly that he was sorry he had not killed Roosevelt and that he hoped he would have another opportunity to do so. Thirty-two years old, single, ill-disposed, unhealthy, and with a burning hatred of the privileged class, Zangara immediately, and unwaveringly, confessed to attempting to kill the president-elect and proclaimed his desire to kill all the torture agents of capitalists. All the while he rubbed his stomach in a circular clockwise direction.

At the jail that night, Zangara was stripped, searched, photographed, and interrogated. Reporters seized on the opportunity to ridicule his pubescent physique and mimic his foreign accent.

"Why do you want to kill?" reporters asked him.

"As a man I like Meester Roosevelt. As a president I want to keel him. I want to keel all presidents."

The jail was on the top six floors of the South's tallest building, a twenty-four-story granite tower that housed Dade County government. Around ten p.m., Zangara, battered and bleeding from the blows of the spectators and policemen who had set upon him, was whisked from the basement to the top level were he was stripped.

"When we arrived at the jail," Zangara said, policemen "threw me on the stone pavement like a dog. After a while they took all of my clothes away and left me nude." He was cooperative and cheerful except when the subject turned to the capitalist oppression of the working class, which set him off on a tirade. Most of his interrogation was conducted by Sheriff Dan Hardie, who claimed to speak Italian. The *Miami Herald* described Hardie as "something of a linguist," though in fact he knew only a couple of words in Spanish, which he inserted into his questions. The prisoner recounted his horrific Italian childhood, his immigration to America, and his steady work from the time of his arrival in 1923 until 1929, when the construction industry in New Jersey dried up. He had taken a bus to Miami in August 1932 and stayed at various hotels and cottages on the beach before settling in a third-floor apartment in the boardinghouse near Bayfront Park. He was paying two dollars a week in rent for the run-down attic space at 126 Northeast Fifth Street. He idled about on the wharves, gambled on the horse races, and played shuffleboard in Lummus Park.

On Thursday, February 16, 1933, Zangara was charged with four counts of attempted murder for the botched assassination of Roosevelt and the wounding of three other victims who suffered minor injuries. He was not initially charged in connection with the wounding of Cermak or Mabel Gill, as the severity of their condition was not yet apparent. Rumors of a planned vigilante attack on Zangara by a lynching party prompted county officials to tighten security in the sixth-floor courtroom of Judge E. C. Collins. Observers were searched for weapons, and armed guards were stationed at all entrances to the courthouse. Zangara, wearing a checked shirt and dress trousers, was swept in by a mass of brawny policemen who engulfed the tiny prisoner. Seated in a massive leather chair that enveloped him, Zangara announced that he did not want legal representation. Still, Collins appointed three defense attorneys in order to guarantee that the Dade County justice system could not be accused later of railroading the defendant.

The defense team made a request for the appointment of a lunacy commission to determine Zangara's mental stability. The county physician, Dr. E. C. Thomas, had conducted a physical examination of Zangara on the night of his arrest. He had diagnosed the stomach pain as gastritis triggered by nervousness and fear, and had pronounced him not only "normal in every respect" but also "sane." Thomas's declaration would be the first in a long line of professional opinions that the assassin was sane. The judge appointed two local psychiatrists, who rushed to the jail to examine him

near midnight. They issued their eighty-three-word finding the following morning, saying that Zangara had a "perverse character" and a "psychopathic personality," but they did not call him insane. Zangara's chief
counsel also declared him to be "a sane man," as did Judge Collins. In any
case, Zangara and his lawyers had no intention of using an insanity defense, apparently leaving that decision to the defendant himself.

The wheels of justice in Miami gave new meaning to the term "speedy
trial," as the criminal process against Zangara proceeded with uncharacteristic dispatch. Even Cermak commented on Florida's unique legal system.
"They certainly mete out justice pretty fast in this state," he said. "If the
law could be enforced this swiftly in other states . . . it would have a great
tendency to check crime." At ten A.M. on February 20—a mere four days
after the shooting—Zangara's trial began. The *Miami Herald* editorialized that morning that the United States should "round up" people of the
"Zangara class" and send them back to their country of origin—"any with
radical opinions must be barred."

Reporters, photographers, and newsreel operators swarmed the courtroom and corridors. Zangara appeared composed and alert, as if his steady
jailhouse diet of milk and eggs was agreeable with his stomach condition.
"The people could not understand how I could take things so calm and
contented," he wrote in his memoir. "They marveled at the way I took it. I
was not worried."

Judge Collins asked Zangara how he wanted to plead to the charges
against him. "Your Honor," one of his lawyers said, standing to address
the court. "My client has insisted on his guilt. He has one gruesome regret. He is sorry he did not succeed in his attempt on the life of President-
elect Roosevelt. He scoffs at the idea he may be insane. After talking with
the doctors and Zangara, we came to the conclusion he could be nothing
but sane."

Before sentencing Zangara, the judge briefly questioned him, hoping
to determine some semblance of motive. Zangara, rambling and over-
wrought, summarized his incentive for killing Roosevelt: Capitalists were
responsible for his father's poverty and oppression. His father reacted by
abusing Zangara, which caused Zangara's physical problems. Hence, capitalists caused his stomach pain, and Roosevelt was the supreme capitalist.
"You see I suffer all the time and I suffer because my father send me to
work when I was a little boy—spoil my life . . . If I was well I no bother the
president." As he told his story, newspaper photographers and newsreel

cameras captured his words and images and flashed them throughout the world.

Collins brought the tirade to a halt and directed Zangara to leave the witness box and approach the bench for sentencing. The prisoner had pleaded guilty to four counts of attempted murder, each one punishable by up to twenty years in prison. Dispensing the maximum sentence, Collins ordered him remanded to eighty years of hard labor in the state penitentiary.

Laughing out loud, Zangara shouted insolently: "Oh judge, don't be stingy. Give me hundred years!"

"Perhaps you'll get more later," Judge Collins replied.

CHAPTER TWENTY-ONE

Old Sparky

AT SIX FIFTY-SEVEN A.M. ON MONDAY, March 6—nineteen days after the attempted assassination—Cermak was pronounced dead. Just hours later, Giuseppe Zangara was indicted on charges of first-degree murder.

"Not my fault. Woman move my hand," Zangara said when informed that Cermak had died. When asked whether he was sorry, he replied: "Sure I sorry, like when die bird, or horse, or cow, I sorry."

Thousands of Miamians turned out to watch the funeral cortege that took Cermak's body from the Philbrick Funeral Home to the railroad depot. American Legion pallbearers carried the bronze, flag-draped coffin as a band played "Nearer My God to Thee" and church bells pealed in the early evening air of March 6. A special seven-car train, swathed in black and purple, would take the martyred mayor back to his beloved Chicago.

When the train arrived two days later at Chicago's Twelfth Street Station, it was met by the city council and swarms of bereaved citizens. Flags were at half-mast, and the open casket was taken to Cermak's home in the Chicago neighborhood of Lawndale, where nearly fifty thousand came to view the body. It then lay in state at City Hall for twenty-four hours, attracting another seventy-five thousand spectators. At Chicago Stadium— where, ironically, Roosevelt had been nominated over Cermak's opposition less than a year earlier—the floor became a "sea of lawn and flowers in the form of a great cross," according to one account. More than half a million souls lined the procession of what was the largest funeral in Chicago history. The fifty-nine-year-old Czechoslovakian immigrant had risen to power in one of America's toughest cities, fighting organized crime and a longtime Irish American stranglehold on the city. He was eulogized as a symbol of patriotism—the man who gave his life for Franklin Roosevelt— but the cause of his death was shrouded in controversy.

Zangara could be charged with murder only if his bullet had directly resulted in Cermak's death. But medical evidence indicated that if surgeons had removed the bullet the night of the incident, Cermak probably would have survived, raising the specter of malpractice. Still, all nine of his physicians signed the autopsy report stating that death culminated "as a result of the bullet causing cardiac failure, gangrene of the lung and peritonitis."

After a Florida grand jury indicted Zangara on charges of first-degree murder, he was rushed before Miami Circuit Court Judge Uly O. Thompson three days later for sentencing. His previous three defense attorneys were reappointed. "These ones take care of me," Zangara said facetiously, apparently referring to their facilitation of his previous maximum sentence. Again he pleaded guilty, and again the judge questioned him perfunctorily, and again Zangara insisted that he did not mean to kill Cermak or anyone else except Roosevelt. "Supposed to kill the chief," he said. "The chief is the boss."

Zangara had remained incarcerated at the Dade County Jail for the intervening three weeks since the shooting, in anticipation of murder charges in the event either Cermak or Gill expired. During that time he began his memoir, which plainly and unrepentantly recorded his hatred for capitalists and desire to kill Roosevelt.

In staccato shouts from the witness stand that were reminiscent of his earlier hearing, Zangara reiterated his intentions. "I want to kill all capitalists. Because of capitalists, people get no bread . . . I feel I have a right to kill him [Roosevelt] . . . It was right. I know they give me electric chair, but I don't care—I'm right."

Judge Thompson used the opportunity to advocate for gun-control legislation. "Assassins roaming at will through the land—and they have killed three of our Presidents—are permitted to have pistols. And a pistol in the hands of the ordinary person is a most useless weapon of defense. No one can foresee what might have happened had Zangara been successful in his attempt."

When Thompson asked him whether he had any final words, the moment at which most capital suspects express remorse and plead for leniency, Zangara was resolute. "I want to kill the president because I no like the government. Because I think it is run by the capitalists, all crooks, and a lot of people make a lot of money. Things run for the money."

Thompson sentenced him to death by electric chair.

"You is crook man too," Zangara yelled at the judge. "I no afraid. You one of the capitalists."

A squad of National Guardsmen armed with machine guns transported him from Miami to the Florida State Prison farm, four hundred miles north at Raiford. His execution was set for Monday, March 20—a mere ten days after his sentencing. He was placed in a tiny steel cell in the "death house," a concrete building adjacent to the execution chamber. Once he was issued his striped prison uniform, he posed for the dozens of press photographers. The Florida governor had ordered that no one could interview the prisoner, but the prison warden, Leonard F. Chapman, was so intrigued by Zangara that he spent hours in conversation with him. Guarded twenty-four hours a day in his metal cage, Zangara worked busily to complete his memoir, which he then gave to the warden.

Chapman had become unusually fond of Zangara in the short time that the prisoner was housed at Raiford. He came to the conclusion that Zangara was sane and was a member of a secret Italian terrorist organization, similar to the Mafia, called Camorra. Chapman described Zangara as "a being utterly unassimilated, a foreigner wandering in a strange land and making no effort to understand that land; practicing the hatreds which came natural to him; bent on the ancient wheel; bringing to flower the code of the Camorra; attempting to correct a fancied wrong by wreaking personal vengeance."

Lashing rains poured from the sky on Monday morning as prison guards retrieved Zangara for his death march to "Old Sparky," as Florida's electric chair was affectionately called by avid proponents of capital punishment. Though more solemn than usual, he went willingly. "I am not making a hero out of Zangara," recalled a psychiatrist who was among the forty witnesses, but he "had more nerve than any man I ever saw."

Chapman had supervised more than 135 executions, but he had never seen such bravery as that exhibited by this little Italian, whom Chapman described as dapper in his striped prison outfit. As he walked to the electric chair, Zangara paused next to Chapman and handed him the three notebooks that contained his thirty-four-chapter autobiography, written in Italian, in longhand. "With a courtly bow, reminiscent of the days of old Italy, even with an almost ironical grace, he handed me these books, making the calm and confident announcement as if he were leaving for the ages a legacy of priceless value: 'This is the book.'"

Having been pronounced sane but "perverse," Zangara would be executed in the swiftest capital punishment in twentieth-century America. His head had been shaved for placement of the fatal electrode, a black hood was tied over his head, and his arms were strapped to the chair. Zangara then spoke his last words, powerfully and defiantly.

"Viva Italia! Viva Camorra! Goodbye to all poor people everywhere!"

Then, as if surprised that he was still alive, he said: "Push the button. Go ahead and push the button!"

"The execution of a man is unbelievably simple," Chapman later wrote. "No smoke, no burning flesh, no odor. Just a rigid body and shortly death. Witnesses quiet. Newsmen taking notes."

An autopsy on Zangara's body revealed a normal brain and a chronically diseased gallbladder. He was buried in an unmarked grave on the prison grounds at Raiford.

J. Edgar Hoover apparently never investigated any of the alleged ties between Zangara and either a national group of anarchists or Chicago organized crime figures. Characteristically, the nation's grandstanding top cop used the event to incite fear and thereby elevate his own stature and build power for his agency. As for the probe itself, Hoover showed no interest in determining whether Zangara acted alone, had accomplices, or was part of a larger conspiracy.

Had Zangara's bullet found its intended target—had Roosevelt been killed and Cermak lived—John Nance Garner would have become president, and there never would have been the New Deal that would revolutionize American government, business, culture, and society. Cermak, the boss of Chicago, was poised to dominate the political scene in that city for years to come. If he had survived, the powerful Richard Daley machine that would shape Illinois politics into the twenty-first century might never have risen.

"Had Giuseppe Zangara had steadier aim and a clearer shot in February of 1933, Franklin Roosevelt would be remembered now as a footnote to history instead of as the greatest President of the twentieth century," historian Geoffrey C. Ward wrote.

PART TWO

To Kill the New Deal

Fascism always comes through a vast pretense of socialism backed by Wall Street money.

—WILLIAM ALLEN WHITE, *SELECTED LETTERS OF*
WILLIAM ALLEN WHITE

A Good Beginning

On Monday, March 6, Roosevelt's first weekday in office, he learned of Cermak's death. That morning he attended the funeral of his attorney general–designate, the elderly Senator Thomas Walsh of Montana, who had died suddenly of a heart attack on the way to the inauguration. A widower, the seventy-two-year-old Walsh had traveled surreptitiously to Havana to marry a beautiful young Cuban woman and had been stricken while returning from Florida to Washington by rail. The deaths of both men came as a shock to Roosevelt at a moment when he needed to focus his full attention on the economic and social crisis at hand. Walsh, a distinguished statesman and brilliant attorney, had been instrumental in convincing the president to invoke the Trading with the Enemy Act, and Roosevelt felt the loss sorely.

That afternoon he hosted a governors' conference in the East Room of the White House, at which eighteen of the attendees signed a pledge expressing their "confidence in the leadership of the President" and beseeching Congress and all Americans to cooperate with the new administration. The body as a whole then adopted a resolution expressing its desire that Congress immediately grant him "such broad powers as may be necessary to enable the Executive to meet the present challenging emergency." In his meeting with the governors, Roosevelt obfuscated about his strategies for solving the bank emergency because he really did not yet know how the proposed legislation was going to shape up. While his advisers worked feverishly behind the scenes to create a banking bill, Roosevelt acted as a clearinghouse for all their ideas. Most of the bankers who had descended on Washington were sequestered with the shy and slight treasury secretary, William Woodin. Many were calling for the nationalization of the banking system, in which all the assets would be assembled into one central, government-owned national bank that would have branches throughout the country. The self-effacing Woodin, who was the former president of the American Car and Foundry Company and had switched parties in order to support Roosevelt, reached out across the aisle to high-level Republicans, former Hoover officials, and Wall Street financiers. He realized that the catastrophe required the best minds and ideas the country had to offer, and in that vein he sought urgent bipartisan cooperation, while keeping Roosevelt's left-leaning advisers "well in the background." Moley later said that they "were just a bunch of men trying to save the banking system," putting party politics on the back burner in favor of the common good. Moley's machinations in the process elicited acrimony among liberal members of the Brain Trust, who accused him of covertly grasping at power within the administration.

Woodin recognized that the underpinnings of the solvency crisis were, as President Hoover had repeatedly contended, a question of confidence. Still, the government couldn't simply issue scrip and expect that to reassure the public. To Woodin, the very concept of state and municipal scrips floating across the country was abysmal. A talented musician who had composed the "Franklin Delano Roosevelt March" for the previous Saturday's inauguration, Woodin quietly plucked his guitar while listening for hours to the proposals put forth by the steady stream of bankers.

By Tuesday morning, Woodin had settled on a plan that, ironically, was based on a draft prepared by Hoover's secretary of the treasury, Ogden Mills, on the last day of the Hoover presidency. In accordance with the Federal Reserve Act of 1913, the government would not simply print more money, but would produce Federal Reserve banknotes that were collateralized by bank assets rather than gold. "It won't frighten people," Woodin told Moley over breakfast. "It won't look like stage money. It will be money that looks like money."

During the frantic days of creating the Emergency Banking Act, which would "rescue the moribund corpse of American finance," as New Deal historian David Kennedy put it, the Roosevelt team worked around the clock, unable to sleep with such a daunting task at hand. "Only Roosevelt," Moley recalled, "preserved the air of a man who'd found a happy way of life." The rest of them had frayed nerves and short tempers, and had reached a level of exhaustion that obstructed clear thinking. "Confusion, haste, the dread of making mistakes, the consciousness of responsibility for the economic well-being of millions of people, made mortal inroads on the health of some of us . . . and left the rest of us ready to snap at our own images in the mirror," Moley wrote. But Roosevelt, with his placid temperament and optimistic fatalism, seemed not to have a care in the world. To him, things were going splendidly.

On Wednesday morning, March 8, Roosevelt held the first of what would be nearly a thousand press conferences, winning over the 125 reporters who made their way to the Oval Office. During the course of the Hoover administration, the relationship between the White House and the press corps had become a chilly standoff. Now, Roosevelt set out to create a lively give-and-take session of conviviality that would serve his political agenda, Americans' right to transparency, and journalists' need for riveting copy. As the newspapermen crowded in, the president greeted them individually, shaking hands and beaming his infectious smile. Seated at his desk, which was adorned with a bouquet of flowers, Roosevelt wore an elegant navy blue suit and stark white shirt. After a series of jokes and banter to lighten the mood, he got down to business and set the ground rules.

"I am told that what I am about to do will become impossible, but I am going to try it," he began, and then revealed his plan to hold twice-weekly press conferences to accommodate the newspapers' deadlines. Following a model he had devised as governor of New York, he set forth the guidelines: No radio coverage was allowed. His comments would be "on background" and reporters could not quote him directly unless they acquired verbal consent. He would not entertain any hypothetical questions. From time to time he would reveal information meant to be totally "off the record." As it turned out, Roosevelt was inadvertently setting journalistic precedents that would shape professional standards for the future, as well as creating the prototype for the modern presidential press conference—"the most amazing performance of its kind the White House has ever seen," enthused a *Baltimore Sun* reporter.

For thirty-five minutes he charmed and flattered them and gave a thumbnail overview of his forthcoming system of currency:

> We hope that when the banks reopen a great deal of the currency that was withdrawn for one purpose or another will find its way back. We have got to provide an adequate currency. Last Friday we would have had to provide it in the form of scrip, and probably some additional issues of Federal Bank notes. If things go along as we hope they will, the use of scrip can be very greatly curtailed, and the amounts of new Federal Bank issues, we hope, can be also limited to a very great extent. In other words, what you are coming to now really is a managed currency, the adequateness of which will depend on the conditions of the moment.

When reminded that he had promised "sound currency" in his inaugural address, he replied: "The real mark of delineation between sound and unsound is when the Government starts to pay its bills by starting printing presses," reasoning that to rescue failing banks with freshly minted scrip would undermine the larger economic recovery program. He stressed that the banking legislation was for emergency purposes—"We cannot write a permanent banking act for the nation in three days"—and when he concluded his press conference, the newsmen gave him a standing ovation.

That night, Woodin polished the final draft of the Emergency Banking Act to be submitted to the special session of Congress when it convened the following day. From eight thirty in the evening until one A.M. the following morning, Roosevelt, Woodin, and Moley discussed the bill with key senators and representatives. The bill conferred on the president nearly total authority over gold and foreign exchange transactions, basically legitimizing the action Roosevelt had already taken under the Trading with the Enemy Act. The U.S. Treasury would gradually reopen banks in the country under rigorous supervision, beginning with the most sound of the depositories. Less-solvent banks would receive support from the Federal Reserve. The most insolvent of institutions—an entire third class of bankrupt institutions—would not be permitted to reopen. The sweeping legislation sanctioned the government guarantee of all deposits in the banks that were allowed to reopen. The bill also expanded the authority of the Federal Reserve, granting it the right to issue currency backed by bank assets rather than by gold. As the governor of the

Federal Reserve of New York wrote in his diary, printed money was to be issued against "all kinds of junk, even the brass spittoons in old-fashioned country banks." Far from the radical alteration of the American capitalist system that many feared, it was, as Moley put it, a desperate effort to keep alive "the last remaining strength of the capitalist system."

At noon on Thursday, March 9—a hasty five days after the inauguration—Congress convened. Within moments it received a message from the president: "Our first task is to reopen all sound banks," he said. "I cannot too strongly urge upon the Congress the clear necessity for immediate action." The House of Representatives passed the bill unanimously on a voice vote without debate and without reading it, since it had not yet been printed and distributed. The Senate took longer, as Huey Long—who had taken to calling Roosevelt "Prince Franklin, Knight of the *Nourmahal*" and referring to Roosevelt's supporters as "his goddamned banker friends"— debated Carter Glass for several hours. Long, the champion of the "little county seat banks," advocated for the small depositors who would lose their life's savings under the legislation, which favored the strong New York banks that Long thought bore responsibility for the crisis. Long found it outrageous that only five thousand of the nation's banks—a mere 10 percent—would reopen, while the government would not protect another fifteen thousand. As ad hominem attacks flew between Long and Glass, who vehemently favored the legislation, the two almost came to fisticuffs, each calling the other a "sonofabitch." At one point, Glass, a caustic Virginian who was chairman of the Senate Banking and Currency Committee, slammed his fist on the desk and yelled at Long to "be more civil!" Finally, Long's nemesis, Majority Leader Joe Robinson, broke it up and called for a vote. The bill passed 73–7.

Never before had Congress acted with such alacrity and decisiveness. An hour after the bill's passage, Roosevelt signed it and immediately announced a schedule for reopening the banks. By the following Wednesday, he said, all of the banks in the country would open their doors, except for those that could not survive the scrutiny of Treasury Department examiners.

"The President drove the money-changers out of the Capitol on March 4," one congressman commented, "and they were all back on the 9th."

Roosevelt had conceived an ingenious scheme to restore confidence in the banking industry, announcing that the unpatriotic gold hoarders' names would be published. The press, he said, would identify anyone who had withdrawn gold coins or bullion in the previous four weeks. By Friday, March 10, more than four thousand people had redeposited three hundred million dollars in gold and gold certificates in New York banks alone to avoid public embarrassment.

The national mood during one of the most momentous weeks in American history "had running through it a broad streak of messianic authoritarianism," wrote Roosevelt biographer Kenneth S. Davis, ". . . a longing for the Leader, the Messiah in whom a passionate communal faith could be invested and who would take responsibility for everything, obviating the necessity for individual thought and decision."

The sense that such a yearning had been fulfilled was palpable, as the nation breathed a collective sigh of relief. Franklin Roosevelt's administration had "superbly risen to the occasion," gushed the *Wall Street Journal*. "It and the country still have incalculable tasks to perform before they can afford so much as to pause for breath. But together they have made a good beginning and there are times when a beginning is nearly everything."

CHAPTER TWENTY-THREE

Time for Beer

PRESIDENT ROOSEVELT HAD PLANNED TO RUSH through the banking legislation and send Congress home. But encouraged by the rapid congressional response, he decided to use the momentum to push his domestic agenda, setting off what would go down in history as the famous "Hundred Days"—the exact period of time between the opening and closing of the special session of the Seventy-third Congress. Roosevelt had borrowed the term, which had the intriguing ring of both victory and defeat, from the famous hundred-day Waterloo campaign in the Napoleonic Wars of more than a century earlier. Even Roosevelt had no idea how prescient the comparison would be, as Napoleon's heroic escape from exile led him into the most severe trial of his life. Exhilarated by how fast, bipartisan, and enthusiastic the legislators were, and pressed by his cabinet, which was urging him to seize the opportunity this presidential honeymoon offered, he decided to keep them in session until his program was enacted. Considering that his program wasn't fully formulated, it was an audacious move, and the challenge thrilled him.

Drawing on the ideas of dozens of academics, economists, sociologists, labor leaders, populists, and reformers, Roosevelt intended to initiate a series of emergency relief programs to stimulate the economy and get Americans back to work. On Friday, March 10, he quickly sent Congress

"A Bill to Maintain the Credit of the United States Government," which would become known as the Economy Bill. Drafted just one day earlier, it proposed cutting all government salaries by 15 percent—including those of the president and members of Congress—and reducing veterans' pensions, which, in 1933, accounted for nearly a quarter of the federal budget being paid out to 1 percent of the population. The legislation would become the centerpiece of Roosevelt's economic recovery policy, which was based on the commitment to federal solvency.

"If the Congress chooses to vest me with this responsibility it will be exercised in a spirit of justice to all, of sympathy to those who are in need and of maintaining inviolate the basic welfare of the United States," Roosevelt promised. The United States had "been on the road toward bankruptcy" for the past three years, Roosevelt said in his message to Congress, and "immediate action" was necessary to avoid economic collapse.

Roundly embraced by fiscal conservatives, the bill provoked outrage among veterans and their powerful American Legion and Veterans of Foreign Wars lobby. Mississippi Democrat "Lightnin'" John Rankin avowed that World War I veterans shouldn't be penalized for the mistakes of bankers. Huey Long, by now predictably antagonistic to the Roosevelt agenda, rushed to oppose it as well. "Talk of balancing the budget! Let them balance the budget by scraping a little off the profiteers' profits from the war." When it became clear that the Democratic caucus was going to abandon him, Roosevelt resorted to the brilliant political instincts that had elevated him to the presidency. Working masterfully with conservative Democrats and fiscally minded Republicans, Roosevelt maneuvered passage of the bill on Saturday—a mere week after his inauguration—by a vote of 266–138.

Meanwhile, Roosevelt's Brain Trust hastily focused on recovery programs for public works, the unemployed, and the agricultural and manufacturing industries. On Sunday evening, March 12, he would take his ideas to the airwaves to rally support from the American public for his amorphous and nascent agenda and to reassure them that the country was back on track. He announced his plan for a national radio address "to explain clearly and in simple language to all of you just what has been achieved and the sound reasons which underlie this declaration."

An estimated sixty million citizens, clustered around seventeen million radios, heard the first "fireside chat." As lore has it, the new president had seen a laborer working outside a White House window and the idea had come to him to write some remarks directed at this man. "I decided

I'd try to make a speech that this workman could understand," he told Louis Howe. "I really made the speech to him." He had selected Robert Trout of the Columbia Broadcasting System's Washington station to be the announcer, given his euphonious voice and friendly demeanor. Welcoming the listeners with his mellifluous delivery, Trout told them that "the President wants to come into your home and sit at your fireside for a little fireside chat." Speaking into the microphones installed in front of a roaring fire in the Diplomatic Reception Room, the president entered the living rooms of millions.

With his rich tenor voice—which Hollywood actress Miriam Howell thought "almost as good as Walter Huston['s]"—Roosevelt explained the intricacies of the banking industry. Neither condescending nor patronizing, like a patient country doctor or loving father, he selected his words carefully to restore confidence, presenting his timetable for reopening the banks and commending both Democratic and Republican members of Congress for their swift and forceful action to save the nation.

> I want to talk for a few minutes with the people of the United States about banking—with the comparatively few who understand the mechanics of banking but more particularly with the overwhelming majority who use banks for the making of deposits and the drawing of checks. I want to tell you what has been done in the last few days, why it was done, and what the next steps are going to be.
>
> Because of the undermined confidence on the part of the public, there was a general rush by a large portion of our population to turn bank deposits into currency or gold—a rush so great that the soundest banks could not get enough currency to meet the demand. The reason for this was that on the spur of the moment it was, of course, impossible to sell perfectly sound assets of a bank and convert them into cash except at panic prices far below their real value.
>
> . . . [We] start tomorrow, Monday, with the opening of the banks in twelve Federal Reserve Bank cities . . . This will be followed on Tuesday by the resumption of all their functions by banks already found to be sound in cities where there are recognized clearing houses . . . On Wednesday and succeeding days banks in smaller places all over the country will resume business . . . I can

assure you that it is safer to keep your money in a reopened bank than under the mattress.

Rather than besmirch all of the nation's bankers, he distinguished between those who were crooked and those who were victimized.

> Some of our bankers had shown themselves either incompetent or dishonest . . . They had used the money entrusted to them in speculations and unwise loans. This was, of course, not true in the vast majority of our banks, but it was true in enough of them to shock people for a time into a sense of insecurity . . . It was the Government's job to straighten out this situation . . . And the job's being performed . . . Confidence and courage are the essentials of success in carrying out our plan. You . . . must have faith; you must not be stampeded by rumors or guesses. Let us unite in banishing fear. It is your problem no less than it is mine. Together we cannot fail.

"Our President took such a dry subject as banking," Will Rogers wrote in the *New York Times*, ". . . and made everyone understand it, even the bankers." A stunning departure from the stuffy and pedantic addresses of his predecessors, Roosevelt's first radio chat signaled a revolutionary use of mass media technology, and the transformative power of the radio was instantly apparent. Forever changing the relationship between the government and the governed, the radio address had the immediate effect of restoring certainty in a jittery nation. "People edge their chairs up to the radio," the novelist John Dos Passos said of the historic drama. "There is a man leaning across his desk, speaking clearly and cordially so that you and me will completely understand that he has his fingers on all the switchboards of the federal government, operating the intricate machinery of the departments, drafting codes and regulations and bills for the benefit of you and me worried about things, sitting close to the radio in small houses on rainy nights, for the benefit of us wagearners, us homeowners, us farmers, us mechanics, us miners, us mortgagees, us processors, us mortgageholders, us bank depositors, us consumers, retail merchants, bankers, brokers, stockholders, bondholders, creditors, debtors, jobless and jobholders. 'Not a sparrow falleth but . . .'"

Accurately gauging the mood of the country and the responsiveness of Congress, Roosevelt capitalized on the good will he was afforded. First he assuaged the fears of a terrified nation, inspiring confidence, hope, and camaraderie. He then moved quickly to send a historic number of bills to Congress—landmark legislation that would mark the beginning of the New Deal. "Consummate politician that he was," his biographer Jean Edward Smith wrote, "Roosevelt feinted right before turning left."

While historians have debated how much of the New Deal Roosevelt had in mind on taking office, those closest to him depicted a period of extreme fluidity. To see policies of the early legislation as "the result of a unified plan," Moley wrote, "was to believe that the accumulation of stuffed snakes, baseball pictures, school flags, old tennis shoes, carpenter's tools, geometry books, and chemistry sets in a boy's bedroom could have been put there by an interior decorator."

For his part, Roosevelt compared himself to a football quarterback who had to make quick decisions based on the results of the first move. In one of his early press conferences he said, "Future plays will depend on how the next one works." Such a remark emblemized the invention and improvisation of the New Deal. A shining example of this innovative approach to governing was the president's sudden repeal of Prohibition. It began with dinner at the White House that Sunday evening, before his first radio chat, as he supped with a few close friends. "I think this would be a good time for beer," Roosevelt said. That, as his friends well knew, meant he was ready to send to Congress a bill to amend the Volstead Act—the National Prohibition Act that, since 1919, had prohibited the production, sale, and transport of alcohol and in Roosevelt's view fostered racketeering.

Yet another adroit political move, Roosevelt's proposed modification of the Volstead Act to legalize beer of 3.2 percent alcoholic content was a bill that the Senate would be eager to pass—thereby preempting the possibility that it might stall on the economy bill. By sending to Congress a wildly popular bill, Roosevelt prevented a drawn-out Senate debate on the controversial economy legislation, knowing that the senators could not turn to the exciting new business at hand until they had dealt with the economy. His brief, seventy-two-word message was greeted with whoops and hollers on the floor of Congress.

> I recommend to the Congress the passage of legislation for the
> immediate modification of the Volstead Act, in order to legalize
> the manufacture and sale of beer and other beverages of such al-
> coholic content as is permissible under the Constitution; and to

provide through such manufacture and sale, by substantial taxes,
a proper and much-needed revenue for the Government.

I deem action at this time to be of the highest importance.

On Wednesday, March 15, the Senate passed the economy bill with a
62–13 vote. The next day, the beer-wine legislation passed into law as
well. Arguably one of the most sweeping and influential acts of 1933—the
opening shot in what would result in the repeal of Prohibition a few
months later—the amendment changed American culture in deep and
abiding ways. With the repeal would come a reassessment of the role that
government should play in moral reform. Even more significantly, it
would shape how government would deal with the gangster interests that
had flourished under the illegal and underground bootleg system—"the
government is going to muscle in on your racket," a fictional Roosevelt
tells a fictional Al Capone in a Hollywood movie.

For now, the new bill mostly served to make the budget cuts, bank failures, and bread lines less dreary. Fascists and Communists were thrown off
the front pages. Newspaper editors estimated that during the first twenty-
four hours of the new legislation "the amount of beer sold in the United
States . . . would float a battleship," as *Newsweek* put it, and bring in federal
income ranging from seven and a half million to ten million dollars on the
first day since 1920 that beer was sold legally.

"In the midst of the Depression it was a note of hope that something
would be better," author Studs Terkel said of the moment.

The nation was giddy in its response to their deliverer. "Roosevelt is the
greatest leader since Jesus Christ," a prominent businessman was quoted as
saying. "I hope God will forgive me for voting for Hoover."

CHAPTER TWENTY-FOUR

A Gang of Common Criminals

ROOSEVELT'S FIRST TWO WEEKS IN OFFICE seemed to herald a new America in which despondency was replaced with gusto, inertia with activity. It was as if the president's inveterate cheeriness had rubbed off on everyone. "For the first time since we can remember we are trying to be a unified people," said Labor Secretary Frances Perkins.

Initially the economy recovered rapidly. By March 15, 1933, 76 percent of the country's Federal Reserve member banks had reopened. The following day, the New York Stock Exchange, which had been dark for ten days, opened for business, marking the beginning of a new bull market in which the Dow jumped a historic 15 percent. More than a billion dollars in cash had been redeposited in the nation's banks and the hoarding had come to a standstill—or so it appeared.

The situation must have galled Herbert Hoover, who, embittered and disheartened, had retreated to his Palo Alto, California, home. "A bank rescue plan introduced by Roosevelt, a man he despised, drafted by Hoover's own people on principles he had originally proposed, had in the space of a week restored confidence that had eluded poor old Hoover in three years of fighting the Depression," said one account.

However, the glowing relationship between Roosevelt and the "banksters" he had just saved would not last. Inevitably, their temporary sense of relief gave way to their characteristic sense of entitlement, and they began to bristle at Roosevelt's dictatorial control of their industry. "The bankers were aware that they had put their heads into the lion's jaws and at first tried to be friendly," wrote Matthew Josephson, a Wall Street insider turned journalist. While at the beginning of the presidency there was "sort of a love fest between Roosevelt and the House of Morgan," by late spring the bloom was off the rose. Recognizing the government bailout as an opening salvo in a battle that would pit government regulation against unfettered capitalism, Wall Street—the bogeyman of the Depression— jostled to return to its pre-crash supremacy.

"White-shoe Wall street suddenly seemed no better than a gang of com- mon criminals, skimmers, double-dealers, and confidence men," said one historian, and Roosevelt, although a member of the same patrician class, could not ignore the populist impulse to hold them accountable. The House of Morgan, more than any other firm, emblemized the greed, chicanery, and rampant corruption of finance capitalism. Promising to restrain the oligarchy that had strangled the nation's economy, Roosevelt threw his sup- port behind a fiery Italian-born lawyer named Ferdinand Pecora. As chief counsel to the Senate Committee on Banking and Currency in its inquiry into the cause of the 1929 stock market crash, the diminutive Pecora was the guiding force behind the most successful congressional investigation in American history. In Pecora's world, no one was above the law, and subpoe- naed witnesses who appeared before the committee "in imposing succes- sion," as he later wrote in his memoir, *Wall Street Under Oath*, were "the demigods of Wall Street, men whose names were household words, but whose personalities and affairs were frequently shrouded in deep, aristo- cratic mystery . . . Never before in the history of the United States had so much wealth and power been required to render a public accounting."

That Roosevelt chose to back Pecora 100 percent—giving muscle to a probe that had foundered under the Hoover regime—signaled a serious- ness of presidential purpose that the Wall Street titans had gravely under- estimated. Heir to the 1913 Pujo Committee investigation into the ruling-class "money trust" believed to dominate the nation's economy, the Pecora Committee had an even broader mandate. U.S. Supreme Court Justice Louis Brandeis had written a series of articles for *Harper's Weekly* that drew from the Pujo findings and charged that a consortium of in- vestment bankers and insurance companies were conspiring to control American industry through the use of "other people's money."

In the twenty intervening years since Louisiana congressman Arsène Pujo's investigative committee first shed light on Wall Street practices, the American economy had drastically worsened. More than half of the fifty billion dollars' worth of stocks sold in the country during the 1920s had been "undesirable or worthless," according to the House Commerce Committee. "Securities houses of the most reputable banks manifoldly increased their profits at the expense of their own clients," according to an official account of the nation's banking and securities condition. "Powerful investment bankers continued to fill key corporations' boards of directors. Overly optimistic loan programs threatened vast banking chains with domino-like collapse. Utility holding companies teetered precariously in an intricate system of interlocking directorates with little regard for corporate efficiency or local requirements. Concurrently, the federal government remained willfully ignorant of stock exchange and private banking operations."

Warning that "we must break the Money Trust or the Money Trust will break us," Brandeis's treatise became a battle cry for political and financial activists of the early 1930s. His articles had been published in book form in 1914 under the title *Other People's Money and How the Bankers Use It*, which became an instant bestseller when it was reprinted in 1933. The new edition was ubiquitous on Capitol Hill, with copies found in various committee rooms as "old and young liberals alike carried its message to Washington with the new Roosevelt Administration."

Although Florida senator Duncan U. Fletcher was chairman of the Banking and Currency Committee, it was the slight but indomitable Sicilian with the flashy black pompadour who would be the committee investigation's namesake. By May 1933, every newspaper in America carried sensational front-page stories about the venality and mendacity of the nation's most prestigious bankers, and Pecora's fame was comparable to that of rock stars of later generations. The press was riveted by the probe, showering Pecora with publicity in his giant-slaying pursuits—the feisty immigrant taking on the dour blue-blooded tycoons. With the full support of Congress and the president himself, Pecora had stronger subpoena powers than had ever been granted in a congressional investigation. If that were not enough—if witnesses balked or stonewalled, as they were wont to do—he "marched his staff directly into the banks and brokerage houses" and gathered whatever material he needed.

He called the financiers before the committee and elicited gripping confessions of depravity, incompetence, self-dealing, and irresponsibility.

Testimony revealed how Wall Street insiders hired publicity agents, journalists, and radio announcers to hawk certain stocks, thereby manipulating
the market; how National City Bank (forerunner of today's Citigroup) sold
worthless bonds; how bankers systematically abandoned their fiduciary responsibilities; and how J. P. Morgan, who wielded extreme personal and
unregulated power over billions of dollars in profits, created elaborate
machinations to dodge taxes. Morgan partners, in what was effectively a
cozy and exclusive men's club, held 126 directorships in eighty-nine corporations. Most infuriating to the Depression-era public were the dispropor-
tionate compensations and bonuses to those who had deceived and thieved
common Americans. Dubbed the "hellhound of Wall Street" for his relentless pursuit and exposé of its underbelly, Pecora and his committee would
change the relationship between Washington and Wall Street—at least for
a few decades.

When J. P. Morgan Jr. took the witness stand on May 23 in the committee's marble-floored conference room, he became symbol and metaphor for
what went wrong in America. His father, the founder of the great Anglo-
Saxon banking firm J. P. Morgan and Company, commonly known as the
House of Morgan, had been called before the Pujo Committee twenty years
earlier and had managed to mockingly evade substantive scrutiny. Now the
son appeared "less than lordly," fidgeting, and "flushed with annoyance and
embarrassment," according to one account. Pecora had uncovered devastating documentation of Morgan's "preferred list" of "our close friends." Morgan offered these well-placed men—including former president Calvin
Coolidge, Herbert Hoover's treasury secretary, Woodrow Wilson's treasury and war secretaries, U.S. Army General John J. Pershing, the president
of the U.S. Chamber of Commerce, and the chairmen of both the Democratic and Republican National Committees—common stock prices at
nearly half their current market value. "It is nothing more or nothing less
than bribery," railed Republican governor Alfred M. Landon of Kansas of
the windfalls that averaged fifteen thousand to twenty thousand dollars
each. Republican senator James Couzens of Michigan was appalled at the
bipartisan financial world that was exposed, with leaders of both parties
groveling to the House of Morgan. "When it comes to money, there are no
Republicans or Democrats. Rich men never fight each other seriously.
There is the finest coalition of all parties when it comes to control of the
Treasury of the United States."

The most headline-grabbing testimony by Morgan was the revelation that neither Morgan nor any of his partners had paid income tax for the past three years, and he intended to rely on loopholes to avoid paying any in 1933. At a moment when Roosevelt was determined to raise $220 million by an increase in individual income tax rates, Morgan's haughty defiance would galvanize the nation in its disgust for the establishment regime and set the stage for authentic reform.

Among those most vocal in pursuit of the Wall Street money changers were Father Charles Coughlin and Huey Long, who both stood ready to hijack the populist agenda away from Roosevelt. Long stridently accused Roosevelt of packing the Treasury Department with appointees from the House of Morgan. In a blistering speech on the floor of the Senate, which he called "Our Constant Rulers," Long lamented the influence that the "bloated masters of fortune and power" enjoyed in the new administration. "Instead of being out of the temple, they not only inject themselves in the temple but they sit in the seats of the mighty and pass judgment on the balance of us who waged that fight to deliver the country back to the American people." Long charged that Morgan owned a hundred suits— "each one stolen from the back of a workingman." Such an allegation was especially ironic considering Long's own sartorial extravagance.

Like Long, Coughlin began to backtrack from his initial support of Roosevelt. He soon trotted out the timeworn conspiracy theories, first put forth by Henry Ford during World War I, that the American and British financiers connived to draw America into the war. Drawing on the anti-European isolationist trends that erupt every few decades in America, Coughlin made the leap from criticizing the debased "international bankers" to the international *Jewish* bankers. At first he praised Roosevelt's New Deal as "Christ's Deal," but once he became convinced that Roosevelt was failing to drive the "shylock banksters"—widely believed to be primarily Jewish—"from the temple," he began referring to it as the "Jew Deal." To the priest from the Church of the Little Flowers, bankers were synonymous with Communists, and he used his radio pulpit—reaching as many as forty million people—to incite fear of a Judeo-Masonic led world domination plot.

CHAPTER TWENTY-FIVE

Traitor to His Class

THE ATTACKS ON ROOSEVELT BY Huey Long and Charles Coughlin were acutely misdirected, as it was Roosevelt who had first singled out the "unscrupulous money changers" for special derision. In his inaugural address, then in the fireside chat, FDR had excoriated the bankers for their dishonesty and incompetence. It was Roosevelt who had complained that "fewer than three dozen private banking houses and stock-selling adjuncts in the commercial banks have directed the flow of capital within the country and outside it," and who had vowed, while campaigning for the presidency, to implode the "economic oligarchy." It was Roosevelt who had emboldened Pecora, thrown his invincible backing behind Pecora's committee, and immensely enjoyed watching the public airing of Wall Street's dirty laundry. It was Roosevelt who had pledged vigorous government intervention, promised to level and democratize the toxic system, and set his team of economic advisers on a course to create reform legislation.

Senator Couzens, who, as a member of the Committee on Banking and Currency, was instrumental in bolstering Pecora, believed that Roosevelt personally urged the Wall Street inquiry to garner congressional and public support for his New Deal legislation. Throughout the probe, Roosevelt, like Pecora, accumulated powerful and vindictive enemies, and his forceful challenge to the patrician powers-that-be would inspire the charge that he was a "traitor to his class." While much would be made of this accusation, in fact it was the other way around: His class would betray *him*. The "captains of Wall Street, still within the shadow of panic and depression, gave utterance to little outspoken criticism of the New Deal," Pecora later wrote. "Their cry then was that we were all victims of a common calamity, due not to bankers' guilt, but to human fallibility." But as Roosevelt's policies and reforms were manifested, these "captains" would regard Roosevelt with captiousness and turn ferociously against him and his New Deal.

The fifty-one-year-old Pecora had officially begun his investigation in February 1933, following the first bank moratorium declared by the governor of Michigan. Once Roosevelt had been inaugurated and the Senate had begun rushing through his first hundred days of legislation, Pecora accelerated the inquiry, which paved the way for the passage of the groundbreaking Glass-Steagall banking reform bill. Amassing more than twelve thousand pages of bank documents, culling private income tax records, and subpoenaing internal data from investment firms, Pecora's staff of attorneys and accountants pored over the material, which was stored in trunks guarded by armed Bureau of Investigation agents. Evidence was overwhelming that depositors were bilked when commercial and investment banks gambled their funds in the stock market, and that unethical manipulation and insidious conflicts of interest had triggered the 1929 crash. Pecora summarized the committee's findings:

> The testimony had brought to light a shocking corruption in our banking system, a widespread repudiation of old fashioned standards of honesty and fair dealing in the creation and sale of securities, and a merciless exploitation of the vicious possibilities of intricate corporate chicanery. The public had been deeply aroused by the spectacle of cynical disregard of fiduciary duty on the part of many of its most respected leaders; of directors, who conveniently subordinated their official obligations to an avid pursuit of personal gain; of great banks, which combined the functions of a bank with those of a stock jobber; of supposedly impartial public markets for the sale of securities, actually operated as private clubs for the individual benefits of their members.

On May 25, while J. P. Morgan was still testifying before Congress, the Senate passed the historic Glass-Steagall Act, requiring banks to eliminate securities operations; guaranteeing individual bank deposits up to $2,500, which provided security to the average citizen; allowing the Federal Reserve Board to set interest rates; and creating the Federal Deposit Insurance Corporation (FDIC). Roosevelt proudly pointed to that legislation and other reform measures, claiming they "had brought about the transfer of the financial capital of the United States from Wall Street to Washington." Thanks to Roosevelt's decree, the supply of hoarded gold had been returned to the central bank and going off the gold standard stripped international bankers of their unchecked power. Meanwhile, the stock market was recovering, the dollar was rising in the international money market, and wheat and cotton prices were climbing as a result of an emergency farm relief bill allowing the administration to subsidize the farm economy—all of which made "a happy springtime for the New Deal," as one Wall Street historian said. Even Morgan congratulated Roosevelt for taking the country off gold, and one Morgan financier wrote the president: "Your action in going off gold saved the country from complete collapse. It was vitally necessary and the most important of all helpful things you have done."

But the bankers who had been so enthralled with Roosevelt when he was rescuing the banks and saving the private enterprise system now intensely opposed his experimental corrective measures. Wall Street critics began calling him a "demagogue" and a "fascist," and his antagonist Al Smith referred to the new currency as the "baloney dollar."

By late May—barely three months after FDR took office—the "happy springtime" was over and the backlash against him was under way. When Roosevelt became president, one out of every four heads-of-household was unemployed. He had vowed to restore the country to prosperity, to put Americans back to work, and to build the nation's infrastructure, and by May 1933 he had already taken numerous steps in that direction—a groundbreaking experiment that spurred his enemies into action.

The nation's reactionary fringe, on both the Left and the Right, began to mobilize to attack him personally and to undermine his presidency. In addition to his predictable Wall Street adversaries, political dissidents rose to challenge him. The Left contended that his policies were not doing enough to redistribute the nation's wealth, with one prominent socialist claiming that Roosevelt's efforts to fix the economy were like "trying to cure tuberculosis with cough-drops" and one of America's top Communists writing that "Mr. Roosevelt is nothing more or less than a lightning rod for capitalism to protect it from danger." The Right, calling him a "Social-ist" or "Communist," claimed that Roosevelt had concentrated too much power in the government rather than the individual and was interfering with free market capitalism. "Although some people mistakenly identi-fied Roosevelt as a Communist or a Socialist," two twentieth-century scholars wrote, "they were usually people who could not have recognized a Communist or a Socialist had they met one in the street. Communists and Socialists never mistook Roosevelt for one of their own. In fact, Roo-sevelt was so unconvincing a liberal . . . that even liberals refused to claim him."

Though stung by the charge that he was a traitor to his class, Roose-velt took the denunciation in stride, telling journalists that public and private attacks against the New Deal had become routine. Undeterred, he remained focused on his domestic agenda, which received an ironic boost with the reappearance in Washington of the Bonus Army veterans.

Nearly all the Bonus marchers had returned to their homes after the routing by General MacArthur the previous summer, vowing as they re-treated that their fight was not over. On May 9, 1933, several hundred straggled into Washington prompted by elements of the right and left wings of the veterans organizations. Within a week, more than three thou-sand had arrived. Desperately poor, disaffected, and angry at their treat-ment at the hands of President Hoover, they were a pathetic lot. Roosevelt instinctively saw a political opportunity at hand and moved adroitly to use his pet project—the Civilian Conservation Corps (CCC)—to solve the veterans' dilemma. The ingenious CCC was Roosevelt's own idea for put-ting a quarter million unmarried men between the ages of eighteen and twenty-five to work. The program was designed to get "the wild boys of the road," menacing itinerant hoboes, and the unemployed and troublesome young men of the cities to work in the national forests—in what became known as Roosevelt's "Tree Army." He was zealous about the concept that would draft 250,000 men into public service to plant trees, blaze trails, fight fires, erect flood control devices in national parks, and improve beaches, parks, and historic battlefields. Roosevelt had impulsively rushed the legis-lation, which combined his love of conservation with his commitment to job creation and full employment, personally ushering it through both houses of Congress—"the way I did on beer," he told Moley.

The U.S. Army, under a civilian administrator, supervised the thousands of young men who were assigned to more than 1,500 camps throughout the country, while Roosevelt delegated authority for employee recruitment to the Department of Labor and for work projects to the Departments of Interior and Agriculture. The men were paid thirty dollars a month and were required to send at least twenty-two dollars back to their families, if they were on relief. The president of the American Federation of Labor, William Green, was initially appalled that the men would only be paid a dollar a day and worried that the program would undermine unions. Calling it "Fascism, Hitlerism, and Sovietism," Green also strongly opposed the military regimentation of the labor force, likening it to that in Mussolini's Italy. Roosevelt dismissed Green's complaints as "utter rubbish" and won Green's eventual support when he appointed a vice president of the Machinists' Union to head the CCC.

The Bonus veterans were resentful that they were too old to qualify for the work project. To add insult to injury, Roosevelt's Economy Act would further reduce their pensions. J. Edgar Hoover brought an alarming report to the attorney general that more than 333,000 armed veterans who were members of an organization called the Oppressed People of the Nation were planning a march on Washington. As Hoover and other law enforcement officials monitored the left wing and right wing within the Bonus Army, whose rifts they feared could escalate into violence, Roosevelt sought a détente. Determined to strike a bold departure from his predecessor's colossal bungling, he directed his personal troubleshooter, Louis Howe, the pragmatic former newspaperman, to arrange for the veterans to be sheltered comfortably at Fort Hunt. At the abandoned Army camp near Mount Vernon in Virginia, the men would be served three meals a day and serenaded by the Navy Band. "See that they have good food and shelter and above all good, hot coffee to drink. There's nothing that makes people feel as welcome as a steaming cup of coffee," Roosevelt told Howe. Under Howe's direction, six hundred tents with latrines, showers, and mess halls were erected at the camp, as was a medical facility.

It was Howe who came up with the innovative idea of sending the First Lady into the camp to greet the men and serve them coffee. Having been revolted by the tear gassing and bayonetting of the penniless veterans by MacArthur's troops, Eleanor was eager to do whatever she could "to prevent a similar tragedy." When Howe "played his master card" and asked her to drive him to the camp in Virginia one rainy day, she readily agreed. Howe told her to go "in there and talk to those men, get their gripes, if any, make a tour of the camp and tell them that Franklin sent you out to see about them. Don't forget that—be sure to tell them that Franklin sent you. Inspect their quarters and get the complete story."

"I got out and walked over to where I saw a line-up of men waiting for food," Eleanor later wrote. "They looked at me curiously and one of them asked my name and what I wanted. When I said I just wanted to see how they were getting on, they asked me to join them." Her Secret Service agents were apoplectic upon learning of the outing, providing her and Howe with pistols to be carried on future excursions into the populace. But she assuaged the bodyguards' fears. The veterans had welcomed her warmly, and soon she was leading them in wartime songs. She visited their living quarters and the makeshift hospital, and apologized to them that she bore no knowledge about their bonuses. They cheered and applauded her as she left the camp. "Hoover sent the army. Roosevelt sent his wife," said one veteran who grasped the significance of the gesture.

In a stroke of genius, Roosevelt waived the CCC age requirement to allow veterans a decade older to enroll in the program. While some of the veterans' leaders rebuffed the proposition—"It's like selling yourself into slavery," said one—more than 2,600 of the 3,000 Bonus marchers chose to enter the CCC. The rest were given free rail transportation back to their homes. Eventually more than 25,000 veterans would accept the government's offer, thus defusing a potentially volatile situation. Howe "had been anxiously heading off trouble for Franklin Roosevelt for 20 years," his biographer wrote. "His most successful coup was his handling of the new Bonus Army."

Ultimately, Roosevelt would ignore the original requirements of the CCC in an effort to stave off poverty for older married men in various walks of life. He extended the benefits to 14,400 Native Americans whose farms had been ravaged by drought and who were allowed to remain at home rather than join one of the CCC camps. He also hired nearly 25,000 unemployed foresters and lumbermen, at civil service wages, to supervise the camps.

The CCC would be one of the New Deal's most successful triumphs, eventually employing three million men—mostly white, urban youths averaging nineteen years of age. They would thin four million acres of trees, develop eight hundred state parks, stock lakes with a billion fish, plant three billion trees, build thirty thousand wildlife shelters, lay 12,000 miles of telephone poles, and clear 125,000 miles of trails from Texas to Canada. Roosevelt was rightfully proud of his brainchild, which reduced crime in the nation's cities by giving young impoverished men a sense of purpose while inspiring hundreds of similar state and federal community projects—"leaving no doubt that the father of national service in the United States was FDR," as one account concluded.

When Roosevelt visited the camps, the workers swarmed to greet him, eager to pay their respects and express their gratitude. "At each camp Roosevelt saw a neat line of army tents set up along a company street and about two hundred tanned young men who stood at attention until an army sergeant dismissed them so they could rush up to the President's car and shake his hand," according to one description of his tour.

"All you have to do is to look at the boys themselves to see that the camps . . . are a success," Roosevelt said with satisfaction.

CHAPTER TWENTY-SIX

A Balanced Civilization

THE WHITE HOUSE, LIKE THE REST of America, came to life when Franklin and Eleanor took over. The somber rooms of the Hoover occupation were now bubbling with laughter, the hallways bursting with frolicking children, and the bedchambers filled with a continuous influx of guests. Not since the previous Roosevelt presidency had the White House been such a vibrant headquarters of gaiety, banter, conviviality, and entertainment. With his mischievous sense of humor and devotion to his sacrosanct cocktail, the president himself set the tone. The staid decorum of previous administrations gave way to an informality reminiscent of the Andrew Jackson era a hundred years earlier.

The Roosevelts brought with them a lifestyle that had been honed at the governor's mansion in Albany, where Eleanor, in particular, constantly strived for a balance between private and public life. It was Eleanor who struggled to maintain a semblance of family normality, while Roosevelt relished the chaos with a more-the-merrier attitude. Both thrived on the intellectual stimulation of the ceaseless socializing, though Eleanor, as the daughter of an alcoholic, eschewed the regular evening mixers. Eleanor oversaw the cuisine, planning meals based on traditional American recipes and instilling the same frugality that restrained other Depression-era housewives. She decided it would be "highly appropriate to serve purely American dishes at the White House," she said in her first interview. "I want to work out some meals that consist entirely of American food, prepared in the American manner, from American products." Gone were the seven-course meals, the formal dinner attire, and the pretentious trappings of footmen and butlers that had attended the Hoover presidency. One guest of the Roosevelts reported receiving a meager dessert consisting of a slice of pineapple topped with whipped cream, two maraschino cherries, and one walnut—three nights in a row.

Roosevelt had asked his wife to cut the White House operating expenses by 25 percent, in keeping with his call for national sacrifice. She efficiently managed to fit her large family—which now included two grandchildren—into the small living quarters and to find space for other friends and employees who would be full-time residents. Marguerite "Missy" Le Hand, Roosevelt's longtime secretary, moved into the former housekeeper's quarters. Eleanor's closest friend, Lorena Hickok, who had resigned from the Associated Press when she felt her personal relationship with Eleanor clouded her objectivity, took over an upstairs bedroom. Resembling a boardinghouse more than a presidential mansion, the place was a twenty-four-hour hub of activity; one Washington traditionalist derisively described the atmosphere as being like "Saturday night at a country hotel." Roosevelt reserved the best guest suite, where Abraham Lincoln had signed the Emancipation Proclamation, to host those he was courting politically.

The president's typical sixteen-hour day involved a firmly structured routine that necessarily revolved around his infirmity. He awakened at eight thirty every morning and took breakfast in bed. After finishing his eggs, toast, and orange juice, he would settle in with five morning newspapers and a strong cup of coffee, and light the first of his forty Camel cigarettes of the day, which he would slip into a long ivory holder. Cartoonists made great hay of the affectation, the caricatured portraits depicting an insouciant Roosevelt gripping the holder between his front teeth, flashing a wide grin with his chin lifted haughtily. Once he had read all the gazettes from Washington, New York, and Baltimore, he would receive Moley and Howe and give them instructions for the day. As his valet helped him with his toilette and into his braces, his press and appointment secretaries would drop by his bedroom to get their marching orders, often conferring with him while he was shaving. His wife and children would stop by as well and chat for a few minutes as he conducted presidential business.

At ten thirty A.M. he would be wheeled to his office, where he would remain at his desk throughout the day and often into the evening, eating a light lunch of hash with one poached egg, which cost the taxpayers nineteen cents. At the beginning of his presidency, he would meet visitors at fifteen-minute intervals. His open-door policy would frequently result in overlapping appointments and an anteroom overflowing with people from all walks of life, which often flustered them but bothered him not at all. Between two and three P.M. he would dictate correspondence, sign official documents, review the letters and telegrams his secretary had culled from the thousands that arrived daily, and make telephone calls to members of Congress. From three until five he would hold cabinet meetings and twice-weekly press conferences. Several afternoons he would swim in the new White House pool, joined alternately by Eleanor, his secretaries, and children—a pastime so vital to his health that it carried a top priority in his scheduling. The celebrated cocktail hour was inviolable; he insisted on lighthearted banter, risqué jokes, and stiff martinis. Dinners were generally relaxed and unceremonious events with a mix of family, friends, journalists, and dignitaries, and they would often be followed by film screenings. He loved movies, especially the romances starring his favorite actress, the steamy and politically liberal Myrna Loy. He would then return to his office for several more hours of work and finally retire around midnight, propped up in bed and surrounded by diplomatic cables, magazines, and murder mysteries.

He leaped at the opportunities for afternoon outings when they arose, summoning the presidential yacht, the *Sequoia*, for jaunts down the Potomac to the Chesapeake Bay. But even those coveted getaways usually included an entourage of staff and advisers, ensuring that his work accompanied him. He absolutely loved being president—"Wouldn't anybody?" he asked a visitor—and ran his operation like a "one-man show." He was surrounded by a gaggle of bright young bachelors who poured into the nation's capital to work for the dynamic new administration and who created an air of youthful exuberance. Many, like Dean Acheson, Lyndon Johnson, Abe Fortas, J. W. Fulbright, Hubert H. Humphrey, and Adlai Stevenson, would become fixtures in Washington for decades to come.

The president's accessibility was unparalleled. He had a list of a staggering one hundred people who were allowed to see him without being required to declare their business to his secretary. He referred to himself as "Frank" and called everyone by his or her first name. He accepted phone calls at all hours from common Americans throughout the country and gave specific orders that anyone who telephoned the White House with a request was to receive assistance. Such responsiveness prompted an unprecedented amount of folksy mail—450,000 letters during his first week in office—from Americans thanking him for saving their lives. One recipient of his help wrote,

> Dear Mr. President: This is just to tell you that everything is all right now. The man you sent found our house all right, and we went down to the bank with him and the mortgage can go on for a while longer. You remember I wrote you about losing the furniture too. Well, your man got it back for us. I never heard of a President like you.

Those first, charmed one hundred days in the White House were exhilarating and buoyant, as Roosevelt sent measure after measure to Congress and each was met with swift passage. Understanding the powers and limitations of the presidency, the tenuousness of political goodwill, the impatience of the populace, and the unknown consequences of his ideas— not to mention that his rivals were champing at the bit—he wisely "opened the New Deal floodgates," as one of his biographers put it, and pushed through every bit of legislation he could. During the Hundred Days, the specially convened Seventy-third Congress broke all previous records for enacting legislation, a whirlwind feat of governing and experimentation.

"No president since [Roosevelt] has faced so desperate a financial situation, and none have enjoyed such mastery of the legislative process," biographer Jean Edward Smith wrote in the *New York Times* seventy-five years later. What Americans saw during the first three months of the Roosevelt administration was a dynamic president, unhindered by his disability, who was using the power of his office to fight tirelessly for the common man. Perhaps, as some believed, it was his physical paralysis that impelled his dynamism. In explaining his newfound admiration for Roosevelt, a friend of Herbert Hoover's told the *New York Times*, "Having overcome that [his physical disability], he is not afraid of anything. This man functions smoothly because he has learned to function in chains." Meanwhile, those alarmed by Roosevelt's swift and effective use of executive decree compared him to Hitler and Mussolini and wrung their hands at his dictatorial action and Congress's rubber-stamping response.

The onslaught had begun on March 9, when he had sent Congress the Emergency Banking Act, which reopened the banks. Then came the Economy Act, which slashed government salaries and department budgets, saving the government nearly a billion dollars. Those were followed by the "beer bill," which set the stage for the repeal of Prohibition; the CCC legislation, which put youths to work; and Glass-Steagall. When Congress adjourned on June 16, 1933, it had enacted all fifteen New Deal economic policies that the White House had submitted. Roosevelt had also delivered ten major speeches, held biweekly press conferences, instituted Wall Street reform, and influenced foreign policy by taking the country off the gold standard, giving the United States greater control over its dollars. Included in the innovative, momentous, and often contradictory legislation were such diverse policies as the Agricultural Adjustment Act and the Home Owners Loan Act.

The Agricultural Adjustment Act (AAA) introduced federal planning into yet another of the nation's major economic sectors. The most blatantly interventionist of all of his policies, the AAA created a new agency charged with raising crop prices and controlling production. Roosevelt had been moved by the plight of the farmers, who had been especially hard-hit by the Depression, and saw them as a cornerstone for rebuilding the economy. Perhaps more significantly, he sought to forestall an Iowa insurrection and impending farmer's strike that could set off explosive unrest throughout the country. He strong-armed the legislation through Congress in time for spring planting. His secretary of agriculture, Henry Wallace, would oversee the production of three hundred million bushels of wheat and eight million bales of cotton, the raising of thirty million hogs, and the harvesting of 106 million acres of corn, also with a mandate of creating scarcity to drive up prices. "To destroy a standing crop goes against the soundest instincts of human nature," Wallace said, but he was quick to blame the previous administration for the current disaster. He was equally reluctant to slaughter six million baby piglets but saw no alternative.

The Home Owners Loan Corporation (HOLC) protected home owners at a moment when more than a quarter million families had lost their homes and the foreclosure rate was a thousand per day. The government agency refinanced mortgages, provided money for taxes and repairs, lowered interest rates, and negotiated flexible repayment plans. It was designed to prevent the collapse of the national real estate market and would assume one sixth of all home mortgages in the country.

Among the measures that brought special pride to Roosevelt was the creation of the Tennessee Valley Authority (TVA), which addressed rural poverty. Based on the belief that all Americans were entitled to affordable utilities, the TVA was designed to bring cheap electrical power to one of the country's most impoverished regions. In a feat of engineering— and a slap in the face to price-gouging utility executives—the TVA would build dams and power plants to benefit seven Southern states.

By executive order, Roosevelt created the Farm Credit Administration, merging nine federal agencies into one to provide emergency refinancing of farm mortgages for the desperate agricultural community. At his behest, Congress established the Federal Emergency Relief Administration (FERA). He placed Harry Hopkins, a New York social worker, as the head of this organization, which would deal with millions of indigent Americans. Entire families were living on less than fifty cents per day, and municipalities, states, and private charities were tapped out. The new legislation gave five hundred million dollars in unemployment-relief aid to states.

The triumphal achievement was the National Industrial Recovery Act (NIRA), a massive economic stimulus package implemented by the National Recovery Administration (NRA) that established the Public Works Administration with a $3.3 billion budget for nationwide construction projects—roads, hospitals, power plants, schools, flood control projects, bridges, sewage plants, tunnels, courthouses, U.S. Navy aircraft carriers and submarines, and fifty U.S. Army airports. The act strengthened organized labor, guaranteeing the right to bargain collectively and setting minimum wage and maximum hours standards to eliminate child labor and women's sweatshops, ushering in a new era of corporate accountability for safe and humane working conditions. The NIRA bill also provided employment for two million people. When he signed the bill into law in June 1933, Roosevelt grandly proclaimed it "a supreme effort to stabilize for all time the many factors which make for the prosperity of the Nation, and the preservation of American standards." He believed that history would prove it to be "the most important and far-reaching legislation ever enacted by the American Congress."

Other New Deal laws that emerged from the Roosevelt barrage included the Truth in Securities Act, which regulated stocks and bonds and put "the burden of telling the whole truth on the seller," as Roosevelt saw it; the Railroad Coordination Act, which reorganized the railroad industry and was, in stark contrast to the other legislation, a paean to the powerful industry at the expense of the workers; and the abolition of the gold clause in public and private contracts. "Roosevelt is an explorer who has embarked on a voyage as uncertain as that of Columbus," British statesman Winston Churchill wrote, "and upon a quest which might conceivably be as important as the discovery of the New World."

Most of the New Deal was aggressively defensive, a hodgepodge of reforms to keep America from falling apart. But a significant part of the legislation was also driven by Roosevelt's dream to build a "balanced civilization," to confirm that government had an obligation to its citizenry, and to eliminate the possibility of a future depression. He had a Jeffersonian agrarian nostalgia—harking back to his tranquil childhood—in which he envisioned a world where Americans thrived in peaceful landscapes rather than industrialized cities. As governor of New York he had sought to shift "the population balance between city and countryside," Arthur Schlesinger wrote in *The Coming of the New Deal*, "taking industry from crowded urban centers to airy villages, and giving scrawny kids from the slums opportunity for sun and growth in the country." He saw himself as steward of the land and, in Jeffersonian terms, as guardian over a government that provided the greatest good for the greatest number. Simply put, he wanted to shape a better life for all Americans while conserving the land for future generations.

Much of the legislation was also directly paradoxical. Some programs were deflationary while others were inflationary, for instance. Roosevelt was aware of the "contradictory character of some of his policies," according to his son Elliott. "The administration was wedded to no economic philosophy. It was pragmatic in outlook. What it sought was to put people back to work, to raise prices, and to lighten the debt load." The overall effect was one of *emergency*, and more carefully considered bills would supersede much of the legislation down the road, once the economy stabilized.

The Hundred Days was a breathtaking period in which American society and government was restructured. Steeped in regulation and federal expenditures, the new bills changed the balance of power and gave Roosevelt unprecedented and virtually unbridled authority. Declaring a state of national emergency and assuming full responsibility for the government, the patrician reformer forever altered the role of the U.S. president and signed the largest peacetime appropriations bills in the country's history. We were "confronted with a choice between an orderly revolution—a peaceful and rapid departure from past concepts," wrote Tugwell, "and a violent and disorderly overthrow of the whole capitalist structure." The seamlessness with which the executive and legislative branches collaborated—under dire circumstances and a perilous time constraint—was unmatched. Roosevelt thanked the exhausted representatives profusely, and in the wee hours of June 16, 1933, the most productive Congress in American history adjourned.

No one would ever know "how close were we to collapse and revolution," U.S. Army General Hugh S. Johnson later said. "We could have got a dictator a lot easier than Germany got Hitler."

CHAPTER TWENTY-SEVEN

Hankering for Superman

THE MOTION PICTURE INDUSTRY AND COMMERCIAL newsreel firms jumped on the Roosevelt bandwagon, exploiting his on-screen charisma—and calling him "the Barrymore of the capital"—to produce propaganda films and short documentaries about America's savior. Even before his inauguration, the industry had begun preparing the country for a radical takeover of government. Spawned by the fear of violent mobs of unemployed men blanketing the nation, this dictator craze, fueled by Hollywood and right-wing media moguls, set off an idealistic yearning for a benevolent despot—what Walter Lippmann called a "hankering for Superman" and another described as "a rage for order."

Hollywood was at the ready with a string of politically charged features about economic injustice, governmental fraud, revolutionary fervor, class hatred, mob hysteria, and the tyrannical white-knight heroes who came to the rescue. Frank Capra's *American Madness* depicted a frenzied mass of depositors rushing a bank in what the *New York World Telegram* described as "one of the most excitingly realistic mob scenes ever pictured on the screen." In *Wild Boys of the Road* a roving quartet of teen-age misfits thrown into destitution and rootlessness by economic conditions wander the country looking for redemption. As their road trip unfolds, hundreds of juvenile hoboes join them, sending the unmistakable

149

message that America has abandoned its children. Rousted about by police and railroad "bulls," the hungry, unemployed teens are a heartbreak-
ing lot.

In Cecil B. DeMille's *This Day and Age*, an ominous collection of teen
vigilantes, disgusted by the depravity of adult politics and culture, form a
bloodthirsty gang. Most discomfiting were the rousing cheers of movie-
goers during a scene when the mob's target is bound by rope and lowered
into a pit of rats. "The public has been milked and are growing tired of
it," DeMille proclaimed in justification of his gratuitously violent film.
"It is not [financial] speculation alone. There is something rotten at the
core of our system."

The most incendiary of the films was the overnight sensation *The Three
Little Pigs*, with its memorably eerie song, "Who's Afraid of the Big, Bad
Wolf." Screened throughout the spring and summer of 1933 to standing-
room-only crowds, the eight-minute Walt Disney cartoon came to symbolize the threat of the Great Depression and the unshakable hope for
deliverance. "The whimsical tale follows the adventures of a trio of pigs
who experiment with three progressively sturdier options in home building materials (straw, wood, and bricks)," wrote Thomas Doherty in his
academic treatise *Pre-Code Hollywood*, "and their respective resistance to
the lung power of a lupine predator." The unmistakable moral of the fable
was that the huffing and puffing predatory wolf could be kept at bay with
"sound reconstruction policies and honest statecraft." No film in American history had so emblemized the political environment of fortitude in
the face of terror. Its theme song became "an alternate national anthem,"
according to one historian, "sung, hummed, and whistled on trains and
buses, in taxis and hotels." The audience in a Texas movie theater nearly
rioted when management forgot to show the cartoon.

At the same time, breadlines, hunger marchers, mobs of unemployed
veterans, strikers, and hobo camps dominated the newsreels and wire-
photos, inciting the very fear President Roosevelt had warned against in
his inaugural address. After his inauguration—the first to be recorded
with sound—the newsreels played a crucial role in championing both the
president and the New Deal. In Fox Movietone's *The Inauguration of
Franklin D. Roosevelt*, which played in theaters across the land and often
received top marquee billing, the narrator momentously proclaims that
the "hour of destiny has struck." Several melodramatic newsreels came in
the following weeks, including Hearst Metrotone's *Roosevelt: The Man of*

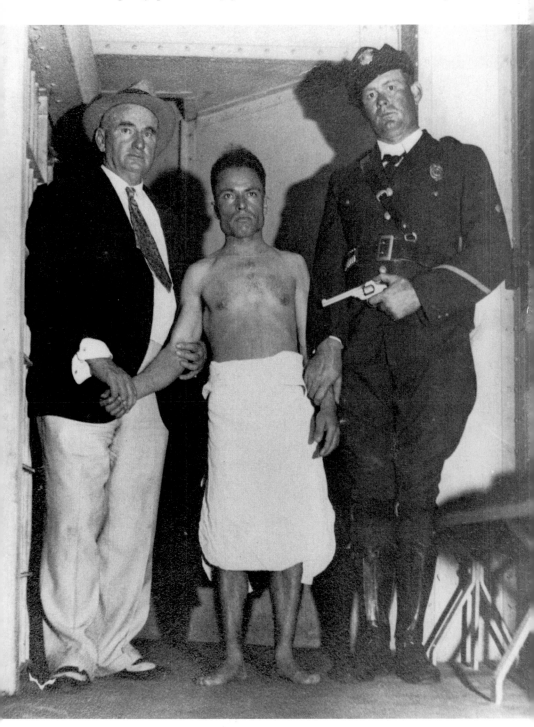

The tiny and defiant assassin, Giuseppe Zangara, railed against capitalists from the moment he was apprehended until he was put to death just weeks later. The anti-Fascist Italian immigrant was battered and bloodied by the crowd at Miami's Bayfront Park after he fired shots at Roosevelt's entourage. Police whisked him to the Dade County Jail, where they kept him nude during interrogation. (*Courtesy of the State Archives of Florida*)

Franklin D. Roosevelt aboard the *Nourmahal*. During the long interregnum between the presidential election and the inauguration, Roosevelt waited impatiently to take office. For nearly two weeks in February 1933, he cruised the Caribbean with five wealthy friends. This is one of the few existing photographs of Roosevelt in a wheelchair. (*Photograph by Robert Cross-Sailor/Courtesy of the Franklin D. Roosevelt Presidential Library and Museum*)

On Inauguration Day, March 4, 1933, Roosevelt and a hostile President Herbert Hoover traveled in an open touring car from the White House to the Capitol. Despite Roosevelt's trademark smile and efforts at conviviality, Hoover remained unmoved. As the spectators cheered and clapped, a beaming Roosevelt broke the tension between the two men and began waving his top hat.

"THE ONLY THING WE HAVE TO FEAR IS FEAR ITSELF--"

1933

MARCH 4, 1933

Addressing one of the largest audiences to ever attend a presidential inauguration, Roosevelt gave his famously powerful first inaugural address. Castigating Wall Street's "money changers," he pleaded with the masses to band together in order to accomplish restoration and recovery. Vowing to put Americans back to work, to prevent foreclosures, and to regulate the nation's banking industry, Roosevelt's speech was a call to action. When he said, "The only thing we have to fear is fear itself," the phrase did not elicit applause. But it would later go down in history as one of the greatest presidential quotes of all time.

Destined to become the most controversial First Lady in the country's history, Eleanor Roosevelt was a political force in her own right. Highly intelligent and fiercely independent, Eleanor bridled at performing the role of official presidential hostess, instead focusing her considerable energy on creating economic and political power for women.

Marine general Smedley Darlington Butler was famous for his daring exploits in China and Central America. But by the end of his career he had come to see himself as "a high-class muscle man for Big Business." He reported to Congress in 1934 that he had been solicited to lead a veterans' army in a Fascist coup d'état against President Roosevelt. Details of the putsch—allegedly conceived and financed by Wall Street brokers who opposed Roosevelt's New Deal policies—shocked the nation. (*U.S. Marine Corps/Courtesy of Wikimedia Commons*)

The "cruelest year," as 1932 was called, epitomized the deepening crisis that had begun three years earlier with the stock market crash. In the absence of substantial government relief programs under the Herbert Hoover administration, free food was distributed by private organizations. Bread lines throughout the country, like this one in New York City, snaked for blocks through city streets.

As Franklin D. Roosevelt ascended to the presidency, a thousand homes per day were being fore-closed. That figure does not even include the half million farm foreclosures. Some farmers especially hard hit by the Depression engaged in "organized refusal" to market products for which they were being underpaid. Moved by their plight, Roosevelt saw them as a cornerstone for rebuilding the economy, and by executive order created an agency to provide desperately needed refinancing of farm mortgages.

The national banking system was beginning its final collapse during the first months of 1933 while Roosevelt waited to take office. Banks were closed, or on the verge of closing, in twenty-one states, unable to meet the demands of depositors trying to withdraw their money. Rumors swept the nation that banks were no longer safe, and panicked depositors, like these in New York City, rushed to retrieve their money.

Roosevelt's Federal Emergency Relief Administration (FERA) brought support to an estimated two and a half million self-sustaining farms. The parents of these children were part of a rehabilitation program in Arkansas designed to bring young farming couples back to the land.

During the Great Depression, with unemployment rising to sixteen million, hundreds of thousands of Americans—like this migrant worker on a California highway—wandered the country in search of jobs.

The ingenious Civilian Conservation Corps (CCC) was Roosevelt's own idea and pet project to combine conservation with full employment. Roosevelt's "Tree Army" was designed to get the destitute and troublesome young men of the cities to work in the national forests. These men working in Idaho were among the quarter million called into public service.

the Hour and Universal's *The Fighting President* (with its tagline "Show Us
the Way and We Will Follow"), complete with robust nationalistic marching music. Hollywood, recognizing Roosevelt and the New Deal as the
box-office saviors, embraced its role as chief booster. Studio executives
formed a committee to bolster the White House by creating propaganda
films and enlisting the support of the nation's movie theaters. "Stand by
your president," trailers intoned at the beginning of film projections.
"President Roosevelt is doing a great job. He is restoring order out of
banking chaos . . . Our lot may be tough, but his is tougher, so let us all
help him as best we can."

The only film to capture the first hundred days during which America
wobbled on the verge of anarchy was *Gabriel Over the White House*. Media
mogul William Randolph Hearst bought the rights to the script and financed the controversial film, which was an unabashed glorification of
totalitarian dictatorship. Written by a British novelist, it was adapted as a
screenplay with a Rooseveltian figure and released in theaters shortly after Roosevelt's inauguration. The film's over-the-top propagandistic elements were alternately decried as Fascist, Socialist, liberal, or reactionary,
capturing the radically fluid nature of the moment. "Just as American
communists looked dewy-eyed toward Joseph Stalin and the future that
worked in the Soviet Union," wrote one scholar, "homegrown authoritar-
ians yearned for potent stewardship and doted on images of ordered men
marching together in sharp uniforms." Hearst was just such a man, one
who firmly believed that America needed a dictator and took seriously his
self-appointed mandate to shape public opinion. Having first backed Roosevelt's Democratic opponent the previous summer, he moved swiftly to
curry favor with the new president and help him chart a despotic course.

Hearst enlisted Roosevelt's creative input, sending him a copy of the
script, complete with Hearst's own annotated edits, before the movie
went into production. The plot begins benignly enough, with a hack
politician ascending to the presidency. Played by Walter Huston—father
of John Huston and grandfather of Anjelica Huston—the fictional president Jud Hammond is a handsome lightweight who is the genial front
man for behind-the-scenes party powerbrokers. He makes no pretense of
wielding real power, as scenes show him playing on the floor with his
young nephew, oblivious to the background radio blaring reports of poverty and unemployment. Elected to office on promises he has no intention of honoring, Hammond smiles blankly when an aide reminds him,

"Oh, don't worry, by the time they realize you're not keeping them, your term will be over." A feckless playboy, Hammond directs his passion toward his secretary—a thinly veiled reference to Roosevelt's extramarital affair with his wife's secretary, Lucy Mercer—and driving fast cars, an analogy to Roosevelt's enthusiasm for sailing and yachting.

The story takes a dramatic turn when the boyishly irresponsible Hammond drives speedily away from a pack of motorcycle-riding journalists. His car careens out of control after a tire blowout at a hundred miles per hour, landing him in a coma with a terminal prognosis. Given up for dead back in his sumptuous White House bedroom, he receives a visit from Gabriel—the archangel of revelations—at the moment of his passing. Like Roosevelt overcoming polio, Hammond arises from his deathbed a changed man. His previously vacant eyes are now brimming with intensity, symbolizing his metamorphosis from empty suit to divinely inspired autocrat. In a dizzying series of executive actions, he seizes control of the government; calls Congress into a special session and orders it to take "immediate and effective action"; declares martial law; prohibits the military from attacking the fictional version of the Bonus Army; muscles in on the liquor racket of an Al Capone–like hoodlum by nationalizing the sale and distribution of alcohol; oversees the execution by firing squad of the Capone gang after a court-martial conviction; creates an "Army of Construction" to put the unemployed to work; rallies the public with a series of radio addresses; threatens to destroy any European nation that reneges on its war debt; fires his cabinet of old, white Wall Street patsies; allocates billions of dollars in New Deal–style social and public works programs; and disarms the world, bringing about global peace.

Understandably, he falls away exhausted. In a final scene, Hammond can barely summon the energy to raise the quill pen Abraham Lincoln used to sign the Emancipation Proclamation. Taking pen to paper to sign the historic legislation that has been enacted under his direction, he is struck by a fatal heart attack as the famous quill scratches across the page. He is eulogized as "one of the greatest presidents who ever lived."

"The good news: he reduces unemployment, lifts the country out of the Depression, battles gangsters and Congress, and brings about world peace," reads the Library of Congress description of the presidential character in the film. "The bad news: he's Mussolini . . . Depending on your perspective, it's a strident defense of democracy and the wisdom of the common man, a good argument for benevolent dictatorship, a prescient anticipation of the New Deal, [or] a call for theocratic governance."

Hearst had intended the movie to prepare both Roosevelt and the nation for the necessity for decisive executive action. The original screenplay included a scene in which the president was shot at, but after the Miami assassination attempt, it was deemed to be too close to reality and was deleted. "I want to send you this line to tell you how pleased I am with the changes you made in 'Gabriel Over the White House,'" President Roosevelt wrote to Hearst in April after he had viewed the film in a private screening. "I think it is an intensely interesting picture and should do much to help."

Left-leaning magazines dismissed it as an instructional effort to convert Americans to the benefits of Fascism. Nascent Hollywood censors declared, "Its reality is a dangerous item at this time," and MGM boss Louis B. Mayer was infuriated upon viewing the film that his studio had produced. "Put that picture back in the can, take it back to the studio, and lock it up," he reportedly told an associate, though it was already in distribution.

While Hearst saw the film as a fantastic primer, Roosevelt ultimately came to regard it as fantasy entertainment, and the American public—riveted by Roosevelt's movie-star looks and larger-than-life exploits—felt no need for a dramatized version. Despite its backing by the tycoon, the film was a box-office flop throughout the country. The deifying of Roosevelt through newsreels continued in Hollywood, but Hearst soon broke with the president, disappointed that his "protégé" had a mind of his own and had failed to follow the script to its letter.

CHAPTER TWENTY-EIGHT

That Jew Cripple in the White House

IN A FEW SHORT MONTHS, those who had been begging Roosevelt to become a dictator had turned against him. At first it was the predictable resistance: "It is socialism," sniffed Republican congressman Robert Luce of
Massachusetts about the New Deal legislation. "Whether it is communism
or not I do not know." But by summer the criticism was reaching a crescendo. Nine million workers were employed in NRA programs, and wage
codes had been signed by a million employers. Businessmen—nervous that
Roosevelt's legitimizing of collective bargaining would strengthen the
labor movement—denounced the omnibus NIRA as creeping socialism or
business fascism. Northern sweatshop owners and Southern planters
feared they would lose their cheap labor to the "dole," as the recovery and
public works projects were dubbed, and started calling Roosevelt a Communist. Herbert Hoover publicly denounced the NIRA as totalitarian.

The massive government-industry collaboration lauded as a godsend
in May seemed radically anti-capitalist as panic receded and business
leaders contemplated the scope of Roosevelt's program. "The excessive
centralization and the dictatorial spirit are producing a revulsion of feeling against bureaucratic control of American life," Walter Lippmann
said. Erstwhile Roosevelt supporter Hearst charged that NRA stood for

"Nonsensical, Ridiculous, Asinine interference." He aggressively opposed "Stalin Delano Roosevelt's Raw Deal" and compared the president to "the Mussolinis, the Hitlers, the Lenins and all of those who seek to establish a dictatorial form of government."

Wall Street, bridling at the new securities regulations and distressed by the burgeoning federal expenditures, began rumbling about "dictatorial powers." Much of the negative reaction swirled around the gold standard and a deep-seated belief—"rooted in suspicion," as historian William Manchester put it—that gold and empire were synonymous. Gold was sacred, seen as the "hallmark of Western culture." To rabid anti-Semites, Roosevelt, as a Wall Street puppet, had taken America off the gold standard to allow the Jews to control the world's gold while the Gentiles were left with the less valuable silver.

If pundits and advisers were stunned by the swiftness with which the backlash took hold, Roosevelt saw it coming. The fissures in Congress were just beneath the surface in the special session's waning days, but Roosevelt had managed to keep them from splitting open. Critics on both sides of the aisle had begun to question the constitutionality of NIRA, prompting Roosevelt to accelerate his timetable to send Congress home. "We're going at top speed in order to adjourn early," one Democratic senator confided to his sons. "Roosevelt wants the Congress out of the way. He is losing a little bit of his astounding and remarkable poise . . . There is a revolt in the air in the Congress, too. Men have followed him upstairs without question or criticism . . . These men have about reached the limit of their endurance. Roosevelt, clever as he is, senses that fact, and before there is an actual break, he wishes us out of the way." FDR had rammed through his policies until his impeccable intuition told him it was time to stop. He possessed a heightened sense of timing and the practicality to stay apace with the populace, never getting too far in front at the risk of losing their confidence. He knew the necessity of appearing calm and assured, knew that projecting the image of serene leadership was as important as the policies themselves. He had successfully maneuvered the newspapermen at his twice-weekly press conferences to explain his reasoning for various ideas and to prepare the public to accept them.

Even as prices rose, purchasing power increased, homes were saved, bank deposits were restored, millions went back to work, and recovery was proceeding, an undercurrent of dissatisfaction among the country's elite took hold. Contemporaneous observers thought the griping was really about jealousy of Roosevelt's success, bitterness at having been manipulated, anxiety about the long-term results, apprehension of change, and an inherent resistance to government interference.

"Businessmen of 1929 had enjoyed privileges and were delighted to receive them in 1933," wrote a historian of the period, "but did not like being told by Roosevelt that they must shoulder responsibilities, especially toward their workers." A South Carolina newspaper editor had little empathy for their plight. "The 'captains' of finance and industry have been exposed as empty-pates . . . The 'captains' are bare in their nakedness as greater fools even than knaves."

Elite extremists posing as liberty lovers and constitution defenders cropped up and became increasingly vociferous throughout the summer. "This is despotism. This is tyranny. This is the annihilation of liberty. The ordinary American is thus reduced to the status of a robot . . . The President . . . has not merely signed the death warrant of capitalism, but has ordained the mutilation of the Constitution unless the friends of liberty, regardless of party, band themselves together to regain their lost freedom," a U.S. senator wrote in an appeal to arouse his constituents.

One target of special enmity was Roosevelt's close relationship with Sidney Hillman—a Jewish refugee from czarist Russia. The onetime rabbinical student had been a fabric cutter in what was known as New York's "needle trades" and had gone on to form a new union, the Amalgamated Clothing Workers of America, to organize the nation's most notorious sweatshops. Throughout America, women and children were being paid less than three dollars a week for a fifty-hour workweek; in New York City, the garment industry—which employed more than fifty thousand women—was sometimes paying as little as sixty cents an hour. Thousands of workers took home less than a dollar after a nine-hour day. As a Roosevelt insider, Hillman helped design the New Deal unemployment and public works policies, which were committed to transforming America's benighted working class into a modernized workforce with economic security and fair labor practices.

The dissatisfaction vented by Wall Street was not felt by ordinary Americans, who rushed to hang portraits of Roosevelt over their fireplaces and proudly displayed the famous "Blue Eagle" NRA poster. With an insignia modeled after a Native American thunderbird—and a concept derived from a wartime patch by which soldiers could recognize each other—the poster bore the legend "We Do Our Part." In his most soothing and convincing way, Roosevelt had launched the Blue Eagle during a fireside chat: "In war, in the gloom of night attack, soldiers wear a bright badge on their shoulders to be sure that comrades do not fire on comrades. On that principle, those who cooperate in this program must know each other at a glance." Effusive and grateful letters and telegrams poured into the White House by the truckload from poor Americans who saw their lives improving. While the Far Right and Far Left abandoned him, the "vast army of the center" was firmly in the president's camp.

Meanwhile, Roosevelt's us-against-them rhetoric and references to "comrades" inflamed the upper class, and the stirrings of anti-Rooseveltism, which had begun even before he had taken office, were escalating. Soon these sparks would ignite into full-fledged hatred, dividing the country and emboldening powerful enemies. "Through the channels of the rich— the clubs, the banks, the brokerage offices, the Park Avenue salons, the country club locker rooms, the South Carolina shoots, the Florida cabanas— there rushed a swelling flood of stories and broadsides, many unprintable, depicting Roosevelt as a liar, a thief, a madman given to great bursts of maniacal laughter, an alcoholic, a syphilitic, a Bolshevik," according to Arthur Schlesinger's account. It was from this fertile field of loathing that the "traitor to his class" epithet was born, and the publishers of the country's most influential newspapers, themselves members of the noble class, eagerly fanned the flames.

The rapport between Roosevelt and the press was initially based on mutual benefit, in which he used them to disseminate his philosophy and float his designs and they relied on him for a steady stream of copy. But an element of wariness and suspicion existed, especially between Roosevelt and the wealthy publishers—as opposed to the working press, for whom he had respect. He thought the *Chicago Tribune* under the helm of reactionary Republican Robert McCormick "the rottenest newspaper in the whole United States." He thought Arthur Krock, editor of the *New York Times*, "terrible" and consistently inaccurate, and he derided the *Times* newsroom as a "rarefied atmosphere of self-anointed scholars." He reproached syndicated columnist Frank Kent for having both a "poison pen and poison tongue," and considered Lippmann painfully out of touch with the reality of America. "I wish sometime that he could come more into contact with the little fellow all over the country and see less of the big rich brother!" He accused *Time* magazine's Henry Luce of having a "deliberate policy of either exaggeration or distortion." And he reserved a special animus for his onetime friend and promoter of dictatorship, Hearst: "I sometimes think that Hearst has done more harm to the cause of Democracy and civilization in America than any three other contemporaries put together." He condemned the fat-cat newspaper owners for caring more about their personal social and economic status than about fostering an independent American press. He sympathized with the working journalists whose bosses ordered them to write certain stories and ignore others. "I think they [the publishers] have been more responsible for the inciting of fear in the community than any other factors," Roosevelt said.

The feeling of distrust and animosity was reciprocal. In addition to Hearst, Roosevelt's most vicious critics were McCormick and H. L. Mencken, who steadily portrayed the president and his advisers as "Reds." The Roosevelt haters lapped up the visceral, often-illogical, and irrational attacks. Not since the hostility heaped on Andrew Jackson a century before had a president been so savagely pummeled by the press—their screeds betraying "a certain streak of madness in American political criticism," as two twentieth-century scholars saw it.

"Colonel" McCormick rebuked Roosevelt for spending billions on "men who have been parasites their entire lives, have never produced anything and never intend to produce anything, who have always lived at the expense of others, and plot to live better than the others who support them."

Likewise, the tremendously influential Mencken could not abide Roosevelt's freewheeling spending on the nation's indigent and unemployed. "The republic proceeds toward hell at a rapidly accelerating tempo," Mencken wrote to a libertarian author when the New Deal was finalized in June 1933. "I am advocating making him a king in order that we may behead him in case he goes too far beyond the limits of the endurable. A President, it appears, cannot be beheaded, but kings have been subjected to the operation from ancient times." While Mencken's remark was certainly in jest, such chatter by respected pundits had the power of provoking deranged individuals into action. Loose and inflammatory talk of assassination and other violent acts became eerily prevalent, and the Secret Service went into high gear as threats multiplied. "What that fellow Roosevelt needs is a thirty-eight caliber revolver right at the back of his head," a respectable citizen said at a Washington dinner party.

While Mencken thought the New Deal laboratory just that—a wild experiment that was unplanned, untried, and unwise—Hearst and Mc-Cormick saw a more sinister hand in it, subscribing to the theory that Roosevelt was the puppet for a Communist takeover. Both took seriously their mission to stop him, for only with a gullible public and a malleable press could Roosevelt's coup be successful.

In addition to the mainstream establishment critics, there arose an extremist element with its own methods for propagating hatred, name-calling, and character assassination. One shadowy organization began spreading the canard that Roosevelt—on behalf of an international Jewish conspiracy—was protecting the Jewish killer of the "Lindbergh baby." The toddler son of celebrity aviator and Nazi sympathizer Charles Lindbergh had been kidnapped from the nursery of his parents' upscale New Jersey home on March 1, 1932—in what became known as the "crime of the century." Footprints, a ladder, and a chisel were left beneath the nursery's second-story window. A fifty-thousand-dollar ransom payment was made before the boy's murdered remains were found three months later. The case came to epitomize the fears plaguing America's ruling class—which Roosevelt had so legendarily betrayed—about an angry Jewish proletariat. In the convoluted, far-fetched scenario that would eventually find its way into a published pamphlet with nearly a million copies distributed, Roosevelt was a de facto collaborator with the kidnappers.

Much of the Far Right suspicion centered on the New Deal as being a Jewish conspiracy, and there developed a cottage industry for those determined to prove that Jewish blood coursed through Roosevelt's veins. William Dudley Pelley and his legion of Silver Shirts worked feverishly to prove that Roosevelt was the installed head of a Jewish dictatorship. Pelley and others intent on exposing Roosevelt's Jewish bloodlines inevitably trotted out the infamous *Protocols of the Learned Elders of Zion*, the crackpot 1905 alleged transcripts from a secret World Zionist Conference, which were gaining popularity among American anti-Semites in 1933. "Often characterized as a blueprint for world domination by Jews," wrote religious scholar James Carroll, "the *Protocols* is a mishmash of commentary on the press, finance, government, and history . . . The diabolical center of the plot, of course, was the international cabal of Jewish financiers, and world domination would be achieved by Jewish control of money." It was published in the United States by the automobile titan Henry Ford, the inventor of the assembly line and an advocate of a "biblical capitalism" personified by German Fascism.

Citing the fact that Jews had received 15 percent of the senior appointments in his government, compared with a national Jewish population of only 3 percent, critics sought irrepressibly to tarnish Roosevelt by claiming he was pursuing international Jewish interests. The conspiracists might have been handily dismissed if not for Adolf Hitler's disturbing machinations in Germany. The fanatics charged that Roosevelt was the head of a Communist conspiracy to take over the world. Such indictments would have been laughable if not for the suggestion of violence they contained and the unhinged population to which they appealed.

"If you were a good honest man, Jesus Christ would not have crippled you," said a letter to the president that was typical of correspondence from the disaffected. In the whisper campaign of 1933, Roosevelt was denigrated as a cripple and falsely labeled a Jew, and zealots prepared petitions for his removal on the grounds of treason.

CHAPTER TWENTY-NINE

We Don't Like Her, Either

"PEACE TIME CAN BE AS EXHILARATING to the daredevil as wartime," Eleanor Roosevelt told an interviewer. "There is nothing so exciting as creating a new social order."

While Roosevelt set out to remake America, his wife led a parallel revolution. Eleanor fast became a political force in her own right, and a lightning rod as well: She would become the most controversial First Lady in the country's history. Far more liberal than her husband, she focused her considerable energy on creating economic and political power for women. During the interregnum, while Roosevelt had been scheming with his Brain Trust and dodging bullets in Miami, Eleanor began writing two books: one about her father, *Hunting Big Game in the Eighties: The Letters of Elliott Roosevelt, Sportsman*, and the other, *It's Up to the Women*, intended to motivate her gender into the world of political activism.

Urging women to seize real power, to create their own political-machine bosses, and to boldly and courageously compete in that male-dominated sphere, Eleanor was the first straightforward feminist to operate from within the White House. Such blatant grasping for power by a woman was groundbreaking. Women had only had the right to vote in all states for a slight decade and had not yet fully embraced their individual or collective authority. If President Roosevelt was a threat to the American status quo, his wife was a terrifying specter.

Whatever the context and complexities of their marriage—their physical relationship had irretrievably broken off twenty years earlier when Franklin fell in love with Eleanor's social secretary, Lucy Mercer—there existed between them an unbreakable bond. Eleanor's manner with her husband was "at once intimate, informal, natural and deeply respectful," one of her closest friends later wrote. By all accounts, he admired her intelligence and courage, relished her sense of humor, and remained devoted to her and their deeply unorthodox marriage even as he maintained his affair with Mercer. While their marriage was not conventional, it was one of Washington's most successful. "Fueled by power," wrote Eleanor's biographer Blanche Wiesen Cook, "they were each dedicated to making life better for most people. Together they did more than either could have done alone." Evidence of the rather impersonal bond that existed between them can be glimpsed in a letter he wrote to her on March 17, 1933, their twenty-eighth wedding anniversary, in which he directed her to choose her own gift.

"Dearest Babs," he wrote, using his pet name for her. "After a fruitless week of thinking and lying awake to find whether you need or want undies, dresses, hats, shoes, sheets, towels, rouge, soup plates, candy, flowers, lamps, laxation pills, whisky, beer, etchings or caviar . . . I GIVE UP! And yet I know you lack some necessity of life—so go to it with my love and many happy returns of the day." Included with the note was a personal check.

The head housekeeper made each of their favorite desserts that evening—angel food cake for Eleanor and fruitcake for Roosevelt—and, together with their guests, they watched *Gabriel Over the White House*. The film prompted an argument between those who admired the fictional president and those who admired real-life President Herbert Hoover's aggression against the Bonus Army. They would call "soldiers out if a million unemployed marched on Washington," Eleanor said, summarizing the reaction of her guests, "& I'd do what the President does in the picture!"

Fiercely independent, strong-willed yet self-effacing, Eleanor realized straightaway that performing the role of official presidential hostess would not sustain her for long. "I'm just not the sort of person who would be any good at that job," she told a friend. "I dare say I shall be criticized whatever I do." Rebellious against protocol, which she found superfluous in a democracy, she made early headlines with her bold changes. First, she allowed women to smoke in the White House because she found it ridiculous that, in the modern decade of the 1930s, it was still considered an unladylike vulgarity. Next, though she had long been a Prohibitionist, she began serving beer as soon as Congress amended the Volstead Act, having come to believe that moderation in all things trumped abstinence. "She shattered precedent in ways that helped her husband dispel every last wisp of the gloom, the funereal formality, that had characterized 1600 Pennsylvania Avenue when Herbert Hoover lived there," one historian said.

She did not arrive at the White House from a distant vacuum but as a fully formed forty-eight-year-old woman with an impressive set of accomplishments. She wrote a monthly column for *Women's Democratic News*, had owned a crafts factory, co-owned and taught at a New York girls' school, and had worked closely for many years with the women activists within the Democratic Party.

Americans who retained the belief that a proper First Lady was to be seen and not heard, to stare adoringly at her husband, to smile sweetly and withhold her opinions were in for a rude awakening. Eleanor was informal and active, teeming with ideas, thoughts, and judgments and eager to express them. She was informed and animated on subjects ranging from politics to the economy to the environment to child care to war. One of her earliest innovations was to institute her own press conferences—the first of their kind ever held by a First Lady. On March 6, 1933, a mere two days after her husband had taken office, she greeted thirty-five newspaperwomen in the Red Room of the White House. In stark contrast to Roosevelt, she set only one ground rule—that she would not answer questions of a political nature—and she agreed to be quoted directly. At a moment when Washington journalism was overwhelmingly a man's domain, Eleanor's press conference was a great morale-booster in addition to a radical change. She had hoped it would encourage newspaper publishers to hire more women reporters. As with all things progressive, it was not met with unanimous acceptance. One newspaperwoman snidely implied that the homely and oft-neglected Eleanor was seeking attention. "Mrs. Roosevelt doesn't hide her light under any bushel; if she had a bushel she'd burn it to add to the light."

The gesture, begun as an experiment, was enormously popular, second only to the president's own historic press conferences. As the New Deal got under way the forbidden boundaries of political questions became increasingly blurred, and her commitment to economic and social justice set the tone. Her role as Roosevelt's eyes and ears—which started after his paralysis in 1921—was widely known, as was the deep influence she exerted with her husband, prompting many to attempt to gain access to him through her. "That I became . . . a better and better reporter and a better and better observer," she later wrote, "was largely owing to the fact that Franklin's questions covered such a wide range. I found myself obliged to notice everything." It was an immense amount of power she wielded, for Roosevelt had nearly total faith in her perceptions, and it resulted in one of the most extraordinary political partnerships in history.

One of her initial outings as First Lady was in March, when she toured the scandalous slums of Washington where thousands of black people lived in squalor and disease within sight of the gleaming Capitol. She drove through the ghetto in her own roadster, accompanied by an eighty-one-year-old female friend, stopping frequently to enter back alleys and speak with the residents.

In 1933 alone, she traveled more than forty thousand miles, usually in coach class, in airplanes or trains, or by driving herself. Her crusades were focused on women, children, and the nation's poor, and she reported her results and recommendations not only to Roosevelt but also to his advisers in their relevant capacities. She pressed Harry Hopkins to provide for unemployed women schoolteachers through his Emergency Relief Administration. She pushed Louis Howe, by now her loyal comrade in the White House, to launch a program to help the poverty-stricken families of West Virginia coal miners. In her ceaseless campaign for social justice and to improve the status of women, she took her cause directly to the president, who in turn urged members of Congress and Democratic Party leaders to hire more women in substantive positions. She vociferously fought the Hoover-era policy of firing married women from government jobs and threw her support behind Labor Secretary Perkins, who advocated its reversal. She enthusiastically championed the aviation pursuits of Amelia Earhart, with whom she flew one spring day. By the summer of 1933, Eleanor was already considered the pioneer leader of a women's movement that had not yet been formally hatched. She was receiving five hundred ebullient letters a day. "For some time I have had a collection of statesmen hanging upon my wall," one woman wrote to her, "but, under the new administration, I have been obliged to start a new collection and that is one of stateswomen. Now it is ready and you are the very center of it all." By the time the New Deal legislation was enacted, Eleanor was already seen by Americans to be a potent force in her husband's administration. She too had come to see the value in her exploits. "The only thing that reconciles me to this job is the fact that I think I can give a great many people pleasure & I begin to think there may be ways in which I can be useful," she wrote to Lorena Hickok.

Her work on behalf of women's rights would spark J. Edgar Hoover of the Bureau of Investigation to create a secret intelligence file documenting her activities through the use of confidential sources and covert surveillance. Such action was extraordinary; never before in American history had a First Lady been the subject of a surreptitious government probe. Reactionary forces had labeled her "un-American," and in keeping with Hoover's zealous covenant to sniff out the unpatriotic, he eagerly targeted her. Publicly expressing her contention that Fascism was far more threatening to world peace and U.S. domestic stability than Communism, Eleanor incurred further suspicion from the rabidly anti-Communist Hoover, who marked her as a "subversive."

"Those who attacked the New Deal as a Jewish conspiracy were frequently (and almost automatically) anti-Negro as well," according to an assessment of the fever-pitch criticism of the Roosevelts. And no one was more publicly associated with the plight of the "Negro" than Eleanor Roosevelt. Racist ditties and doggerels became ubiquitous. Not since Rachel Jackson had a First Lady been so vilified, ridiculed, and slandered.

Caricatures of her were savage, emphasizing her tall ungainliness and protruding teeth, her sensible shoes and shapeless dresses. "Eleanor can bite an apple through a picket fence" was one slur that made the rounds. Columnist Westbrook Pegler, her most avid and sustained critic, dismissed her as a do-gooding busybody. But just as they ignored the scorn heaped on her husband, the majority of Americans dismissed the criticism of Eleanor, and soon she would be known as the most popular First Lady of all time.

"Despite a lithe, graceful figure, she is not beautiful," Rita S. Halle wrote in a 1933 *Good Housekeeping* magazine story on one of Eleanor's public speeches. "She does not charm by her personal appearance. Yet, as she spoke, the wearied audience uncurved its collective spine until, all over the large room, men and women were sitting forward on their chairs in intent response to the magnetism of her simple sincerity."

CHAPTER THIRTY

The Shifty-Eyed Little Austrian Paperhanger

"During the Hundred Days, while Congress debated farm subsidies and banking legislation, Jews were being beaten on the streets of Germany," wrote historian William E. Leuchtenburg. "While Roosevelt's 'forest army' planted trees on western hillsides, Hitler was rebuilding the *Reichswehr*. All of the New Deal was to be carried on under the shadow of the menace of fascism."

Indeed, during the spring of 1933, Hitler's aggression was gathering velocity as he evicted Jews from government and private industry, instituted a boycott of Jewish businesses, and relegated them to ghettos. He had eradicated his opposition, assumed dictatorial powers, amassed the largest army in Europe, and seemed to have his eye set on war. His "Proclamation to the German People" revealed his totalitarian Fascist designs. The ratification of Hitler's chancellorship occurred the day after Roosevelt's inauguration. Reports of Hitler's persecution of Jews and the infamous book burnings in massive public bonfires slowly made their way to the United States, though most Americans had little interest. Most of Washington considered Hitler more of an oddity than a threat, and the American people were far too entangled in their own problems to turn their attention to Europe.

During the campaign Roosevelt had backpedaled from his Wilsonian internationalist stance, but he was now wary of Germany's escalating armament. In May he hosted the bizarrely named Hjalmar Horace Greeley Schacht—German president of the Reichsbank and Hitler's Washington envoy—to discuss preparations for the upcoming World Monetary and Economic Conference in London. At a congenial luncheon in the Blue Room, complete with a Marine Band adaptation of the German national anthem, Roosevelt masked his disgust for Schacht, Hitler, and their ilk, whom he later described as warmongering "bastards." After lunch, Roosevelt and Schacht retreated to a private conversation in which Roosevelt, as he reported it, insisted that Germany stop its rearming. "I intimated as strongly as possible that we regard Germany as the only possible obstacle to a Disarmament Treaty," Roosevelt wrote in a memorandum to the secretary of state, referring to disarmament negotiations going on in Geneva, Switzerland.

Schacht apparently received a quite different "intimation." "After dinner, exactly half an hour remained for a private conversation between the President and me," he reported to the German Foreign Ministry. "He began with the Jewish question . . . not out of particular sympathy for the Jews, but from an old Anglo-Saxon sense of chivalry toward the weak." Schacht wrote that Roosevelt had expressed the fact that the American people were put off by newsreel depictions of "marching, uniformed columns of Nazis." In his memorandum Schacht made no reference to Roosevelt's discussion of armaments and concluded his report with what he claimed was Roosevelt's endorsement of Hitler's actions. "He once made use in his conversation of the expression that when it came to the speedy execution of governmental measures, there were not everywhere such efficient managers as (literally) Mussolini, Hitler, and Roosevelt."

Given Roosevelt's concern over Germany's rearmament and his commitment to an international treaty, Schacht's interpretation of their meeting seems intentionally ambiguous at the least, if not outright mendacious. By this time Roosevelt despised Hitler and was overtly apprehensive about Germany's saber rattling, and it would have been highly uncharacteristic for him to compare himself favorably to Hitler. The relationship between Roosevelt and Hitler, who came to power a day apart, was "openly hostile from the first," according to Roosevelt biographer Conrad Black. "They represented two diametrically different views of how to govern and of what human society and international relations should be . . . Apart from policy matters, Roosevelt detested Hitler's racism, militarism, [and] totalitarianism."

As it turned out, the London conference—"a much-ballyhooed event that was expected to cure the global Depression and bring peace on earth in one sweet package," as Jonathan Alter put it—was a bust for Roosevelt. In what would be called the "bombshell message," Roosevelt sent an undiplomatic and aberrantly arrogant cable to the conference. He scorned the leaders' emphasis on international monetary stabilization, calling it "old fetishes of so-called international bankers"—a euphemism for the cabal of gold nations trying to force the United States back to the gold standard. The statement exploded over London—hence the term "bombshell"—and effectively ended the conference. Roosevelt's first foray onto the world stage had seemingly backfired, as European leaders denounced his presumption, and Roosevelt realized that the rubber-stamping he had enjoyed from the American Congress was not universal. "No such message was ever before sent by the head of a government to representatives of other nations," wrote a British official. "It will be filed for all times as a classic example of conceit, hectoring and ambiguity."

For his part, Roosevelt claimed victory, explaining that the gold bloc nations that dominated the conference were trying to force a return to the gold standard when it was not in the best interest of the United States to do so, and that these same nations were "unwilling to go to the root of national and international problems." In any case, the bombshell destroyed the conference that had been designed to establish secure trade agreements and stabilize the world's currency. Roosevelt was left without the Disarmament Treaty and with a lot of disaffected and distrustful former allies. The only foreign leader apparently pleased by Roosevelt was Hitler. The Nazis praised Roosevelt "because they see the end of any united front against Germany," the *New York Times* reported.

"You have opportunities for experiment which we do not have here," British prime minister Ramsay MacDonald wrote to Roosevelt. ". . . To pull out a brick, to see what is behind or to get at some rotten bit of structure, is as dangerous in the State as I have just found out it is in my own delightful old house which is beginning to show signs of its two centuries of years."

Roosevelt's cable landed like a bombshell at home as well. Eleanor was disappointed in her husband. "As ER feared most, a great opportunity for international leadership had been lost," her biographer wrote. "Her husband had failed to take a risk for peace. Rearmament and economic nationalism would forevermore rule the day."

Throughout the spring of 1933, Eleanor had clipped articles about Hitler's escalating war on Jews for her husband. Jewish men and women were randomly beaten in the streets. Union leaders were being arrested. Nazis made funeral pyres of books written by Jewish, liberal, and Communist authors, including Albert Einstein, Upton Sinclair, and Thomas Mann. Jewish shop owners were seized by Nazi storm troopers, stripped of their clothes to reveal their circumcisions, and brutalized. Nazis had burned the Reichstag and raided Jewish-owned stores. Jewish judges and lawyers were evicted from the courts and professors ejected from universities while Hitler instituted new classes in "science and race." The first concentration camp had been constructed at Dachau. More than fifty thousand people poured into the streets of New York City to protest Hitler, and American Jews called for a boycott of German goods.

American journalists were slow to respond to the Nazi persecution of Jews. "Our ignorance was inexcusable," a wire-service correspondent in Germany later said. "All of us in the west, our political leaders and our newspapers above all, had underestimated Adolf Hitler and his domination of this land and its people." One of the first American writers to take Hitler seriously was muckraking *Philadelphia Record* reporter I. F. Stone, who warned about Hitler's rise as early as 1932: "Today or tomorrow the shifty-eyed little Austrian paperhanger, Hitler, may step into the mighty shoes of Bismarck as Chancellor of the Reich." In the spring of 1933, Stone wrote that the "danger to Europe and the world is that he may seek a way out in war." Stone's unease was in stark contrast to the response of Walter Lippmann, called America's "most stately Jewish pundit" by *Time* magazine, who depreciated Hitler's bellicosity as "Europe's problem." Had Lippmann—one of the most powerful and widely read journalists in the country, and one who wielded great influence with Roosevelt—turned his attention to Hitler, he might have molded public opinion in a decisive way while also nudging the president toward a more internationalist policy. "Lippmann had no illusions about Hitler's territorial ambitions or his ruthlessness," wrote his biographer Ronald Steel. "Yet he showed a surprising insensitivity to the human dimension of the Nazi threat, especially as it concerned the Jews." Following Lippmann's lead, *Time* also urged calm, explaining comfortingly that a "dictator, once he feels secure in the saddle, always tries to curb and discipline his followers who have invariably run more or less amuck."

The owner of the *New York Herald Tribune*, Helen Rogers Reid—a dear friend of Eleanor's, who was a liberal and a feminist despite being a Republican—was one of the first American publishers to give the Nazi crisis priority coverage. In March 1933, the paper's magazine section carried a lengthy analysis called "Hitler's War on Culture" by a leading German intellectual. "The universities of Germany have been transformed into hotbeds of extreme nationalism," wrote the German-Jewish novelist Dr. Lion Feuchtwanger. "The apostles of Fascism . . . have made man's worst instincts their god and they have stirred senseless racial hatred to fever pitch. They declare that the Jews are to blame for everything. Hitler declares that 'the Jews have conquered Europe and America,' and are now embarked on an effort to conquer Asia." Eleanor was intensely affected by Feuchtwanger's article and its revelations of hatred, racism, and anti-Semitism, and she relentlessly urged her isolationist husband to make peace and disarmament the centerpiece of his foreign policy.

Despite his reticence to challenge Hitler during these earliest days of the Nazis, Roosevelt was one of the first world leaders to recognize the global menace that Hitler posed. In 1933 alone he dispatched at least two emissaries to Germany to assess Hitler and the Nazis. On a flyleaf of an American edition of Hitler's *Mein Kampf*, published in 1933, Roosevelt wrote: "This translation is so expurgated as to give a wholly false view of what Hitler really is or says." Years later, Rex Tugwell told an interviewer that "from the moment Hitler came into power, Roosevelt regarded him with a strong, almost religious, dislike . . . [and thought him] a dangerous character standing against everything in which the United States believed." In the spring of 1933, Roosevelt told Treasury Secretary Henry Morgenthau that he considered it "a strong possibility" that Hitler planned to start a war in Europe. Roosevelt's appeal to world leaders to halt construction of offensive weapons systems was a direct response to the aggressions of Hitler's new Nazi government. He already envisioned the possible necessity of a future pact with other European nations to eventually contain Hitler. For now, he saw disarmament as a first crucial step toward that end.

"I am concerned by events in Germany," Roosevelt wrote to Prime Minister MacDonald after the economic conference collapsed. "For I feel that an insane rush to further armaments in Continental Europe is infinitely more dangerous than any number of squabbles over gold or stabilization or tariffs."

CHAPTER THIRTY-ONE

A Rainbow of Colored Shirts

HITLER'S BROWN SHIRTS AND MUSSOLINI'S Black Shirts inspired America's right wing to form its own paramilitary organizations. J. Edgar Hoover had repeatedly and consistently warned President Roosevelt that the Bonus Army was a dangerous collection of Socialists and Communists intent on taking over the government. While both the American Fascist and Communist movements were burgeoning in response to the crisis of the early 1930s, whatever radical elements had existed within the Bonus Army had coalesced into a Fascist rather than Communist movement.

Calling themselves the Khaki Shirts, and openly emulating the Brown Shirts and Black Shirts, this reactionary core of veterans posed an actual threat to the U.S. government and the Roosevelt administration—J. Edgar Hoover's myopic assessment notwithstanding. The self-styled "general" of the Khaki Shirts, alternately referred to as the U.S. Fascists, was enamored with the autocratic leaders of Germany and Italy. Arthur J. Smith founded the Khaki Shirts in Philadelphia, recruiting pro-Mussolini immigrants and vowing to build "the strongest army, navy and air corps in the world." Espousing Fascism as the only escape from economic injustice and global depression, Smith in June 1933 claimed to have assembled one and a half million men who were prepared to take control of Washington, remove Roosevelt, and establish a dictatorship.

When word spread that he planned to lead his army in a takeover of Pennsylvania's National Guard arsenal, Philadelphia police moved in. Smith met what a historian called his "slapstick Waterloo" when the police stormed the Khaki Shirts headquarters and "captured the entire putative army." Smith fashioned a dramatic escape through a window. One of his followers was killed, which provided Smith with the pro-Fascist martyrdom he sought. He "staged a well-publicized funeral," according to one account, and moved his "army" north.

On July 14, 1933, Smith led a rally in New York City in preparation for a Mussolini-style march on Washington. A group of anti-Fascists disrupted the protest and violence erupted. "Amid flying chairs and flashing knives," the Khaki Shirts first "smashed the bleeding head" of a young anti-Fascist student and then fatally shot him. Smith eventually received a short prison sentence in connection with the killing. He ultimately disappeared with twenty-five thousand dollars from the Khaki Shirts' coffers and reinvented his organization as the Christian Front—a group with equally anti-Semitic and pro-Nazi sympathies. Meanwhile, other extremist groups were erupting and sputtering throughout the country, organizing under various flags and shirt colors.

The Silver Shirts—a divinely inspired and apocalyptic Christian militia impelled into formation when Hitler became German chancellor— hoped to save America from Roosevelt in the same way that Italy and Germany had been saved by Fascist leaders. Described by the founder, the religious mystic William Dudley Pelley, as a "preventive and protective Militia working under cover" in forty-six states, the group was patterned on the notoriously corrupt, brutal, and xenophobic Texas Rangers. The Silver Shirts stockpiled weapons at its headquarters in Oklahoma— "the heart of the old Indian territory"—where former military and law enforcement officers taught recruits street fighting and other warrior tactics. Its elite unit, known as the Storm Troopers, drilled in California with Springfield rifles stolen from the Naval Air Station in San Diego. Referring to Roosevelt as "President Rosenfeld," Pelley avidly spread the rumor that Roosevelt was descended from Dutch Jews and that his election "had been planned and prophesied by the Elders of Zion."

Ku Klux Klansmen in Georgia formed an American Fascists group called the Black Shirts, named after Mussolini's paramilitary forces. Anti-Communist, anti-atheist, and anti-Negro, the white supremacists described themselves as "Friends of the New Germany." The Gray Shirts, based in Glen Falls, New York, were commanded by a New York stock-broker and school superintendent and were focused on eliminating "idealistic or Communistic college professors" from the nation's educational institutions. The White Shirts of Chattanooga, Tennessee, were a "military organization armed with wooden staffs." Crusaders for Economic Liberty, an extremist band of Christians, drilled in accordance with Army regulations, their white shirts bearing a Crusader cross and flag on the left breast. Their mission was to first take control of local government and then proceed to Washington to establish a new monetary system based on the "Golden Rule."

What united this "rainbow" of colored shirts was a theatrical outpouring of pageantry and patriotism, flamboyant uniforms and lofty military ranks, a love of discipline and intimidation, and a melding of church and state. These flag-waving and cross-bearing white people paraded to the music of military marching bands, riling up enthusiasm in numerous towns and cities. The fervor revealed a disturbing obsession by some parts of America for "playing soldier and arraying [themselves] in panoplied garb calculated to inspire respect," Charles W. Ferguson wrote in his 1930s assessment of America's lodges and clubs, *Fifty Million Brothers*. Whether or not the "various shirts and fancy breeches" signified anything larger in the American political process or psyche was not yet clear that summer of 1933. "The real threat of these bodies lies in the fact that, disunited though they may be at the moment, they have a common fund of pernicious doctrines," Ferguson said. "They are all eloquently alarmed; they are dissatisfied with the present system. They incline to the totalitarian state with its corollary of a gagged press and stifled speech . . . Most of them seek to exclude Jews and other distasteful minorities from public life and economic competition. They agree on the necessity of direct, unparliamentary action."

How deeply the reactionary impulse ran in America was not readily apparent, but the German and Italian Fascist upheavals clearly resonated with an element of the populace. Dangerous or not, America was awash with right-wing groups overtly bent on government takeover outside the bounds of the democratic electoral process. Government officials were sufficiently worried that they created congressional investigative committees and initiated undercover probes.

Democratic congressman Samuel Dickstein of New York City represented thousands of Lower East Side immigrants whose families, like his own, had escaped the anti-Jewish pogroms of Europe. His district bordered the East River from Chatham Square to East Houston Street. In 1930 he had participated in a congressional investigation into the dissemination of Communist propaganda in the United States. Later he inquired into religious persecution in Russia, and in 1933, after the assassination attempt on Roosevelt, instigated an inquiry into anarchist organizations. In the summer of 1933, Nazi-sympathizers held goose-stepping rallies in his own district. In the East Side ghetto he represented, where Jewish men had their beards pulled, "their wives insulted, their sons beaten," Dickstein was naturally provoked into action. As chairman of the House Immigration Committee, he conducted an unofficial inquest into American Nazis, and when Hitler seized absolute power in Germany, Dickstein convinced his colleagues in the House of Representatives to create the Special Committee to Investigate Nazi Propaganda Activities in the United States. Even before the committee went into effect, Dickstein began amassing a body of information that he predicted would "shock the nation."

Meanwhile, J. Edgar Hoover, ever on the lookout for new public enemies to incite fear and "to justify his increasingly large budget requests," as his biographer Curt Gentry put it, found a captivating one in American Fascism. The issues at hand were so compelling and menacing that on July 30, 1933, Attorney General Cummings announced his appointment of Hoover as head of a new Division of Investigation that would absorb the former Bureau of Investigation. Hoover "did not have to look far for a new 'menace,'" wrote Gentry. "He found two, in fact. One, communism . . . an old menace, newly resurrected . . . [and] the other, fascism." That the Roosevelt administration would place as controversial and offensive a figure as Hoover to head the new overarching investigative agency shocked many in the media. "Despite all this burlesque and bombast," wrote Ray Tucker, the Washington bureau chief of *Collier's* magazine, "there is a serious and sinister side to this secret federal police system," which he described as Hoover's "personal and political machine." The first published account to insinuate that Hoover was a pantywaist, if not a homosexual—pointing out his fastidiousness in dress and other feminine qualities—the *Collier's* story said that Hoover was "short, fat, business-like, and walks with mincing step." The implication stung, and Hoover would adopt a strident manliness to impede any suggestion that he was not tough enough for the job. Hoover and his agency—destined to go down in American history as one of the most powerful and often-chilling government agencies—would turn its considerable command toward rooting out subversives.

Against the backdrop of an America that had come unglued, in a climate of restless uncertainty, frenzied protest, conspiracies and intrigues, surreptitious probes, mutinous masses, and charismatic dictators, a plot to overthrow Roosevelt seemed plausible. So when a U.S. general claimed that he had been asked by a group of powerful businessmen to lead an army of veterans in a coup d'état against President Roosevelt, J. Edgar Hoover and Samuel Dickstein took him seriously.

CHAPTER THIRTY-TWO

Maverick Marine

"ONE OF THE REALLY GREAT GENERALS in American history" is how General MacArthur described the wiry Smedley Darlington Butler. Inspired by the ideals of Manifest Destiny and the Monroe Doctrine, and the image of Teddy Roosevelt and his Rough Riders, Butler began his soldiering career as a sixteen-year-old enlisted Marine in the 1898 Spanish-American War. "A splendid little war," Butler called the conflict for Cuban independence, which was fought and won in ten weeks.

The first of three sons, he was born on July 30, 1881, in West Chester, Pennsylvania, to Thomas Butler and Maud Darlington, both descended from a long line of notable Quakers. Butler was "vigorously brushed and combed and soaped to acquire the cleanliness next to godliness before going to the Friends' Meeting twice a week," and he recalled a childhood peppered with the archaic *thee*s and *thou*s. Though pacifists, both grandfathers had served in the Union Army and the teenage Butler was enamored with all things military. Steeped in the law, politics, farming, and religion, his father was a judge in Chester County—where a Butler had sat on the bench for seventy-five years—and then served as a Republican congressman for three decades. Butler took the predictable route to the serene campus of Haverford College, the Quaker equivalent of Harvard, where an elocution teacher determined to make him a "first class orator" styled after William Cullen Bryant.

When the American warship the U.S.S. *Maine* was sunk in the Havana Harbor, setting off war between the United States and Spain, Butler, eager to defend his Pennsylvania home against the Spaniards in Cuba, thought school "seemed stupid and unnecessary." He lied about his age and enlisted with the Marine Corps, newly expanded to assume tasks in "sunny tropic scenes," according to a history of the Corps. His father strongly opposed his enlistment, but Butler convinced his mother to accompany him to the Washington headquarters to sign up. "If thee is determined to go, thee shall go," the elder Butler said, finally giving his blessing. After six weeks of basic training, in which he learned how to use a 6-millimeter straight-pull rifle, a Gatling gun, and a Hotchkiss revolving cannon, Butler was sent to Guantánamo, Cuba, where a sniper's bullet barely missed his head one night. He was commissioned a first lieutenant and sent the following year with three hundred soldiers to the Philippines to defend the American occupation of the islands against native insurgents. By now fully enamored with the exploits and bravery of the Marines, he had a Japanese tattooist imbed the Marine Corps emblem across his minuscule chest, causing a life-threatening infection and high fever.

In 1900, he joined a Marine force being sent into China's Boxer Rebellion to rescue the U.S. legation stationed in Peking. He saw his job simply as protecting Americans on foreign soil, uninterested in the cause of the strife and oblivious to such provocative slights as the "Forbidden to Dogs and Chinese" signs that hung over the posh American private clubs. After one particularly harrowing battle in Tientsin, Butler and five other soldiers carried a wounded officer seventeen miles through a hail of enemy fire. Butler was shot in his leg and chest and contracted typhoid, and when he dropped below ninety pounds, his commander sent him to a hospital in San Francisco. Allied forces in China, numbering only 19,000, defeated 140,000 Boxers, and the relatively tiny 600-member Marine unit was extolled for special bravery.

After recovering, he returned to Philadelphia, where he was welcomed as a hero at the age of nineteen. Made a captain and now firmly identified with the Marine Corps, which considered itself the proud and "Always Faithful" elite of the U.S. military forces. Butler was now on an upward trajectory in his military career.

From 1902 until 1914, Butler served in several campaigns in Caribbean countries where he saw firsthand the role of American imperialism that would shape his increasingly contemptuous view of the Navy, politics, and the "opera bouffe" of Central American revolutions. He helped "liberate" the isthmus of Panama from Colombia, protected American businesses in Honduras, and engaged in what he thought were ludicrous rebellions in Nicaragua, in which American forces interchangeably sided with dictators and insurgents. "It wasn't exactly clear to me what all the fighting was about," Butler later recalled. He developed a patronizing attitude toward these banana republics, which he thought behaved like unruly children, and a disdain for the U.S. military bent on putting them down while propping up governments that were even worse.

In 1914, Mexican rebels broke out against the repressive and murderous dictator Victoriano Huerta. The United States had a billion dollars invested in Mexico, managed by forty thousand Americans living there. President Woodrow Wilson dispatched a naval squadron to the Caribbean coast to protect Veracruz and Tampico, and the admiral of that operation sent Butler on a spy mission into the interior. Posing as a public-utilities expert, he traveled by rail from Veracruz to Mexico City, reviewing strategic installations along the way. Back in Veracruz, Butler was assigned command of a battalion of Marines who had arrived to help intercept a German ship loaded with weapons and bound for Mexico. The fighting was ferocious, and Butler—a fierce warrior, excellent shot, and precise bayonetter—earned his first Medal of Honor for bravery. "Military engagements during his pre–World War I era mainly pitted soldier against soldier," according to an account in *Smithsonian* magazine. "The winner in such fluid skirmishes was the force that personally killed, wounded, captured or dispersed the most enemy soldiery."

Next came what one historian called "Butler's most bizarre exploit," when the Marines attempted to secure Haiti, which had been plagued by one revolution after another since its 1904 independence from France. There had been seven presidents in an eight-year period, and the U.S. Navy had "visited" the country nineteen times before World War I. One of the oldest independent nations in the western hemisphere, second only to the United States, Haiti had a tumultuous history of anarchy, and in the fall of 1915 was fighting off the indigenous Caco rebels who were fighting against the U.S.–sponsored Haitian government in what was one of the theaters in the "Banana Wars." As in Mexico, Americans were heavily invested in Haiti, owning the only railroad and the nation's largest bank. President Wilson, worried that Germany might exploit the chaotic situation to install a submarine base on the northwest coast of the island, sent in the Marines, and as the ranking officer in the country, Butler assumed powers equivalent to those of the minister of the interior.

Roaming bands of guerrillas scuffled with the Marines. Butler led a dramatic attack against the rebels that earned him the undying devotion of his four companies of twenty-four men, as well as a second Medal of Honor—for which he was nominated by Franklin Roosevelt, then assistant secretary of the navy whom Butler had squired around the island. Butler's men respected him "as much for his care as for his daring," according to one account. "I'd cross hell on a slat if Butler gave the word," said one man of their collective admiration. The feeling was mutual and impelled Butler to throw himself into veterans affairs with his trademark swaggering passion. Haiti was the turning point for Butler, in which he fully grasped that the Marines were being used to subjugate native populations around the world to protect American investments. Once recognizing that they were no more than colonial legionnaires, collecting foreign debts and providing glorified bodyguard services, he lost his zeal for leading young men into wars driven by profits rather than national security. In 1916 he registered his first official complaint with Washington about injustices at the hands of American occupiers, and when he received no reply, he slid further into disillusionment.

He went on to serve in World War I as a commander in France, where the U.S. Navy and Army, as well as the French Order of the Black Star, awarded him medals. Back in the United States, he became commanding general of the Marine barracks at Quantico, Virginia. He was posted to Shanghai, China, in 1927 as a brigadier general commanding a force of five thousand Marines. Sent to protect Americans and their enterprises in the midst of a bitter civil war between Chiang Kai-shek's forces in the south and vicious warlords in the north, Butler was once again baffled by the mission. He wrote his congressman father, who had been a ranking member of the U.S. House Naval Affairs Committee, asking him for an explanation of events transpiring in China. "I do not think that anyone knows our State policies, concerning the situation in China," his father replied. "I do not believe there are any." Policy or not, the American-sponsored Chiang Kai-shek was victorious, and Butler returned to yet another hero's welcome.

His distrust of the rationale for sending U.S. troops around the world coincided with a mounting postwar isolationist sentiment on the home front, and he was drawn to the pacifist disarmament movement supported by Quakers that was springing up as the Great Depression took hold. Antiwar novels were in vogue, and Butler found himself identifying with the protagonists more often than not. While he still believed wholeheartedly in the Marine duty to follow orders at all costs, he questioned the role of the U.S. military and his place in it. In his various deployments throughout the world, he was increasingly drawn to native cultures and customs and couldn't help developing empathy toward the downtrodden masses that the Marines were in the business of subduing. The man who had dedicated his life to the U.S. Marine Corps was riven with ambivalence. While his patriotism never wavered, he found it progressively difficult to stifle his doubts about the direction America had taken.

CHAPTER THIRTY-THREE

I Was a Racketeer for Capitalism

BUTLER'S CRUSTY CANDOR, WHICH ENDEARED him to his soldiers, alienated his superiors. He had been promoted to major general at forty-eight—the youngest Marine to hold the rank—and was assigned to command the Marine base at Quantico. Instead he took a leave of absence—personally approved by President Calvin Coolidge—to take over Philadelphia's fire and police departments as part of a good-government reform movement to root out corruption.

When he returned to active duty, waiting for retirement, he focused his energy on the plight of the Bonus veterans, whom he thought were getting a raw deal from the country they had served. In December 1929, in response to a groundswell of criticism, the U.S. Senate had begun an investigation of Latin American atrocities at the hands of U.S. Marines. Responding to an interviewer's question about corruption in the Corps, Butler claimed that the 1912 Nicaraguan elections were rigged and that he had been ordered to use strong-arm tactics to disrupt the electoral process so that America's puppet leader would not be overthrown. Herbert Hoover's secretary of state, Henry L. Stimson, was outraged by Butler's public allegations: "There is nothing that can do this Government more disservice than such a misstatement of our policy in a Latin American country." Called on the carpet "like an unruly schoolboy," as he described it, and apparently at the behest of President Hoover himself, Butler made a final break from what he saw as the failed policy of gunboat diplomacy.

In January 1931, on the verge of retirement, the renegade Marine gave a speech at a banquet at the influential Contemporary Club of Philadelphia that would spark an international firestorm. In an address about the inhumanity of dictators that he believed was off the record and that was meant to diminish the allure of Fascism that was au courant in the country, Butler singled out Benito Mussolini for special condemnation. "A friend of mine said he had a ride in a new automobile with Mussolini, a car with an armored nose that could knock over fences and slip under barbed wire," Butler told the audience. "He said that they drove through the country and towns at seventy miles per hour. They ran over a child and my friend screamed. Mussolini said he shouldn't do that, that it was only one life and the affairs of the state could not be stopped with one life." Calling Mussolini one of "the mad dogs who are about to break loose in Europe," Butler said he was "one of those fellows who are waiting to start another war. He is polishing up all the brass hats in Italy. He is getting very Roman."

The audience was naturally horrified by the tale. Unbeknownst to Butler, an Italian diplomat was in attendance, and he immediately cabled Rome. The outraged consul filed a protest with the State Department against a high-ranking U.S. military official, in full regalia, publicly insulting Il Duce—at the moment a staunch American ally. Mussolini adamantly denied that his auto had ever killed a child and that he had taken a ride through the Italian countryside with an American.

Headlines throughout the country shrieked GENERAL CALLS MUSSOLINI A HIT AND RUN DRIVER. When Butler refused to back down, confirming that he had indeed made the remarks and believed them to be true, Secretary Stimson issued a formal apology to Mussolini, and President Hoover ordered Butler court-martialed. Hastily drawn charges for "conduct unbecoming" were filed against Butler, and he was placed under arrest—the first such arrest of a general officer since the Civil War.

The man who wore eighteen decorations and was one of only four military men in American history to be awarded two Medals of Honor—"the only man that ever got a double header," said Will Rogers—who had risen from teenage lieutenant to major general, was bolstered rather than chastened by the arrest. "Handed a loaded 'pineapple,'" Butler wrote in his memoir, ". . . the thrust intended to disgrace me and shove me into

oblivion acted as a boomerang on those who were howling for my scalp."
Thousands of anti-Fascist Americans and veterans rushed to show their
support for the beleaguered fighting Quaker. Their letters poured into
Marine headquarters. "General," wrote a veteran, "the stamp on this letter
cost me the two of my last four cents, but I wanted you to know that I am
for you." Then–New York governor Franklin Roosevelt was among many
prominent men who offered to appear as a character witness for Butler.
With public opinion firmly rooted on his side, the press took up his cause.
"Unless we are mistaken the American people are likely to consider these
Cabinet officials guilty of a strange timidity toward Mussolini on one hand
and of an unwarranted harshness toward a splendid American soldier on
the other," Washington's *Daily News* editorialized. Even Mussolini, worried about the anti-Fascist backlash, called it an "unfortunate error" and
urged the federal government to quietly dismiss the case against Butler.

At first, Butler—with distinctive pride and self-righteousness, "preparing to fight to the end"—refused a settlement, eager for the public theater
such a court-martial would provide. When the charges were dropped a few
weeks later, the headlines said it all: YOU'RE A VERY BAD BOY. The affair "cemented my decision to get out in to civil life where I could do something
for powerless juniors degraded by the autocratic action of their department
superiors," Butler wrote of his retirement. "It was not easy for me to leave
the men . . . But I realized . . . it was best to retire while I still had time to
build another life."

Butler was now in great demand as a public speaker. Despite the attempts to muzzle him, or maybe as a result of them, he became ever more
outspoken. He resisted attempts by right-wing military and patriotic organizations to entice him to their cause. He embarked on a lecture circuit, espousing isolationism to huge crowds of veterans and arguing for
the establishment of a powerful Navy that was prohibited from venturing
more than two hundred miles from the U.S. coastline. He told an American Legion audience in Connecticut that during his "thirty-three years
and four months [in] the Marine Corps . . . I spent most of my time being
a high-class muscle man for Big Business, for Wall Street, and for bankers. In short, I was a racketeer for capitalism. I helped make Mexico . . .
safe for American oil interests in 1914. I helped make Haiti and Cuba a
decent place for the National City Bank boys to collect revenues . . . I
helped purify Nicaraguans for the international banking house of Brown
Brothers in 1909–1912. I brought light to the Dominican Republic for

American sugar interests in 1916. I helped make Honduras 'right' for American fruit companies in 1903." Calling it a "swell racket" for which he "was rewarded with honors, medals, promotion," he said he felt as if he "might have given Al Capone a few hints. The best HE could do was to operate his racket in three city districts. We Marines operated on three CONTINENTS."

Sharing the dais with Huey Long in New Orleans, Butler spoke to a gathering of the Veterans of Foreign Wars, claiming to be "the greatest bill collector Wall Street ever sent into the Central American republics, using my marines to collect, taking orders direct, not from Washington, but from Wall Street."

After a short-lived and failed bid for the U.S. Senate seat in Pennsylvania, Butler turned his attention to writing his memoir, *Old Gimlet Eye*, and speaking around the country on behalf of the Bonus Marchers. When Alber Lecture Bureau of Cleveland contracted him for a highly lucrative sixty-city, hundred-thousand-mile tour of America—touting him as "one of the most picturesque and dynamic personalities in American life today"—he used it as an opportunity to meet firsthand the veterans so close to his heart. A lifelong Republican, as were many generations of his forbears, Butler switched parties after Hoover's violent treatment of the marchers. He donated the earnings from that tour to unemployment relief in Philadelphia and to the Salvation Army, which he thought particularly responsive to the needs of the World War I doughboys.

During the 1932 presidential campaign, he called himself "a member of the Hoover-for-Ex-President League because Hoover used gas and bayonets on unarmed human beings."' He became a devoted Roosevelt supporter, giving forty speeches for him around the country and promoting his candidacy to the four and a half million veterans who looked to Butler for leadership. He advocated for taxing the rich to finance unemployment, the establishment of government-financed school and road construction programs, and creating government subsidies for inventive and entrepreneurial industries. Without such measures, the maverick combatant warned, violent revolution was inevitable. Onstage he flailed his arms and raged against the money tyranny, against the "treasury raiders" who had pocketed "millions of dollars worth of patriotism . . . on a ten per cent plus cost basis." The soldiers' general, as he was called, railed against vested interests, entrenched corruption, and the class-driven hierarchy within the U.S. military as epitomized by the American Legion. Since its formation in

1919, the Legion had been the instrument of big business and was notorious for its anti-Semitism and reactionary policies against labor unions and civil rights. Butler cautioned veterans to be wary of Wall Street's flag-waving "Royal Family of financiers" that controlled the American Legion and that, Butler contended, was maneuvering the Legion into supporting the gold standard. He saw the Legion as a paramilitary organization out of touch with the nearly five million rank-and-file men. He thought of the veterans in populist terms and fueled class conflict among them, believing they were a potent political force that could, along with their families, deliver a voting bloc of nearly twenty million. He felt that the Legion was a militaristic reactionary force, in keeping with its roots, that was manipulating the veterans. Don't be taken in by these Wall Street machinations, he inveighed. "What the hell do you know about the gold standard? . . . I believe in making Wall Street pay for it [the veterans' bonuses]—taking Wall Street by the throat and shaking it up."

Iconic hero to every soldier in America, Butler had a complete affinity for, and commitment to, the veterans. So it was with a dose of skepticism that he greeted two elite American Legion emissaries at his Pennsylvania home during the summer of 1933.

CHAPTER THIRTY-FOUR

We Want the Gold

On the morning of July 1, 1933, just as he finished breakfast at his secluded home in Newtown Square, Pennsylvania, General Butler's telephone rang. A man identified himself as "Jack" and said he was an official with the American Legion in Washington. Butler remembered meeting Jack in connection with the veterans' movement, but did not know him well. Jack told Butler that two veterans were on their way from Connecticut to meet with Butler on a pressing matter, and he urged Butler to receive them. Butler responded affirmatively.

"About five hours later a Packard limousine came up into my yard and two men got out," Butler would later tell a U.S. congressional committee. "This limousine was driven by a chauffeur. The well-dressed men entered the house and introduced themselves." One said his name was William H. Doyle, commander of the Legion in Massachusetts. The other identified himself as Gerald C. MacGuire of the Connecticut department of the American Legion. Both were absolute strangers to Butler.

He welcomed them into his house and led them down a hallway to his study. The overweight and perspiring MacGuire guided the conversation, first making small talk in which he claimed to have been a combat Marine who had been disabled with a head wound during World War I. He boasted of his Purple Heart and complained about the silver plate imbedded in his skull. Butler, ever sympathetic to aggrieved veterans, was patient as MacGuire rambled. Finally, the man got to the reason for their visit. Claiming to represent an untold number of rank-and-file Legionnaires who were dissatisfied with the higher-ups in the organization, MacGuire and Doyle were planning to unseat "the royal family in control of the American Legion" at the upcoming Legion convention in Chicago, to be held at the Majestic Hotel in early October, as Butler recalled the conversation. They desperately tried to convince Butler to run for the post of national commander to lead a revolt against the elite leadership, telling him it was of the utmost consequence. The two men were highly disconcerted about President Roosevelt and his New Deal treatment of the veterans.

MacGuire said that he had already made arrangements—as chairman of the Distinguished-Guests committee of the Legion—to have Butler invited to the convention. But when he had submitted Butler's name to the White House to be a Distinguished Guest, as was pro forma since the American Legion was a quasi-governmental organization, Louis Howe had angrily crossed Butler's name off the list and declared that the president was opposed to Butler's invitation, according to MacGuire. "We represent the plain soldiers and we want you . . . to come there and stampede the convention in a speech and help us in our fight to dislodge the royal family."

Butler's suspicions were aroused—by their chauffeur-driven automobile and tailored suits, and by their effort to drive a wedge between him and Roosevelt, whom he admired and considered a friend. He was especially put off by their aspersions against Roosevelt's treatment of the veterans, which, in Butler's opinion, had been in stark contrast with the brutality of the previous president's. He "smelled a rat" but sat silently as he tried to figure out their purpose. "So many queer people come to my house all the time," Butler would later say, "and I like to feel them all out."

Luckily, MacGuire enthused, the men had conceived a subterfuge for sneaking Butler into the convention without the White House stopping them. They had arranged for him to be credentialed as a delegate from Hawaii. Butler refused, telling them he had no intention of using a pretext to attend a veterans' convention. He sent the two disappointed envoys on their way.

A month later they returned. They repeated their appeal, and before Butler could turn them down, MacGuire announced that they had changed tack. Butler was right to have objected, MacGuire told him, for it was beneath his dignity and prestige to attend as a common delegate under false pretenses. Their new plan entailed Butler gathering together several hundred Legionnaires from around the country and traveling with them by train to Chicago. The veterans, who would all be welcome at the gathering, would be strategically seated on the convention floor, and when Butler appeared in the spectator's gallery, they would be roused to a frenzy, cheering and applauding and stomping their feet, demanding a speech from Butler. The Legion leadership would have no choice but to let Butler "make a speech," despite the rejection of him by Louis Howe.

"A speech about what?" Butler asked. MacGuire and Doyle exchanged a satisfied look and placed a document on the table in front of Butler. "We will leave it here with you to read over."

As they rose to leave, they asked Butler to try to round up a few hundred veterans to make the trip. Butler objected, telling them that even if he could interest some veterans, that these impoverished soldiers could never afford to travel back and forth to Chicago and stay in hotels for several days. When he estimated it would cost each man at least one hundred and fifty dollars, MacGuire quickly assured him that he had already made arrangements for the veterans' expenses to be paid. Withdrawing a bankbook from his jacket pocket, MacGuire flipped the pages to show Butler deposits totaling more than a hundred thousand dollars to go toward the veterans' expenses. He refused to identify the source of the money, which naturally piqued Butler's curiosity, but said there was plenty more available.

Butler had been speaking out against the Legion leadership for several years, and he felt strongly that the "royal family" should be ousted. But he also felt that there was something amiss with these two allegedly disabled veterans and their big bank account. He sent them on their way and said he'd be in touch with them once he had read the speech that had been drafted for him to deliver.

As soon as they drove away Butler eagerly picked up the document. It was a highly polished, well-written speech ardently beseeching the Legionnaires to pass a resolution demanding that the United States return to the gold standard. Such a move was imperative, according to the address, so that when the government paid the soldiers their World War I bonuses, they would receive hard currency rather than worthless paper money. So, Butler surmised, someone sought to use the Legion as an instrument to pressure the Roosevelt administration into restoring the gold standard, and Butler was their pawn. But who were they, and was that their only motive?

Butler met MacGuire a third time in September 1933 in Newark, New Jersey, where Butler was addressing a convention of the Twenty-ninth Division. MacGuire appeared unexpectedly and alone and knocked on Butler's hotel room door. Wearing a black derby over his "bullet-shaped head" with its "close-cropped hair," MacGuire inquired anxiously about the progress Butler had made in rounding up veterans. Realizing that MacGuire was simply the front man for powerful backers, Butler demanded to know the source of his money. Nine very wealthy men had put up the funds, MacGuire replied, including his employer—Legionnaire and Wall Street financier Colonel Grayson Meller-Provost Murphy, who operated a brokerage firm in New York City. A West Point graduate and veteran of the Spanish-American War, Murphy in 1919 had been one of twenty men who provided the necessary start-up funding—to the tune of $125,000—for the creation of the American Legion. In addition to owning a prestigious Wall Street stock brokerage firm, Murphy had extensive financial interests in Anaconda Copper Mining, Goodyear Tire, Bethlehem Steel, and numerous J. P. Morgan–owned banks. Mussolini had decorated Murphy, making him a Commander of the Crown of Italy, MacGuire claimed. Given Butler's recent contretemps with Il Duce, MacGuire's boast could hardly have improved the Marine's opinion of Murphy.

MacGuire would only identify one other investor in the scheme—Robert Sterling Clark, an heir to the Singer Sewing Machine fortune and a multimillionaire Wall Street broker famous for his art collection of modernists and masters. Butler remembered Clark as the "millionaire lieutenant" whom he had served under during the Boxer Rebellion in China. He later described the eccentric Clark to Congress as a "sort of batty, sort of queer" man who "did all sorts of extravagant things. He used to go exploring around China and wrote a book on it. He was never taken seriously by anybody. But he had a lot of money. An aunt and uncle died and left him ten million dollars."

Butler decided to force MacGuire's hand, telling him that he had no intention of going to Chicago and didn't believe that MacGuire had any money behind him. Then, Butler recalled, MacGuire whipped out his wallet and threw a stack of thousand-dollar bills on the bed.

"What's all this?" Butler asked. MacGuire responded that it was eighteen thousand dollars for Butler's "expenses."

Now, insulted that he was being bribed, Butler got agitated. "Don't you try to give me any thousand dollar bill . . . I know you people and what you are trying to do. You are just trying to get me by the neck . . . You put that money away . . . because I don't want to be tied up with it at all." MacGuire nervously asked whether he was intending to go to Chicago.

"I do not know," Butler replied. "But I know one thing. Somebody is using you. You are a wounded man. You are a bluejacket . . . I want to know the fellows who are using you. I am not going to talk to you any more. You are only an agent. I want some of the principals."

A few days later Butler—apparently seeking to create a paper trail as he drew out the identity of the sponsors of the plot—wrote to MacGuire and said he had given the proposal more thought and now considered it "a great idea." He agreed that he could easily mobilize a hundred Legionnaires as long as there was "positive assurance of financial support" and no "slip-up in the arrangements, particularly in the matter of paying their expenses and treating them properly." Butler reiterated that he did not want to appear on the convention floor posing as a delegate from Hawaii. "If I am to be of any value to the cause you sponsor, I would necessarily have to have some position. All of this would be lost if I force my way into this part through an imitation delegateship."

MacGuire agreed to set up a meeting with Robert Sterling Clark. A week later, Clark called Butler and arranged to travel to Newtown Square to see him.

Although he had not seen Clark for thirty-four years, Butler recognized him immediately as he stepped off the train. On the drive to Butler's home, they reminisced about the Boxer campaign. After a pleasant lunch, Clark launched into business. He had made plans to travel to the American Legion convention in a private railway car that would retrieve Butler at the Paoli, Pennsylvania, rail station. He had reserved a suite for Butler at the Palmer House in Chicago and had made arrangements for Butler to address the convention to demand the restoration of the gold standard. "There is something funny about that speech, Mr. Clark," Butler said, describing it as too refined to have been written by the clumsy MacGuire and calling it a "big-business speech" that was contradictory to the veterans' interests.

Clark was silent for a few minutes and then was astonishingly candid. "That speech cost a lot of money," Clark admitted, saying that the author was John W. Davis—the 1924 Democratic candidate for president who was currently chief counsel for J. P. Morgan and Company—and implying that the millionaire had paid Davis to write it. "We want the soldiers' bonus paid in gold. We do not want the soldier to have rubber money or paper money. We want the gold. That is the reason for this speech."

"I have got 30 million dollars and I don't want to lose it," Clark told Butler. "I am willing to spend half of the 30 million to save the other half." Clark said he felt certain that if Butler made the speech in Chicago, the Legion would follow his directive and force Roosevelt to return to the gold standard.

When Butler asked Clark why he believed that Roosevelt would be responsive to a veterans' resolution, Clark replied that when Roosevelt realized that it was his own patrician class directing the pressure, that he would willingly succumb. "You know the President is weak. He will come right along with us. He was born in this class. He was raised in this class, and he will come back," Clark said. "He will run true to form. In the end he will come around. But we have got to be prepared to sustain him when he does." Butler was shocked by what he thought a wishful fantasy that Roosevelt was a malleable aristocrat.

When Butler told Clark he would not participate in the plan, Clark stiffened and then berated him. In what Butler considered a thinly veiled bribe, Clark implied that Butler's home mortgage would be paid and there would be additional financial benefits as well: "Why do you want to be stubborn? Why do you want to be different from other people? We can take care of you." He then tried to goad Butler into acquiescing by telling him that he was not the only person being considered for the job to lead the veterans. "Although our group is for you, the Morgan interests say that you cannot be trusted, that you are too radical ... They are for Douglas MacArthur," Butler said MacGuire told him. "You know as well as I do that MacArthur is [Edward] Stotesbury's son-in-law ... Morgan's representative in Philadelphia." Stotesbury, an investment banker worth more than a hundred million dollars, was a partner in J. P. Morgan and Company and a Philadelphia Quaker. Butler later realized that the "Morgan interests" to which Clark referred also included Thomas Lamont and Grayson M.-P. Murphy. Butler told Clark that they had better choose MacArthur and angrily drove him back to the train station.

A few weeks later, Butler read in the newspaper that the American Legion convention had received a flood of telegrams urging delegates to endorse a return to the gold standard. A resolution to that effect was passed. He noted that MacArthur did not address the convention.

CHAPTER THIRTY-FIVE

Coup d'État

In November 1933, shortly after the American Legion convention in Chicago, Gerard MacGuire turned up "like a bad penny," as Butler put it, and informed Butler that a group of Boston veterans were hosting a dinner in his honor. They would transport Butler from Philadelphia by private car, and he would receive a thousand dollars for making remarks in support of the gold standard. Butler testily rebuffed him yet again, but MacGuire remained strangely unflappable, saying, "Well, then, we will think of something else." MacGuire's perseverance flabbergasted the reluctant general, as the sweaty bond salesman continued his overtures. He was relentless in trying to convince Butler that it was pointless to support the soldiers' bonus until the country had a sound currency.

There followed a string of proposals over a period of months in which Butler was offered exorbitant fees for speaking before veterans' organizations. After Butler's lecture agent contracted for a national speaking tour for appearances before numerous Veterans of Foreign Wars (VFW) groups, for which Butler would be paid $250 per speech, MacGuire suddenly materialized and offered him an additional $750 per speech if he would insert an endorsement of the gold standard in each one. Again, Butler brushed him off.

The fall of 1933 saw an increase in the vitriolic anti-Roosevelt rhetoric, which reached a crescendo with FDR's November 17 diplomatic recognition of the Soviet Union. The United States had supported the White Russians in their civil war and had then ignored the victorious Bolsheviks since 1917. The Soviet Union had had an economic office in the United States for several months, but the actual exchange of embassies set off alarm bells in America's anti-Communist circles. It had been Roosevelt's personal initiative, begun with a letter to Soviet president Mikhail Kalinin stating that he had "contemplated the desirability of an effort to end the present abnormal relations between the hundred and twenty-five million people of the United States and the hundred and sixty million people of Russia." A survey showed that 63 percent of the nation's 1,139 newspapers supported it, with the hopes of opening a market for American exports. But an even greater resolve took hold of Roosevelt when Hitler withdrew from the League of Nations, and Roosevelt sought the Soviet Union as an ally in the event of German expansion.

During a series of covert negotiations over a nine-day period, Roosevelt and Soviet emissary Maxim Litvinov, who had traveled to Washington at Roosevelt's invitation, exchanged eleven letters and one memorandum signaling the countries' agreement with each other. "A great many people at the time regarded this event as of earthshaking importance," wrote one Roosevelt biographer.

Roosevelt's right-wing enemies were not among those who saw the move as a great boon for America. Already furious at his "Socialist" leanings, they were now confirmed in their suspicions that the president was a full-blown "Red" who was instituting the Bolshevik experiment in the United States. Business leaders saw a dangerous shift toward Soviet-style Communism at a moment when they were looking enviously at Italy and its dictator, if not also at Germany and Hitler. Their Italian counterparts had financed Mussolini's rise and staged a bloodless coup, and the end result was a highly efficient corporate Fascist state enjoying economic prosperity in the midst of a global depression. Just weeks later, as part of the "Good Neighbor" policy he had mentioned in his inaugural address, Roosevelt announced that the United States would no longer be sending troops to Latin America to protect private investments. The new policy sent more shock waves to America's business community, which had vast financial interests in Latin America and had long depended on U.S. military protection in the region. But Roosevelt unequivocally abandoned the policy of military intervention in the affairs of any other state.

On December 1, 1933, as yet unbeknownst to Butler, MacGuire left for Europe to study how veterans' organizations had brought about dictatorships. He spent two months in Italy evaluating the Black Shirts and their role in installing Mussolini. From there he went to Germany to witness the Nazi phenomenon firsthand. Robert Sterling Clark was the sponsor of his junket, he would later tell Congress. He sent enthusiastic postcards to Butler from Italy, Germany, Spain, and France. He had determined that the Italian and German examples were not feasible to institute in the United States because American veterans were too freedom-loving and would never embrace such absolute rigidity. But in France he had found a perfect model: the right-wing veterans' group called the Croix de Feu (Cross of Fire). He wrote a letter back to his benefactors. "Gentlemen," he addressed them anonymously. "I just returned from a trip to Brussels, Rotterdam, Amsterdam, Hamburg, Copenhagen, Berlin, Prague, Leipzig, Vienna, Munich, Zurich, Basle, Geneva, and thence back to Paris." He reported, "There is a Fascist Party springing up in Holland under the leadership of a man named Mussait, who is an engineer by profession and he has approximately 50,000 followers . . . It is said that this man is in close touch with Berlin, and is modeling his entire program along the lines followed by Hitler in Germany." In a second letter to the "Gentlemen," MacGuire said, "Everywhere you go you see men marching in groups and company formation."

Upon arriving back in the United States in the spring of 1934, MacGuire excitedly related his findings to Butler when the two men met in a remote corner of the lobby at the Bellevue-Stratford Hotel in Philadelphia. MacGuire told him about the "superorganization . . . an amalgamation of all other French veteran organizations . . . composed of officers and noncoms." An insurrection by this Croix de Feu had successfully toppled the government of Prime Minister Édouard Daladier, MacGuire claimed, and could be duplicated in the United States. It was time to "get the soldiers together" for a peaceful military takeover of the Roosevelt presidency, MacGuire told Butler.

MacGuire claimed to already have three million dollars available to launch the effort and said the promoters were prepared to spend as much as three hundred million. The men behind the putsch projected that it would take a year for Butler—the most popular and charismatic military leader in the nation—to assemble five hundred thousand veterans who would be paid between ten and thirty-five dollars per month, depending on their rank. They had chosen Butler, MacGuire told him with an apparent lack of irony, because Butler's unrelenting anti-capitalist, anti-imperialist criticism would strike a chord with the angry half million Bonus Army veterans who would do anything Butler told them to do.

The plot was stunning in its presumption and simplicity. "Did it ever occur to you that the President is overworked?" MacGuire asked Butler. He explained that it did not require a constitutional change to authorize a "Secretary of General Affairs" to take over the details of the office of the presidency. The man the plotters had in mind for this task was Brigadier General Hugh S. Johnson, Roosevelt's head of the National Recovery Administration, who, according to MacGuire's purported inside information, was about to be fired by Roosevelt. "We have got the newspapers. We will start a campaign that the President's health is failing. Everybody can tell that by looking at him, and the dumb American people will fall for it in a second."

The veterans' army, led by Butler, would march on Washington and induce Roosevelt to step aside because of bad health. Vice President Garner, in the line of succession, would refuse the office because he didn't want to be president, and Secretary of State Cordell Hull—next in line—would decline based on his age, or so the plotters' reasoning went. After the "coup," General Johnson would take Hull's place as a sort of "Super Secretary" who would be the de facto president and immediately reinstitute the gold standard. America needed a "man on a white horse," MacGuire told Butler, ". . . a dictator who would come galloping in." It was the only way to "save the capitalistic system." It was all perfectly "constitutional," as MacGuire and his cohorts saw it.

James Van Zandt, the national commander of the VFW, had already agreed to serve as a leader in the veterans' army, according to MacGuire—a charge that Van Zandt would later vehemently deny, although he would later corroborate Butler's story and reveal that he too had been approached by "agents of Wall Street" intent on overthrowing the government. In addition to this "superorganization," an elite paramilitary group would be created, which would be led by General MacArthur.

Staggeringly, MacGuire portrayed the zany plot as an attempt to "support" Roosevelt in his hour of need. Butler challenged him: "The President doesn't need the support of that kind of an organization; and, besides, since when did you become a supporter of Roosevelt? The last time you were here you were against him."

"Don't you understand?" MacGuire responded. "The set-up has got to be changed a bit. We have the President with us now. He has got to have more money . . . Eighty percent of the money now is in Government bonds and he cannot keep this racket up much longer . . . He has either got to get more money out of us or he has got to change the method of financing the government, and we are going to see to it that he isn't going to change that method. He will not change it. He is with us now."

If Roosevelt acceded to their demands, they would allow him to remain as a powerless figurehead "analogous to Mussolini's handling of the king of Italy," as one account put it. If Roosevelt "was not in sympathy with the Fascist movement," then he would be "forced to resign."

"We want to ease up on the President," MacGuire told Butler.

"You want to put somebody in there you can run; is that the idea?" Butler was incredulous at both the naïveté and grandiosity of the scheme. "The President will go around and christen babies and dedicate bridges and kiss children? Mr. Roosevelt will *never* agree to that himself."

Butler was by now convinced that the prospective putsch, wacky and delusional as it was, constituted treason. He considered whom or which government agency he should alert. If such powerful financial magnates and high-level military officials were truly conspiring, as MacGuire alleged, he needed to be careful in how he proceeded. "His protagonists in the present scrap—Wall Street brokers, their legal counselors, and shrewd political operatives—were backed by a supporting network that extended into veterans affairs, politics, and the rightwing press," said a military historian of Butler's dilemma. He considered taking the story to J. Edgar Hoover at the Division of Investigation, to a carefully chosen member of Congress, to the media, or directly to the White House.

MacGuire asked Butler for a commitment. Stalling for time, Butler said he needed to think about it a little longer.

MacGuire said that an umbrella organization had already been created to support the objectives of the plotters and that widespread publicity about the group would soon emerge. "You watch," MacGuire told him, "in two or three weeks you will see it come out in the paper. There will be big fellows in it . . . These are to be the villagers in the opera." At that point it would be imperative for Butler to decide whether he was in or out.

Two weeks later, Butler read in the newspaper about the creation of the American Liberty League—a heavily funded organization formed "to combat radicalism, to teach the necessity of respect for the rights of persons and property, and generally to foster free private enterprise" and to oppose the destruction of America by New Deal policies. Formed by displeased moguls of finance and industry, the Liberty League attacked Roosevelt for "fomenting class hatred" by using such terms as "unscrupulous money changers," "economic royalists," and "privileged princes of these new economic dynasties."

Butler read the list of the Liberty League's 156 sponsors with a combination of disbelief and trepidation. All the founding supporters contributed sizable cash amounts to the new organization and together controlled assets worth nearly forty billion dollars. The first name he looked for on the long list was "treasurer." He was unsurprised: Grayson M-P. Murphy— Gerald MacGuire's boss. The rest of the names read like a who's who of American capitalism and reactionary politics, of organizations and individuals long associated with avowed anti-labor and pro-Fascist policies: Robert Sterling Clark, John W. Davis, Irénéé and Lammot du Pont, Alfred E. Smith, Sewell Avery, Alfred P. Sloan, S. B. Colgate, Elihu Root, E. F. Hutton, John H. Raskob, and J. Howard Pew, among many others.

For the first time it struck Butler that MacGuire's revelations about a "plot to seize the White House were no crackpot's fantasy."

CHAPTER THIRTY-SIX

The Bankers Gold Group

"THERE WAS DEFINITELY SOMETHING CRAZY ABOUT the whole affair," wrote J. Edgar Hoover's biographer Curt Gentry. "Butler, who had gained prominence for speaking out *against* fascism, [was] being asked to become an American *duce*."

Butler decided that it was premature to take the information to either the president or Hoover until he had more evidence. It would be Butler's word against Clark's and MacGuire's, and Butler could end up looking like the crazy one. Suspecting that the entire "plot" might be nothing more than an attempt to discredit him and neutralize him as a critic of Wall Street and Fascism, Butler chose to share the story with a journalist first. He contacted Tom O'Neil, city editor of the *Philadelphia Record*—a liberal newspaper owned by J. David Stern, who also published the *New York Evening Post*. He told O'Neil the bizarre story and asked him to assign his star reporter, Paul Comly French, a fellow Quaker, to explore the legitimacy of the conspiracy. O'Neil agreed and Butler told French everything about what he had come to call the "bankers gold group."

French set out to determine whether the plot was an attempt to extort money from a cabal of rich right-wingers "by selling them political gold bricks," as Butler wondered, or whether a cabal of rich right-wingers, "enraged by Roosevelt and his New Deal policies, was putting up big money to overthrow F.D.R. with a putsch."

French was fired up about the story but worried too that it was so improbable that, short of ironclad evidence, he and Butler both would be disbelieved and ridiculed. He knew that much depended on the credibility, integrity, and patriotism of his main source, Smedley Butler, so he first probed into Butler's background and interviewed the retired Marine extensively. What French found was a highly controversial figure, a whistle-blower whose salty language and "irrepressible temper and tongue kept him in the headlines," whose candor and courage unsettled his enemies and landed him "in hot water with his superiors," and whose blunt truth telling was generated by an idealized love of America and democracy.

Once satisfied that Butler had no history of, or known proclivity for, lying and that his zealous outbursts were inspired by honorable motives, French began to investigate Butler's claims that a group of wealthy Americans was arming and financing Fascist plots.

MacGuire agreed to be interviewed by French after Butler vouched for French's dependability. Posing as a reporter who was sympathetic to the anti-Roosevelt forces, French gained MacGuire's trust and was invited to visit him at his suite at the Grayson Murphy New York brokerage firm. They met in MacGuire's twelfth-floor office at 52 Broadway for a two-and-a-half hour conversation. MacGuire told French the same story that he had told Butler except for one significant amplification: that the weapons and ammunition they needed for a coup would be supplied by "Remington Arms Company on credit through the DuPonts," who owned a controlling interest in the firm. "We need a Fascist government in this country," MacGuire insisted to French, "to save the Nation from the communists who want to tear it down and wreck all that we have built in America. The only men who have the patriotism to do it are the soldiers and Smedley Butler is the ideal leader. He could organize a million men overnight." MacGuire told French of his fact-finding mission to Europe, and how he had "obtained enough information on the Fascist and Nazi movements and of the part played by veterans, to properly set up one in this country." At first MacGuire and his sponsors had planned to have Butler ask each of the million veterans to contribute a dollar to the effort, MacGuire said, but they decided instead to raise funds from wealthy simpatico financiers and industrialists.

Throughout the interview, MacGuire emphasized the patriotism of those desirous of a Fascist government to stop Roosevelt's Socialist plot to redistribute the wealth. They all agreed, he said, that bonds would soon reach 5 percent, creating an economic crash requiring the soldiers to save the country. MacGuire volunteered names of individuals and organizations that had pledged more than a million dollars each. He provided French with the identities of potential leaders of the Fascist plot, including a former national commander of the American Legion. MacGuire was obsessed with the "unemployment situation," saying that Roosevelt had "muffed it terrifically" but that an ingenious plan he had witnessed in Germany would "solve it overnight." French listened, dumbfounded, as MacGuire suggested that the United States follow Hitler's "ideal" prototype of "putting all of the unemployed in labor camps or barracks—enforced labor."

Butler abhorred all the dictator talk, which he thought merely a euphemism for a big-business, corporate takeover of government. "I have been in 752 different towns in the United States in three years and one month, and I made 1,022 speeches," Butler would later testify. "I have seen absolutely no sign of anything showing a trend for a change of our form of Government."

The next, and final, time that MacGuire approached Butler to see whether he would agree to lead a veterans' march on Washington, the ex-Marine was unsparing. "If you get 500,000 soldiers advocating anything smelling of Fascism, I am going to get 500,000 more and lick the hell out of you, and we will have a real war right at home."

His true sentiments now exposed to MacGuire, and with the story confirmed by Paul French, Butler went to see J. Edgar Hoover in the fall of 1934. "Hoover knew a loaded gun when he saw one," Gentry wrote. "This sounded to him like a plot to overthrow the government of the United States. However, if the Division of Investigation investigated Butler's charges, he would risk alienating some of America's most powerful corporation heads." In characteristic fashion, Hoover sought to use Butler's information to expand his own power while avoiding a delicate probe that might jeopardize his ambitions. He told Butler that he thought the plot a grave situation, but that lacking an apparent federal offense, he was powerless to pursue an investigation. Behind the scenes Hoover quickly used the opportunity to justify a larger role in national law enforcement. Indeed, the Butler exposé would, "with Hoover's skillful handling," as Gentry wrote, "help the director grasp control of all domestic intelligence in the United States."

What Hoover neglected to tell Butler was that his agency was already investigating American Fascism at the personal directive of President Roosevelt. Roosevelt had called a secret White House conference with Hoover six months earlier—just weeks after MacGuire's return from his European Fascist research tour—to discuss the growing Nazi movement in the United States. Present at the meeting with Roosevelt and Hoover were Attorney General Homer Cummings, Secretary of the Treasury Henry Morgenthau, Secretary of Labor Frances Perkins, and Secret Service Chief W. H. Moran. In an internal memorandum, Hoover wrote that Roosevelt requested that the Division of Investigation work with the other agencies to conduct "a very careful and searching investigation" of Nazi organizations and, especially, "any possible connection with the official representatives of the German government in the United States."

Since Roosevelt, Hoover, and several other high-level government officials in the administration were obviously concerned about an internal Nazi threat, it seemed highly likely that they knew about the "Business Plot," or the "Wall Street Putsch"—as the Clark-Murphy-MacGuire-veterans scheme would eventually be dubbed by the press.

For his part, Butler reasoned that even though Hoover didn't have the jurisdiction to investigate the charges, the nation's top cop would undoubtedly see that the explosive information got into the right hands. If Butler considered taking his story to the White House, he didn't need to. Suddenly Washington was abuzz with gossip that the American Legion was organizing a Fascist army to seize the capital. John L. Spivak, a veteran muckraker and foreign correspondent, an admitted Communist but one with impeccable high-placed sources, had begun digging into the rumors of a coup. At the same time, the U.S. House Un-American Activities Committee had learned of the plot—undoubtedly from Hoover—and a committee investigator called Butler to see whether he would be willing to cooperate with Congress. Indeed, Butler responded. He had been praying for just such a call.

In the fall of 1934, the political atmosphere was highly charged heading into the midterm elections of Roosevelt's first term in office. The newly formed American Liberty League—well funded and ubiquitous—blanketed the country with incendiary anti-Roosevelt propaganda. It sent out more than five million pamphlets denouncing Roosevelt's "socialist" agenda, hinting darkly at his Machiavellian plots to dismantle the Constitution and referring to the president as "King Franklin I." Supposedly nonpartisan, the professional patriots of the Liberty League were a collection of wealthy Democrats and Republicans concerned that the new administration's work projects and regulations of industry were interfering with the labor market and upsetting the natural method of supply and demand. "Five Negroes on my place in South Carolina refused work this Spring . . . saying they had easy jobs with the government," an official with the DuPont company wrote to the former chairman of the Democratic Party. "A cook on my houseboat at Fort Myers quit because the government was paying him a dollar an hour as a painter."

The group, hoping to encourage Americans to work and to get rich, had agonized over its name. One founding member suggested Association Asserting the Rights of Property, which was then shortened to the National Property League. Just before filing official papers for the organization, John W. Davis lighted on the catchy name the American Liberty League. The new patriotic sounding name "hid the fact that it was really about rich men protecting their interests," as the biographer of founder Alfred E. Smith wrote after reviewing correspondence between the wealthy board of directors. Claiming widespread support from a cross-section of business and finance, its leadership actually drew exclusively from a minuscule group of extremely wealthy individuals. Its thirty-two-room headquarters in the National Press Building in Washington emblemized its provenance as well as its income, which exceeded that of the national Republican Party. In fact, fewer than two dozen bankers and businessmen had contributed more than half the Liberty League's funds, and, notably, its founding members included more conservative "Jeffersonian Democrats" than Republicans. "The financial community," reported the *New York Times*, "sees in the movement the nucleus of a new force for conservatism."

Ultimately, the gap between rich and poor had become too wide, too starkly apparent for the League of multimillionaires to have credibility with most Americans. As George Wolfskill wrote in *The Revolt of the Conservatives*, "New Deal spokesmen did not have to refute the views of the League; they only had to call the roll."

Socialists or not, Roosevelt and the Democrats won both Houses in an unprecedented landslide, increasing the Democrats from 60 to 69 in the

Senate and from 309 to 322 in the House of Representatives. Not since Civil War Reconstruction had one party gained such an overwhelming majority. Roosevelt was now assured of a responsive and productive Seventy-fourth Congress of the United States—Wall Street's worst nightmare.

CHAPTER THIRTY-SEVEN

The Investigation

In November 1934, the House Committee on Un-American Activities met in a secret executive session in New York City. Chairman John W. McCormack and vice chairman Samuel Dickstein were the only committee members at the hearing. They called General Smedley Butler, Gerald MacGuire, and Paul Comly French to appear. Butler spoke first, providing detailed testimony about everything that had occurred beginning with the first visit from MacGuire and Doyle on July 1, 1933, through all his meetings with MacGuire and Clark.

"To be perfectly fair to Mr. MacGuire," Butler testified, "he didn't seem bloodthirsty. He felt that such a show of force in Washington would probably result in a peaceful overturn of the government." After he had been asked dozens of times by both MacGuire and Clark to accept the leadership of the coup d'état, Butler said, he had decided to enlist the assistance of French to gather corroborative evidence. Butler named the alleged conspirators whom he believed the committee should call as witnesses, although these names were stricken from the official record of the hearings that would be released to the public. During his appearance Butler sought especially to spark the indignation of committee chairman McCormack—a Massachusetts Democrat who, though a Legionnaire, was an avid supporter of Roosevelt and the New Deal.

Next came French, who confirmed and verified Butler's story to the letter, adding the Remington Arms connection. The congressmen, by all accounts, were stunned by the allegations raised, by the dangerous implication of an impending coup d'état, and by the sheer political and economic power of the alleged participants. They broke for lunch and reconvened in the afternoon to interrogate MacGuire. Not surprisingly, MacGuire denied all of Butler's allegations implicating MacGuire in bribery, in an effort to unseat the American Legion leadership, and in a Fascist military coup. The bond salesman who earned $150 per week insisted that all his contacts with Butler were to enlist Butler's support of a Clark-funded group called the Committee for a Sound Dollar and Sound Currency and that he merely wanted Butler to speak in support of that movement. That committee, MacGuire testified, was organized to support President Roosevelt and "his position on sound money . . . We were against the inflationists and the people who were trying to bring about inflation in the country."

MacGuire denied attempting to get Butler to attend the Chicago convention and speak on behalf of the gold standard. He denied providing Butler with the speech written by John Davis and claimed never to have discussed money with Butler, nor to have shown him evidence of deposits totaling a hundred thousand dollars. He admitted that Robert Sterling Clark had paid for his trip to Europe so MacGuire could "study securities," but denied that he'd had any discussions with Butler about European Fascist takeovers supported by veterans' armies or of any "superorganization" of veterans in the United States. He denied offering Butler eighteen thousand dollars and repudiated French's claims that he had discussed a Fascist coup.

MacGuire was "hanging himself by contradictions and admissions," Dickstein admitted to reporters after the committee adjourned at the end of the day. McCormack refused to comment to the *New York Times*, explaining that the testimony had been given in executive session, but promised that a public hearing would be held "if the facts warrant." Paul French had broken the story two days earlier in both the Philadelphia and New York newspapers under the headline: $3,000,000 BID FOR FASCIST ARMY BARED, which was reprinted in the country's major newspapers.

Calling Butler's allegations "a damned lie," Grayson M.-P. Murphy told French, "I haven't been able to stop laughing. I hope you come in armed, because I may start shooting, even if this is going to be a bloodless revolution. To say a thing like this about a man who has a record like mine in the Spanish-American War, in the Philippines, in the World War, to say that a man who would serve his country like that would turn around and try to overthrow the Government, is hitting below the belt." French reported that the tall, silver-haired Murphy, his blue eyes shining, had smiled throughout the entire interview.

Robert Sterling Clark, who had been subpoenaed by the committee, was traveling in Europe when the story broke. Reached by telephone in Paris, he told the press that he had "strongly urged" Butler "to use his influence in favor of sound money and against inflation." But he adamantly denied that he was the sponsor of an "American Fascist movement." Still, vice chairman Dickstein announced that both Clark and his New York attorney, who had accompanied Clark to Europe, were under surveillance in Paris. "I believe that Clark has cold feet," Dickstein told the *Chicago Daily Tribune*. "It looks as if he were afraid to appear before our committee. But we will get his testimony. Any one can see there is something wrong in this matter." Dickstein pointed to MacGuire's inability to explain to the committee financial transactions involving more than a hundred thousand dollars. "MacGuire is shielding somebody I believe. Probably a lot of people."

Newspapers reported the "immediate emphatic denials by the purported plotters." Leading the charge was General Hugh "Old Iron Pants" Johnson, who "barked" at the *New York Times* reporter. "He had better be pretty damn careful," Johnson said, referring to Butler. "Nobody said a word to me about anything of this kind, and if they did I'd throw them out the window. I know nothing about it." Thomas Lamont, Liberty League contributor and J. P. Morgan partner, called it "perfect moonshine. Too unutterably ridiculous to comment upon!" General MacArthur was unavailable for comment, but his aides "expressed amazement and amusement."

The committee examined various financial transactions between MacGuire and Clark and concluded that MacGuire had been the cashier for the plotters. Dickstein vowed that as many as sixteen people who had been identified by Butler, including Clark, would be subpoenaed. But as days passed without further scheduled hearings, gossip began spreading through Washington that a cover-up was under way. Despite assurances from both McCormack and Dickstein that the committee planned a full investigation of the plot, they apparently only called one more witness—Frank N. Belgrano, a San Francisco banker and president of the Transamerica Corporation who would soon become national commander of the American Legion—but apparently sent him home without taking his testimony. The committee released its eight-thousand-word "Public Statement on Preliminary Findings" on November 24, 1934. Signed by McCormack and Dickstein, it began, "This committee has had no evidence before it that would in the slightest degree warrant calling before it such men as John W. Davis, General Hugh Johnson," and then went on to list some of the other men who had been named by Butler as accomplices. Both congressmen insisted that they were pursuing the inquiry and planned to call Clark and others. The committee "still intends to get to the bottom of a Wall Street plot to put Major Gen. Smedley D. Butler at the head of a Fascist army here," Dickstein told the *New York Times*. "The committee's statement of the evidence . . . was intended only to satisfy the great public interest in the plot." The newspaper account indicated Dickstein was eager for the statement to be seen "neither as whitewash . . . nor as sensationalism."

"The press . . . handled the Butler affair with its tongue in its journalistic cheek," one historian wrote of the marginalization of the story. The press campaign against Butler got off to a quick start, with *Time* magazine leading the way with a caricatured version of the plot called "Plot Without Plotters." In *Time*'s satirical imagining, Butler is carried to Washington by an imaginary white horse, where he then forces his way into Roosevelt's office—"his spurs clinked loudly"—and orders the president to relinquish his office to Butler and his five-hundred-thousand-man army. "Such was the nightmarish page of future United States history pictured last week in Manhattan by General Butler himself," *Time* reported. "No military officer of the United States since the late tempestuous George Custer has succeeded in publicly floundering in so much hot water as Smedley Darlington Butler."

"What can we believe?" asked the *New York Times*. "Apparently anything, to judge by the number of people who lend a credulous ear to the story of General Butler's 500,000 Fascists in buckram marching on Washington to seize the Government. Details are lacking to lend verisimilitude to an otherwise bald and unconvincing narrative . . . The whole story sounds like a gigantic hoax . . . It does not merit serious discussion."

No American newspaper published the entire testimony, many newspapers suppressed the story altogether, and the large majority ridiculed it. The nation's leading newspapers' dismissal of allegations by a U.S.

marine general that an alliance of Legionnaires, bankers and stockbro-
kers had tried to hire him to overthrow the government was mystifying.
While neither the public nor much of the press seemed to take Butler seriously, the McCormack-Dickstein Committee apparently did. The few
Washington newsmen who had been following the story were not satisfied
with the brief initial findings and closely pressured the committee to release the hearing transcripts. When it finally published its 125-page report
three months later, it was vividly marked "EXTRACTS." Stunningly, the
committee stated that it "was able to verify all pertinent statements made
by General Butler, with the exception of the direct statement suggesting
the creation of the organization. This, however, was corroborated in the
correspondence of MacGuire with his principal, Robert Sterling Clark, of
New York City, while MacGuire was abroad studying the various organizations of Fascist character." The committee summarized its conclusion:
"Evidence was obtained showing that certain persons had made an attempt
to establish a fascist organization in this country. There is no question but
that these attempts were discussed, were planned, and might have been
placed in execution when and if the financial backers deemed it expedient."

As shocking as the findings were, the committee added a further announcement attached to the end of the document in boldface type:

> In making public the foregoing evidence, which was taken in
> executive session in New York City from November 20 to 24,
> inclusive, the committee has ordered stricken therefrom certain
> immaterial and incompetent evidence, or evidence which was not
> pertinent to the inquiry, and which would not have been received
> during a public hearing.

Rumors immediately swirled through Washington that the investigation was halted and the testimony redacted because it threatened national
security. Some speculated that the committee bowed to pressure from
the conspirators themselves, who were not only among the richest men in
America but who were high-level political figures as well, such as John
W. Davis and Al Smith, who had each headed the Democratic Party and
were onetime presidential candidates. Deleted from the official report
were references to the American Liberty League as well as the identities
of nearly all the alleged plotters. While the committee's desire to protect
the reputations of innocent people was considered laudable, the destruction

of evidence and testimony only served to fan the flames of suspicion for decades to come. If not for French's copyrighted exposé, the only conspirator to ever be publicly identified would have been the low-level Gerald MacGuire.

Despite the committee's findings that a Fascist plot had been confirmed, no further action was taken. "The Congressional Committee investigating un-American activities has just reported that the Fascist plot to seize the government . . . was proved," Roger Baldwin, the director of the American Civil Liberties Union, said in a publicly released statement. "Yet not a single participant will be prosecuted under the perfectly plain language of the federal conspiracy act making this a high crime." When the committee's authority to subpoena witnesses expired at the end of 1934, the U.S. Justice Department did not initiate a criminal investigation. When the committee asked the House of Representatives to extend its term to January 1937, the House refused and the committee died in January 1935. The untimely death of MacGuire at thirty-seven eliminated the only witness who could have testified against the alleged plotters in the event that the investigation continued.

After the committee died, John Spivak began writing a series of articles about the investigation, and Dickstein provided him access to the official files. Apparently inadvertently, the committee's secretary turned over Butler's complete testimony as well as other internal documents and evidence that had been deleted from the committee's published findings. But Spivak's sensational exposé, although meticulously researched and informed by the committee's evidence, was predictably ignored, appearing as it did in the Communist publication *New Masses*.

For his part, Butler was satisfied that the coup had been thwarted, but he never missed an opportunity to blast the committee for "bowing to the power of Wall Street and for censoring his remarks." In a radio broadcast in 1935 he denounced the committee for suppressing his testimony and failing to follow up with interviews of the conspirators.

Historians disagree about the veracity of Butler's claims, though not about his personal or professional credibility. He had reasons for hating Wall Street, and his increasingly defiant self-righteousness was off-putting. By 1933 he was sounding a perpetual cry about class conflict and seemed to thrive on drama. After retirement he wrote to a former aide that "you and I were cut out to be pirates and the civilized drone-like life is not to my liking."

Even though MacGuire contradicted or denied Butler's testimony, the committee found corroborating evidence through bank records, MacGuire's letters from Europe discussing Fascist organizations, and other circumstantial details confirming MacGuire's claims about the inner workings of the American Liberty League. Butler's claims were also corroborated by Paul French, who had extensively interviewed MacGuire. Even so, French's testimony was heavily reliant on what MacGuire had told him, and MacGuire was a problematic witness who had perjured himself numerous times and whose credibility was slippery from the start. Still, Butler's personal integrity and trustworthiness were never challenged. Though a firebrand, Butler's patriotism and pro-defense stand were not doubted, and he maintained an admirable independence from partisan organizations that sought his support.

"The committee found that Butler was telling the truth," Robert T. Cochran wrote in *Smithsonian* magazine years later. "Nothing much happened because few people really *wanted* to believe him, and because some prominent people were implicated, the story was hushed up." The conspiracy "quickly and quietly fizzled," as *Military History* magazine put it. After the committee issued its final report, *Time* published a mock photograph of General Butler and Jimmy Durante with the caption: "Schnozzle, Gimlet Eye. Fascist to Fascists?" A small footnote buried on the same page, printed in five-point type, reported that the committee was convinced "that General Butler's story of a Fascist march on Washington was alarmingly true."

Once the story made the national newspapers after the release of the expanded report in which the committee confirmed the existence of a plot, letters came in from around the country directed to the committee, the White House, and the Division of Investigation. A letter from an official of Six Companies Inc. in Boulder City, Nevada—the colossal engineering and construction firm that was building Hoover Dam—alerted Congressman McCormack to the Fascist plot hatched within the American Legion. The letter, which McCormack forwarded to Hoover, and which has never before been cited or published, corroborated Butler's story. "Dear John," the letter began, addressing Congressman McCormack with apparent familiarity. The author described how two men claiming to be representatives of an Eastern-based organization called the "American Fascist Veterans Association" planned to overthrow Roosevelt and had tried to recruit him to head up a Western division. "They told us . . . that General

Butler would line up the Marines . . . that the Veterans of Foreign Wars Department heads were all members . . . and that the Republican National Committeeman was treasurer." The author of the letter wrote that since the Hoover Dam project was a "Republican contractors' job" and because the Six Companies consortium had been "strong for Hoover," he had been afraid to speak out sooner. Further, his workforce was composed of untold hundreds of previously unemployed and hungry veterans whom he legitimately feared could be incited to join a veterans' uprising.

Some Americans who had read the news stories about the coup plot began asking Roosevelt to make a public statement in response to the Dickstein-McCormack Committee findings. A letter from a longtime supporter of Roosevelt who resided in Santa Barbara, California, suggested that "the President take the people into his confidence and openly state what his relations are with regard to those Fascist groups supported by powerful financiers." Roosevelt's reaction and response to the alleged plot has never been published, although Spivak reported that the president had personally intervened to bring the committee to a standstill—and the plot to a halt.

Contemporaneous and contemporary historians largely neglected the "Business Plot." While it has been written about over the past seventy-five years—mostly in endnotes of Roosevelt biographies—and was reportedly the basis for Fletcher Knebel's 1962 political thriller *Seven Days in May* and Sinclair Lewis's 1935 novel *It Can't Happen Here*, it has been mostly marginalized or ridiculed by historians. "No one quite knew what to make of the Butler story," historian Arthur M. Schlesinger Jr. concluded. "No doubt MacGuire did have some wild scheme in mind, though the gap between contemplation and execution was considerable and it can hardly be supposed that the republic was in much danger." Nicholas Fox Weber, Robert Sterling Clark's biographer, deemed both the plot and Clark's alleged role in it to be credible. "The Fascist plot which General Butler exposed did not get very far," according to one account. "But that plot had in it the three elements which make successful wars and revolutions: men, guns and money." Butler biographer Hans Schmidt reviewed all the available evidence and found "little reason to doubt" that Butler was telling the truth, but he questioned MacGuire's motives and wondered if he was "working both ends against the middle," as Butler had suspected. The scholarly Schmidt concluded that Butler may indeed have "blown the whistle on an incipient conspiracy" to overthrow the government, though the depth and breadth of the plot would never be thoroughly examined.

Whether the plot was what New York mayor Fiorello La Guardia dismissed as a fanciful "cocktail putsch" or what the secretary of war, secretary of the Navy, Commander James Van Zandt of the VFW, and numerous U.S. senators and representatives concluded was a real threat to the Roosevelt presidency, it is a fascinating tale of intrigue that sheds light on the power struggles of 1930s America. What is clear is that some of the nation's wealthiest men—Republicans and Democrats alike—were so threatened by Roosevelt's monetary policies that they actually flirted with antigovernment paramilitarism and sought to manipulate the American Legion to support the gold standard. How serious they were, and how far they went or were willing to go, would be debated over the next century. Perhaps at no other time in American history since the Civil War had the very stability of the nation been in play. The country's richest and most powerful men feared the collapse of capitalism and were willing to go to extremes to save it. Political parties were shifting allegiances and the nation's dispossessed were inflamed with anger and frustration. Those on the Right genuinely feared a Communist takeover of the republic, while those on the Left felt threatened by totalitarian schemes. "History is littered with governments destabilized by masses of veterans who believed that they had been taken for fools by a society that grew rich and fat at the expense of their hardship and suffering," said a twenty-first-century secretary of veterans affairs, lending credence to the possibility of a veterans' rebellion. If the Butler charges did nothing else, they successfully identified the Liberty League as a group of right-wing fanatics and effectively neutralized the group's anti-Roosevelt smears.

Years later, after McCormack had become Speaker of the House, he told an interviewer that legal technicalities had precluded the committee from subpoenaing Robert Sterling Clark. "There was no doubt that General Butler was telling the truth . . . Millions were at stake when Clark and the others got the Legion to pass that resolution on the gold standard in 1933. When Roosevelt refused to be pressured by it, and went even further with the gold standard, those fellows got desperate and decided to look into European methods, with the idea of introducing them into America. They sent MacGuire to Europe to study Fascist organizations . . . If General Butler had not been the patriot he was, and if they had been able to maintain secrecy, the plot certainly might very well have succeeded . . . When times are desperate and people are frustrated, anything like that could happen . . . If the plotters had got rid of Roosevelt, there's no telling what might have taken place . . . This was a threat to our very way of government by a bunch of rich men who wanted Fascism."

CHAPTER THIRTY-EIGHT

Are You Better Off Than You Were Last Year?

THE HISTORICAL RECORD OF President Roosevelt's reaction to the "Business Plot" is conspicuously silent, although he doubtless possessed a strong opinion on the matter. The Dickstein-McCormack Committee sent a copy of its findings to Roosevelt, who responded, simply: "I am interested in having it. I take it that the committee will proceed further."

General Butler's motive baffled serious journalists, historians, and scholars, who pursued the story in years to come. Having railed against capitalist profiteers since World War I, Butler could not have been expected to be a reliable ally for Wall Street interests. He had classic macho military values, albeit as a maverick warrior who had outspokenly challenged the bureaucratic and political hierarchy of the elitist American Legion. Emotionally anti-war and anti-imperialist, Butler aroused speculation that he was associated with a loose-knit coalition of progressive populists bent on driving a wedge between Roosevelt and the Wall Street titans and other conservative forces in American politics. Proponents of this theory suggested that Butler was aligned with Huey Long and Father Coughlin in a political ploy to move Roosevelt leftward. Others posited a theory that no criminal prosecutions arose from the evidence because some of Roosevelt's own advisers had participated in the plot and it was considered a matter of national security to suppress the details.

The role of the press was similarly confusing. Was the story down-played because of potential embarrassment to influential figures, or was it marginalized because the plot was so absurdly far-fetched that it resembled one of the potboiler adventure stories that Butler wrote for various magazines, if not a Marx Brothers zany comedy? "An apparently serious effort to overthrow the government, perhaps with the support of some of America's wealthiest men, largely substantiated by a Congressional Committee, was mostly ignored," wrote Clayton E. Cramer in *History Today*. "Why?"

Roosevelt's secretary of the interior, Harold Ickes, would charge an alliance between the American Liberty League and the country's major newspapers, which distorted and covered up the news "in the interest of both their advertisers and in defense of the capitalist class." In any event, the Liberty League was fast becoming the most significant anti-Roosevelt organization in the country. With infinite resources, much of it from the du Pont family, it would spend millions to destroy the New Deal. Providing editorials to thousands of newspapers, radio stations, and libraries, it was described as sponsoring "one of the most extensive propaganda campaigns of the twentieth century."

Another formidable Liberty League coalition blossomed as well. By early 1934 the League was providing a large share of money to anti-Roosevelt groups, including, ironically, to Huey Long's Share Our Wealth Movement and Coughlin's National Union for Social Justice, as well as the ubiquitous "rainbow of colored shirts." Uniting malcontents on the Left and Right to "save the Constitution," the Liberty League consortium was the fiercest challenge to Roosevelt and the New Deal by big business.

"Roosevelt's friends took the American Liberty League seriously," said Samuel Rosenman, one of Roosevelt's closest advisers and an original Brain Truster. "So did he."

Whether spurred by the plot or not, Roosevelt did indeed turn leftward, and he went after Wall Street with renewed vigor. "If the First Hundred Days had comforted the afflicted," wrote Roosevelt biographer Ted Morgan, "the Second Hundred Days would afflict the comfortable." Much of the legislation for the Second Hundred Days was directed against the wealthy, including a bill dismantling holding companies, an inheritance tax, and a tax on corporate income. At the heart of what was derisively called the soak-the-rich policy was the Securities Exchange Act, which regulated securities and prohibited exploitative stock market practices that swindled consumers. For the first time in American history, stock exchanges were required to register with the federal government and bow to oversight by the newly created Securities and Exchange Commission. Roosevelt appointed the indefatigable "hellhound of Wall Street" and J. P. Morgan nemesis Ferdinand Pecora to the commission, prompting Will Rogers to exclaim, "There's finally a cop on Wall Street." Further inciting the wrath of Wall Street was Roosevelt's appointment of Joseph P. Kennedy as chairman of the commission—Kennedy being a notorious swashbuckling Irish stockbroker whose anti-Morgan sentiments were legendary. When a hue and cry arose comparing Kennedy at the SEC to the fox in the henhouse, Roosevelt responded: "Set a thief to catch a thief."

Roosevelt also threw his support behind a U.S. Senate inquiry into the munitions industry and World War I war profiteering. Known as the Nye Committee, for its chairman, North Dakota Republican Gerald Nye, the probe targeted the DuPont, J. P. Morgan, and Remington Arms companies. The president sent a message to the Senate urging full cooperation with the committee and pledging executive backing. "The private and uncontrolled manufacture of arms and munitions and the traffic therein has become a serious source of international discord and strife," he wrote.

The evils of the arms makers were the subject of numerous books, including the bestseller *Merchants of Death* and John Gunther's *Harper's* series "Slaughter for Sale." The explosive hearings of the Special Committee Investigating the Munitions Industry were front-page news and continued for weeks as the committee attempted to determine whether Wall Street financiers "had nudged the United States into war in 1917," as one official account put it, to profit from the production of ammunition, weapons, tanks, and other materiel. Dozens of hearings were held and hundreds of observers crowded into the Senate committee room, eager for the wealthy warmongers to be exposed. While the investigators affirmed that the munitions industry "depended to a large extent on 'greasing the palms' of public officials in Latin America, the Near East, and China," they found that such bribery was not exclusive to the gun trade and no criminal prosecutions resulted.

"The time has come to take profit out of war," Roosevelt said, pressing the committee to hold the arms makers accountable. Committee investigators examined the files and interrogated officers of J. P. Morgan and Company—"the financial angel of the Allied government of 1914–1917," as an official history described it—which "brought a thunderous clap from across the Atlantic."

Roosevelt also unleashed his Internal Revenue Service and Justice Department to go after his Wall Street adversaries. The Justice Department established a new division to investigate civil and criminal violations of the tax code, and one of its first high-profile targets was Andrew Mellon—Herbert Hoover's treasury secretary and the third-richest man in the world. The man who had pronounced the economy "sound and prosperous" at the time of the stock market crash in 1929, and who had once been celebrated as the greatest treasury secretary since Alexander Hamilton, was investigated for tax fraud. Although a federal grand jury declined to indict the "caricature of capitalism," as Amity Shlaes called the elderly Mellon, the civil and criminal cases dogged him until his death; he was posthumously exonerated. Widely seen as politically motivated—to counter Huey Long's burgeoning anti–Wall Street movement—as well as driven by Roosevelt's personal animus against his enemies, Roosevelt's David-versus-Goliath battles were heralded in the hinterland.

Roosevelt was by all accounts genuinely baffled by the animosity and venom spewed at him by his "class." He sincerely believed that he had saved the capitalist system and thought the hatred his actions had engendered was a remarkable "lack of appreciation for him and his policies . . . spiteful ingratitude and political and economic Neanderthalism."

While Roosevelt realized that the road to recovery and reform would be long and complicated, he believed he was on the right track. In early 1934 he published a book outlining the course ahead and aptly titled *On Our Way*. In his first fireside chat of his second year in office, he asked simply: "Are You Better Off Than You Were Last Year?" The nation responded with a resounding yes, as evidenced by the Democratic landslide of the midterm elections, prompting William Randolph Hearst to begrudgingly note: "There has been no such popular endorsement since the days of Thomas Jefferson and Andrew Jackson."

The journalist William Allen White said simply, "He has been all but crowned by the people."

The Paranoid Style of American Politics

Now we are face to face once again with a period of heightened peril. The risks are great, the burdens heavy, the problems incapable of swift or lasting solution. And under the strains and frustrations imposed by constant tension and harassment, the discordant voices of extremism are heard once again in the land. Men who are unwilling to face up to the danger from without are convinced that the real danger comes from within. They look suspiciously at their neighbors and their leaders. They call for a 'man on horseback' because they do not trust the people . . .

So let us not heed these counsels of fear and suspicion. Let us . . . devote more energy to organize the free and friendly nations of the world, with common trade and strategic goals, and devote less energy to organizing armed bands of civilian guerrillas that are more likely to supply local vigilantes than national vigilance.

PRESIDENT JOHN F. KENNEDY,
"THE CONSPIRACY SPEECH," NOVEMBER 18, 1961

THE BUSINESS PLOT WAS NOT the end of General Smedley Darlington Butler. He was recruited for yet another bizarre plot, equally outrageous in its audacity and financial backing. In the summer of 1935, Butler received a telephone call from Father Charles Coughlin.

"Smedley," Coughlin said, addressing him by his first name, though the two had never met. Then the bumptious priest, who had become one of Franklin Roosevelt's most vicious and outspoken critics, launched into a tirade against the president. Roosevelt's new "Good Neighbor" policy toward Latin America left Coughlin and his cohorts in the National Union for Social Justice no choice but to treat privately with Mexican president Lázaro Cárdenas. Coughlin claimed that Cárdenas was a Communist who was condemning the Catholic Church. Coughlin boasted that he had the men and the guns necessary to overthrow the Mexican government and wanted General Butler to lead the expedition. The priest claimed, according to Butler, that he had the financial patronage of armament companies, including Remington and DuPont.

Butler told Coughlin that, as a retired Marine Corps general, he remained an officer of the U.S. government and that such a military force against an ally was in violation of American foreign policy and constituted treason. If such a movement was initiated, Butler told Coughlin, President Roosevelt would "call out the standing army to prevent them from getting very far." Coughlin replied that he and his fellow conspirators were not worried about Roosevelt because "they would take care of him on the way down."

Butler was reluctant to report this second attempt by the Fascist right-wing to recruit him, having been roundly humiliated and mocked during the previous fiasco. But his conscience got the better of him, and in August 1936 he met with J. Edgar Hoover, now director of the once-again renamed Federal Bureau of Investigation. "I pointed out to General Butler that his remaining silent might later be misconstrued if the story became known publicly," Hoover wrote in a memorandum to Attorney General Homer Cummings.

Butler further reported to Hoover that he had evidence of the theft of more than a hundred Browning automatic rifles from the Raritan Arsenal in Edison, New Jersey, which were to be used in the Mexican coup. Butler told Hoover that Coughlin also alluded to armed insurrection in the United States, stating that the 1936 presidential election would be the last opportunity for Americans to vote and that a dictator would be installed afterward.

Since Cummings was away from Washington on an extended trip,

Hoover took the matter directly to President Roosevelt on the very day that he met with Butler. Two weeks later Roosevelt summoned Hoover to the White House to discuss "subversive activities in the United States, particularly Fascism and Communism," according to Hoover's internal files.

Roosevelt "apparently promised to place a handwritten memorandum in his safe, containing a summary of his instructions to the FBI chief," wrote Hoover biographer Curt Gentry, although "no such document has been found in the National Archives or among the Roosevelt papers at Hyde Park."

In any case, the Mexican Plot, like the Wall Street Putsch, died a quiet death.

Despite the attacks against Roosevelt and his presidency, his trajectory was unstoppable. In the 1936 election, he and Garner defeated Kansas governor Alf Landon by a 60 percent margin, carrying every state except for Maine and Vermont. Backed by a coalition of forces that would effectively hold firm for three more decades, Roosevelt's mandate was secure and public sentiment solidly behind him.

Roosevelt went on to an unprecedented fourth-term victory in 1944. By then, at sixty-two years of age, his paralysis and years of chain-smoking had led to numerous life-threatening ailments, and he died of a cerebral hemorrhage on April 12, 1945. Americans were grief-stricken at the death of the man who had led the country for twelve years—longer than any other president—and who had taken a nation on the verge of sinking and recharted its course.

IN 2009, CONSERVATIVE online magazine *Newsmax* posted a column suggesting that a military coup to "resolve the Obama problem" was a distinct possibility. "Imagine a bloodless coup to restore and defend the Constitution through an interim administration that would do the serious business of governing and defending the nation," wrote columnist John L. Perry. "Skilled, military-trained nation-builders would replace accountability-challenged, radical-left commissars. Having bonded with his twin teleprompters, the president would be detailed for ceremonial speech-making."

The resulting uproar led to the story's immediate removal from the magazine's Web site. What seemed to twenty-first-century American readers to be the peculiar musings of a right-wing extremist was a plotline directly descended from the ill-fated and little known 1933 intrigues against Roosevelt.

Responding to "several reader complaints," *Newsmax* quickly distanced itself from "unpaid blogger" John Perry and assured its audience that it "would never advocate or insinuate any suggestion of an activity that would undermine our democracy or democratic institutions."

There is not much difference between the forces aligned against President Franklin Roosevelt and those against President Barack Obama, as journalist and biographer Lou Cannon pointed out in *Politics Daily*. Referring to what historian Richard Hofstadter called "the paranoid style of American politics," Cannon wrote that neither the paranoia nor the opposition "has changed as much as we might think."

Acknowledgments

Every writer about Franklin Roosevelt and the New Deal finds an abundance of material from scholars and journalists who have mined the public record. Unfortunately, few have explored the two events that I chose to examine, which I think are crucial to understanding Roosevelt's first term. The works that I found particularly brilliant and insightful about Roosevelt's rise, the first hundred days, and the New Deal are the biographies written by Kenneth S. Davis, Frank Freidel, William E. Leuchtenberg, and Arthur M. Schlesinger Jr. Alan Brinkley's *Voices of Protest* was a valuable resource on Huey Long and Father Coughlin, and George Wolfskill's work on political extremism in America was enlightening, if a bit frightening.

Very little has been written about Giuseppe Zangara and his attempted assassination of Roosevelt, or about the thwarted Fascist coup d'état. Both incidents were further obscured by the fact that case files have been destroyed and vital documents either have been redacted or are missing altogether. Because both the assassination and coup attempts are surrounded in mystery and controversy, I chose to rely on the few primary sources available and selected my secondary sources very carefully. For the assassination attempt and Zangara's background and anti-Fascist, anti-capitalist political motivation, I depended on contemporaneous news accounts, investigative files from the FBI (which I obtained through the Freedom of Information Act), and Zangara's jailhouse memoir (reprinted in Blaise Picchi's admirable account: *The Five Weeks of Giuseppe Zangara*). For the "Business Plot"—whose trail was even murkier than

Zangara's—I again sought the contemporaneous record, especially the hearings and findings of the House committee investigation. Also useful were Smedley Butler's autobiography (as told to Thomas Lowell); Paul Comly French's story about the plot, "$3,000,000 Bid for Fascist Army Bared"; the FBI files obtained through the Freedom of Information Act, including J. Edgar Hoover's personal memoranda; and Jules Archer's *The Plot to Seize the White House*.

I am grateful beyond words to the Woodrow Wilson Center for International Scholars for my research fellowship there. I am not exaggerating when I say that this book could not have been written without the extraordinary support of the Woodrow Wilson Center. Writing is a profoundly solitary venture, especially when done in the hinterland and without academic affiliation. So the community of scholars that welcomed me in Washington, D.C., breathed new life into my research and writing. Deep thanks to Lee Hamilton, Michael van Dusen, Lucy Jilka, Sonya Michel, Lindsay Collins, Kimberly Conner, Janet Spikes, and Dagne Gizaw. Sheldon Garon was helpful in my understanding of the Fascist impulse in 1930s America. Jamie Stiehm made my time at the center socially, as well as intellectually, rich. I especially want to thank my intern, Lennon Wetovsky, whose research and retrieval of key documents alleviated my workload immensely.

A media fellowship at the Hoover Institution at Stanford University also contributed greatly to my initial research on the subject. The Hoover Library is where I found Raymond Moley's notes from his interview with Giuseppe Zangara, as well as Moley's recollections of the attempted assassination. Many thanks to David Brady and Mandy MacCalla for making that possible.

The U.S. Secret Service failed to respond to repeated Freedom of Information requests regarding both the assassination and coup attempts, which was especially disappointing since it was the lead agency charged with both investigations. Meanwhile, the FBI was extraordinarily cooperative, and I would like to thank Curt Cromer for the alacrity with which that agency's files were culled, analyzed, and released.

To my colleagues whose ideas and perceptions informed so much of what is good in this book, I thank you: Scott Armstrong, Sidney Blumenthal, Phil Cook, Kirk Ellis, Bonnie Goldstein, Jim Grady, Mike Green, Ed Grosvenor, Dennis McBride, Virginia Scharff, and Ron Steel.

I am always appreciative of Mark Adams and Peggy Trujillo at the New Mexico State Library, who make it possible for me to live and write in one of the most beautiful places on the planet.

Once again I want to thank Gloria Loomis, my agent and dear, dear friend, who is my unflagging champion. At Bloomsbury Press, Peter Ginna has been everything one wants in an editor: informed, engaged, encouraging, and trusting. Pete Beatty and Nathaniel Knaebel smoothly ushered the book through the production process.

As I finish this—my seventh book—I am yet again overcome with gratitude toward those men, women, and children in my life who make it all possible. The usual suspects are here again, in rare and impeccable form: my New Mexico, Washington, and Nevada girlfriends, my hiking buddies, my martini mates, my parents, and my three sons. Everyone deserves superlatives this time around, as we all rose to meet the material and the majesty of the drama of 1933 America: Charmay Allred, Shaune Bazner, Sandy Blakeslee, Jan Brooks, Maxine Champion, Nancy Cook, Frankie Sue Del Papa, Dan Flores, Felice Gonzales, Joanna Hurley, Judy Illes, Mike and Terri Jerry, Don and Jean Lamm, Caroline Monaco, Carl Moore, Lucy Moore, Jim and Julie Anne Overton, Marla Painter, Nora Pouillon, Ellen Reiben, Bob Samuel, Gail Sawyer, Patty Smart, Phil Smith, and Greg and Barbara Wierzynski.

Finally, to Sara and Ralph Denton, and to Ralph, Grant, and Carson Samuel—my heart runneth over.

Notes

Prologue: A Beleaguered Capital

1 "that which might be found": *New York Times*, March 5, 1933.
2 count on a benevolent dictator: Freidel, 205.
2 "We could have had a dictator": General Hugh S. Johnson, quoted in Wolfskill and Hudson, 80.
2 "When millions": Leuchtenburg, 21.

Chapter One: Lofty Aspirations

5 "a splendid large baby boy": Schlesinger, 1:319.
5 "brought his young bride": Ibid., 318.
6 "little Greek democracy of the elite": Hofstadter, 415.
6 "left out": Eleanor Roosevelt, quoted in Schlesinger, 1:322.
6 "character building": Black, 22.
7 "after all": Sara Roosevelt, quoted in Hofstadter, 416.
7 "Granny:" Elliott Roosevelt and James Brough, 95.
7 "an angel": Geoffrey C. Ward, 314.
8 "I am plain": Elliott Roosevelt and James Brough, 95.
8 "In all countries": James Roosevelt, quoted in Cook, 1:145.
8–9 "fancy dancing" . . . "deeply moved": Ibid., 135–36.
9 "From the ruins": Roosevelt, quoted in Hofstadter, 417.
9 "lair of predators": Elliott Roosevelt and James Brough, 159.
9 "The conservation battle": Schlesinger, 1:336.

Chapter Two: Rebuild His Broken Body

10   "gnomish cynic": Black, 56.
10   "any other position in public life": Roosevelt, quoted in Schlesinger, 1:342.
11   "would not do to ask": Butler to Roosevelt, quoted in Morgan, 176.
12   "I'd never felt": Roosevelt, quoted in Schlesinger, 1:367.
13   "rebuild his broken body": David M. Kennedy, 98.
13   "No matter": Elliott Roosevelt, *F.D.R.: His Personal Letters*, 2:562.
14   "The circumstances": Black, 183.
14   "acrobat": Ibid., 1020.
14   "As 1928 drew to an end": Ibid., 188.
14   "fierce hatred": Mencken, quoted in David M. Kennedy, 99.

Chapter Three: A New Deal for the American People

15   "a breadline for big business": Manchester, 1:54.
15   "There were miles of highways": Vanderbilt, 80.
16   "What this country needs": Hoover to Morley, quoted in *Time*, "The Presidency: Wanted: A Poem." October 3, 1932.
16   "wild-eyed Utopian": Hofstadter, *American Political Tradition*, 383.
16   "During the 1920s": Shannon, ix.
17   "overproduction and underconsumption": Manchester, 1:37.
17   "a demoralized people": Walter Lippmann, quoted in Manchester, 1:36.
17   "altruistic suicide": Manchester, 1:36.
17   "Surely, thought thousands": Shannon, x.
18   "amiable boy scout": Walter Lippmann to Newton D. Baker, quoted in Steel, 291.
18   "a highly impressionable" . . . "dying day": Lippmann, quoted in Steel, 291–92. Steel wrote: "Lippmann's critics never let him forget that phrase, later citing it as evidence of his bad judgment. Yet at the time it was not so far off base."
18   "on the grounds of great intellectual capacity" . . . "a man who thinks" . . . "That they all lived": Ibid., 291.
19   "I regret that I am late" . . . "I warn those nominal Democrats" . . . "I pledge you": For accounts of the acceptance speech, see Schlesinger 1:313. For the convention see *New York Times*, "Official Report of the Proceedings of the Democratic National Convention," June 20–July 4, 1932.

Chapter Four: The Tombstone Bonus

21   "I done it all by my feet": House Committee on Ways and Means, 72nd Cong., 2nd Sess. 382–83.

22 "hunger marchers" . . . "Diamonds were the symbol" . . . "regaled several Cabinet members": Pearson and Allen, 10ff.

23 "Despite all the Red rhetoric": Dickson and Allen, *Bonus Army*, 45. Captain Charles H. Titus of the Army's Military Intelligence Division was the undercover operative. His observations are in the "Military Intelligence Division Correspondence, 1917–41" file at the National Archives, Record Group 165, Box 2856, File 10110-2674. For the most thorough and eloquent depiction of the subject, see Dickson and Allen, *Bonus Army*. Also see Lisio, *The President and Protest*; Ortiz, "Rethinking the Bonus March"; and contemporaneous press accounts.

23 "a force superior": Folliard.

23 "cruelest year": Manchester, 1:35.

23 "rock bottom": Ibid., 1:1.

23 "permitted to rig": *New Yorker* editor Harold Ross, quoted by Josephson, *Infidel*, 87.

23 "If you steal $25": *Nation*, March 8, 1933.

24 "were suffering in a rural gethsemane": Manchester, 1:41. For incisive, and insightful, accounts of the toll of the Great Depression, see Manchester, David M. Kennedy, Frederick Allen, both Leuchtenberg volumes, and the first volume of Cook.

24 "Babies go hungry": Allen, 58.

24 "America was at a standstill": Cook, 2:25.

24 "viability of the country's institutions": Black, 251.

24 For the Red Scare and state militias, see Josephson, *Infidel*, 98.

25 "precarious moment": David M. Kennedy, "The Great Depression: An Overview," a March 2009 essay for the Gilder Lehrman Institute of American History.

Chapter Five: The Forgotten Man

26 "for the most fundamental realignment" . . . "economic constitutional order": Richard Parker, "The Crisis Last Time," *New York Times*, November 9, 2008.

27 "that build from the bottom up": Daniels, 214. The use of the phrase was widely seen as a "bastardized concept originated by William Graham Sumner," as author Jonathan Alter put it (Alter, 90). See also Shlaes, 12.

27 "hatred" . . . "put on his high-button shoes" . . . "was lucky to come back alive": Manchester, 1:61.

27 "We've got to crack him": Hoover, quoted in Alter, 121.

27 "deliberately chose the low road" . . . "a fear": Manchester, 1:61.

28 "Uncle Sam": Eslick, quoted in Dickson and Allen, *Bonus Army*, 126–27.

28 "Every other interest": Dos Passos, "The Veterans Come Home to Roost."

28 model for an integrated society: NAACP writer Roy Wilkins, paraphrased in Dickson and Allen, *Bonus Army*, 7.

28 "made for America" . . . "For Mr. Hoover": Waters, quoted in Winslow, 29.

29 "every kind of cockeyed": Dos Passos in the *New Republic*, June 1932.

29 "stick it out!" . . . "Cunning Communists": Cox and Coughlin, quoted in Dickson and Allen, *Bonus Army*, 106.

29 "body vermin": Ibid., 107.

29 "rag-and-tin-can city": Henry.

30 "ideal American soldier": Teddy Roosevelt, quoted in Dickson and Allen, *Bonus Army*, 151.

30 "I'm here because I've been a soldier": "Butler Tells Bonus Vets to Stick It Out," *Times-Herald*, July 20, 1932.

30 "slip over into lawlessness": Butler, quoted in Dickson and Allen, *Bonus Army*, 152.

30 "carefully advised": Schmidt, 218.

30–31 "desperate summer" . . . HOOVER LOCKS SELF IN WHITE HOUSE: Manchester, 1:1.

31 "most dangerous men in America": Tugwell, *Brains Trust*, 194.

Chapter Six: Warriors of the Depression

32 "Warriors of the Depression": Dickson and Allen, *Bonus Army*, 65.

32 "trained men": Ibid., 211.

32 "incipient revolution was in the air": MacArthur, quoted in Black, 241.

33 "This is political" . . . "MacArthur has decided": Manchester, 1:13.

33 "We thought it was a parade": Witness Naaman Seigle, quoted in Dickson and Allen, "Marching on History."

34 "Men and women were ridden down": *Baltimore Sun* reporter J. F. Essary, quoted in Dickson and Allen, *Bonus Army*, 174.

34 "It was like a scene": Associated Press, quoted in Manchester, 1:15.

34 "was very much annoyed": From the unpublished biography of George Van Horn Moseley, quoted in Dickson and Allen, *Bonus Army*, 179.

34 "did not want either himself": Manchester, 1:16.

34 "It would not be the last time": Dickson and Allen, "Marching on History."

34 "I told that dumb son-of-a-bitch": Eisenhower, quoted by historian Stephen Ambrose in ibid.

34–35 "Come on!" . . . "a blaze so big": Manchester, 180–81.

35 "the most critical situation": Doherty, 43.

35–36 "It is my opinion" . . . "If there was one man": MacArthur press conference, July 29, 1932. War Department transcript, Herbert Hoover Presidential Library, Bonus March, Presidential File, Box 23.

36 "Soup is cheaper": La Guardia, quoted in Manchester, 1:18.

36 "Hounding men": Ibid.

36 "What a pitiful spectacle": *Washington Daily News*, July 30, 1932. Quoted in Dickson and Thomas, *Bonus Army*, 194.

36   "[There] is nothing left inside the man": Roosevelt, quoted in Black, 242.
36   "the deep social cleavage" . . . "a potential Mussolini": Lisio, 285.
37   "Well, Felix": Brands, 259.

Chapter Seven: Happy Days Are Here Again

38   "But the rout": Lisio, 2.
39   "Yes" . . . "It was called the Dark Ages": Keynes, quoted in Manchester,
     1:35.
39   "We are today in the middle": Keynes, quoted in Ahamed, 4.
39   "The way most people feel" . . . "crank candidates": Ibid., 59.
39   "although subjected": Steel, 291.
39   "his mind is not very clear": Ibid., 293.
39   "a vigorous well-intentioned gentleman": "What To Expect," *Time*, November 21, 1932.
40   "What they saw": Manchester, 1:60.
40   "to prevent extortion against the public": Rosenman, *Public Papers*, 740.
40   "the development of an economic declaration of rights": Hofstadter, *American Political Traditions*, 430. "Every man": Ibid.
40   "A glance at the situation": Roosevelt speech to the Commonwealth Club in San Francisco, September 23, 1932. Schlesinger, 2:425–26.
41   "It was a real shocker": Tugwell, 176.
41   "well of pessimism": Farley, 31.
41   "Now I will have no identity" . . . "turmoil": Alter, 134.
42   "This is the greatest moment": Manchester, 1:54.
42   "there was no" . . . "gathering economic storm clouds": Moley, *After Seven Years*, 65.
42   "You know, Jimmy": James Roosevelt and Bill Libby, 142. See also Davis, 2:378.

Chapter Eight: Brain Trust

43   For the origin of the Brain Trust, see Rosenman, *Working with Roosevelt*, 56–59; and Moley, *After Seven Years*, 1–9; Alter 97ff.; Schlesinger, 1:415ff.
44   "notoriously impractical": Rosen, 114.
44   "an amusing hanger-on": Alter, 97.
44   "considered all policy": Black, 227.
44   "a shrewd salty Irishman": Schlesinger, 1:374.
44   "Rex was like a cocktail": Moley, 15.
45   "I have not the slightest urge": Moley, quoted in Schlesinger, 1:400.
45   "a grown-up Boy Scout": Schlesinger, 1:407.
45   "He was a progressive vessel": Tugwell, *Democratic Roosevelt*, 36.

45 "men who rushed forward": Davis, 2:307.

45 "new political landscape": Cook, 2:15.

46 "Your distant cousin is an X": Johnson, 329.

Chapter Nine: Winter of Our Discontent

47 "Winter of Our Discontent": Shakespeare, *Richard III*, act I, scene I.

47 "I wish for you": Hoover to Roosevelt, quoted in Davis, 2:392.

47 "On the subjects": Roosevelt to Hoover, quoted in Freidel, 18.

47 "rang alarm bells": Davis, 2:393.

48 "the boldest alibi": Black, 253.

48 "The bubble burst first": FDR, quoted in Bernstein, 1.

48 "the tar-baby" . . . "To touch it": David M. Kennedy, 105.

48 "enshrined in human instincts": Hoover, quoted in Davis, 2:397.

49 "had all the appearance": David M. Kennedy, 105.

49 "attempt to mousetrap him": Black, 255.

49 "By March 4": Freidel, 73n.

49 "do anything to save America": Eleanor Roosevelt, quoted in Manchester, 1:84.

49 "used Hoover as a foil": Alter, 139.

50 "either did not realize": Moley, quoted in David M. Kennedy, 110.

50 "We now have the fellow": Manchester, 1:84.

Chapter Ten: Year of Fear

51 "The situation is critical": Steel, 300.

51 "reluctant convert" . . . "to obstruct" . . . "The danger": Ibid., 299–300.

51–52 "take control of the government" . . . "Call out the troops": Manchester, 1:65–66.

52 "organized refusal": Davis, 2:366.

52 "glue that holds societies" . . . "Capitalism is on trial": Manchester, 1:65–66.

52 "The farmers will rise up": Schlesinger, 1:4.

52 "They weren't paranoid": Manchester, 1:65.

52 "I want": Hitler, quoted in Wolfskill, 2.

53 "I do not often envy": Reed, quoted in Schlesinger, 1:268.

53 "The word itself": Sharlet, 137.

53 "men of far greater intelligence" . . . "Those rascals in Russia": Manchester, 1:68.

54 "Communist Party members": MacPherson, 119.

54 "Even the iron hand" . . . "on the shelf": Manchester, 1:67–69.

54 "What does a democracy do": David M. Kennedy, 111.

54 "swaggered across Europe and Asia": Cook, 2:26.

54 "people like Hitler and Stalin": Vanderbilt, 104.

54 "told me that what he wanted" . . . "He told me that the only thing": Ibid., 110.

55 "you seize power": Ibid., 120.

Chapter Eleven: American Mussolini and the Radio Priest

56 "Who is that *awful* man": Tully, 324.

56 The legend of Huey Long has been immortalized in Robert Penn Warren's *All the King's Men* and John Dos Passos's *Number One*.

56 "pudgy pixie": Williams, 4.

56 "Incredible Kingfish": "Democrats: Incredible Kingfish," *Time*, October 3, 1932.

56 "one of the two most dangerous men in the United States": Tugwell, *Brains Trust*, 194.

56 "American Mussolini": Davis, 2:352.

57 "Frankie, you're not going to let" . . . "I like him": T. Harry Williams, 602.

57 "The countless visitors": David M. Kennedy, 113.

57 "twin terror": MacPherson, 123.

57 "When I talk to him": Long, quoted in Brinkley, 58.

57–58 "secretly contemptuous" . . . "capitulated" . . . "Huey was a political man": Williams, 801–2.

58 "father of hate radio": Warren, *Radio Priest: Charles Coughlin the Father of Hate Radio*.

58 "laden with appeals": Brinkley, 278.

59 "all wool and a yard wide": Long, quoted in Brinkley, 58.

59 "once pleasant discourses": Ibid., 83.

59 "A priest who was more famous": Wolfskill and Hudson, 78.

60 "Choose to-day!": Coughlin, quoted in Schlesinger, 3:17.

60 "spirit of gold trading": Coughlin's February 19, 1933, sermon, quoted in Brinkley, 270.

60 "I take the road to fascism": Coughlin, quoted in Wolfskill and Hudson, 112.

60 "in normal times" . . . "There is no question": Roosevelt, quoted in Wolfskill and Hudson, 301.

Chapter Twelve: The *Nourmahal* Gang

61 For Roosevelt's affection for China and dislike of Hitler, see Freidel, 123ff.

62 "Wall Street was not merely": Fraser, *Every Man*, 414.

62 "The belief that those in control": Joseph P. Kennedy, 93.

62 "waiting affably": Schlesinger, 1:464.

63   "scion of a family": Davis, 2:420.

63   "1. World is sick": Moley, *First New Deal*, 100ff.

64   "The Hasty Pudding Club": Flynn, quoted in Davis, 2:420.

64   "fascinated by the mystery" . . . "he was doing so much": James Roosevelt and Sidney Shalett, 277.

64   "At Sea with Franklin D.": Flynn, quoted in Davis, 2:420.

64   "could be neither stemmed": Moley, "Bank Crisis."

65   "the last holiday" . . . "getting a marvelous rest": Franklin Roosevelt to Sara Roosevelt, February 6, 1933. Elliott Roosevelt, *FDR: His Personal Letters*, 1:328.

Chapter Thirteen: Magic City

67   "the blow that broke the boom": Stuart McIver, "1926 Miami: The Blow That Broke the Boom," *Florida Sun Sentinel*, September 19, 1993.

67   "Columns of hooded": Picchi, 6.

68   "begging expedition": Gottfried, 317.

68   "those people": James Roosevelt and Sidney Shallet, 277.

68   "I didn't even open": *New York Times*, February 16, 1933. Quoted in Davis, 2:422.

69   Details of the motorcade are contradictory. Moley contended that he was accompanied in the *second* car by Vincent Astor, Kermit Roosevelt, and William Rhinelander Stewart. Other accounts, including Blaise Picchi's study of the assassination, contend that it was Judge Kerochan, Astor, Roosevelt, and Moley in the *third* car.

69   "It would be easy": Astor, quoted in Moley, "Bank Crisis."

70   "one of those improbable": Ibid.

70   "I remember T.R.": Roosevelt to Garner, December 21, 1932, quoted in Elliott Roosevelt, *F.D.R.: His Personal Letters*, 313.

70   "Sono gli incerti del mestiere": William Manchester, *The Death of a President* (New York: Harper & Row, 1963), 35.

70   "We welcome him to Miami": Picchi, 13.

Chapter Fourteen: I'm All Right

71   "Where do you think" . . . "I go right down" . . . "It no look" . . . "There are many people": Donovan, 160.

72   "After the speech, Mr. President": Gowran, "Shot Aimed at FDR Took Cermak's Life," *Chicago Tribune*, November 23, 1963.

72   "I have had": Roosevelt remarks, quoted in Freidel, 169.

72   "the talking picture people": Roosevelt, quoted in Davis, 2:429.

72   "But you've *got* to" . . . "I'm sorry": Ibid.

72   "The President": Gottfried, 324.

73   "get him the hell out of here": Picchi, 16.

73   "It was providential": Davis, 2:430–31.

73   "I saw Mayor Cermak": *New York Times*, February 17, 1933.

73   "I'm all right": Roosevelt, quoted in Schlesinger, 1:465.

73   "I don't think he is going to last": . . . "It was surprising" . . . "Tony, keep
      quiet" . . . It won't hurt you": *New York Times*, February 17, 1933.

74   "Open the door": Picchi, 25.

74   "F.D.R. had talked to me": Moley, "Bank Crisis,"

75   "These things are to be expected": *New York Times*, February 16, 1933.
      Quoted in Davis, 2:431.

75   "must of have been awfully hard": Eleanor Roosevelt quoted in Cook, 2:27.

76   "Roosevelt's nerve": Moley, "Bank Crisis, Bullet Crisis," *Saturday Evening
      Post*, July 29, 1939.

76   "The President-elect, feeling the bullets": James A. Hagerty, *New York
      Times*, February 16, 1933.

77   "Tony, I hope you'll be up": Roosevelt, quoted in Picchi, 35.

77   "I'm glad it was me": Ibid. While this phrase from Cermak to Roosevelt has
      been widely repeated throughout history, legend has it that a Chicago re-
      porter falsely attributed those words to Cermak.

Chapter Fifteen: Too Many People Are Starving to Death

78   "I have the gun": Zangara.

78   "conducted only minor": FBI "Franklin D. Roosevelt Assassination Attempt"
      file.

79   "among the bonus diehards": Dickson and Allen, 330, n.61.

79   "an Italian anarchistic": Telegram from agent in Houston, Texas, to J. Edgar
      Hoover, February 16, 1933. FBI "Zangara" file.

79   "was the representative": Memorandum from V. W. Hughes of the U.S.
      Bureau of Investigation to J. Edgar Hoover, February 20, 1933, FBI "Franklin
      D. Roosevelt Assassination Attempt" file.

79   "dances conducted": Letter from J. Zajic to J. Edgar Hoover, February 17,
      1933, FBI "Franklin D. Roosevelt Assassination Attempt" file.

79   For more information regarding Zangara's ties to the cases, see FBI "Franklin
      D. Roosevelt Assassination Attempt" file.

79   "When I fired the first shot": Zangara confession. Quoted in Picchi, 252.

80   "Someone sent me here" . . . "to be quiet": Zangara, quoted in Picchi, 85.

80   "Don't do that please" . . . "He is going to kill the president!": Cross, quoted
      in Picchi, 17.

81   "two Legionnaires" . . . "like a ton of bricks" . . . "I want to kill the president!":
      Ibid., 19ff.

81   "I sprang": Armour affidavit, quoted in Picchi, 29–30.

82   "Nobody take my arm": Zangara, quoted in Picchi, 28–29.

82   "deprive Mrs. Cross": Ibid., 163.
82   "little lecture on manners": Donovan, 160.
82   "The fact remains": Ibid., 163–64.
82   "I'm such a little fellow": Zangara testimony.

Chapter Sixteen: Typical of His Breed

83   "The little Italian": Reporter Jack Bell, quoted in Picchi, 47.
83   "a swarthy Italian": *Miami Herald*, quoted in Picchi, 45.
84   "I was figuring to go": Zangara, quoted in Donovan, 156.
84   "I want to keel all presidents": Zangara, quoted in Key, 14.
84   "I see Mr. Hoover": Zangara testimony.
84   "You don't need no school": Donovan, 150.
84   "hate very violently": Zangara, quoted in Davis, 2:433.
84   "like a dog": Zangara, quoted in Picchi, 48.
85   "the stomachache": Zangara, quoted in Picchi, 66.
85   "I needed it": Zangara, Ibid., 243.
85   "The guards got in front of me": Ibid., 241.
86   "an anarchist, socialist" . . . "lunch-hour orator" . . . "governments and men in power": Rosario Candrilli, quoted in Picchi, 72.
86   "fostered and founded": Hynes quoted in Picchi, 77.
87   "not a maniac": *New York Times*, February 16, 1933.
87   "a lonesome morose character": "Zangara Planned Attack All Alone," *New York Times*, February 17, 1933. The motivation behind this dissembling by the Secret Service cannot be determined, as that agency refused to release documents under a Freedom of Information Act request by this author.
87   Di Silvestro accusation against Zangara: "Di Silvestro Links Zangara in Bomb Death: Phila. Attorney Tells Mussolini That Assassin Has Been Identified as Dynamite Terrorist." *Philadelphia Inquirer*, March 18, 1933. Also see FBI "Zangara" file.
87   "against the lives" . . . "With my most sincere regrets": "Five Jailed as Suspects in Roosevelt Plot Quiz," *Los Angeles Times*, February 19, 1933.
88   "I am friend of Zangara": Newspaper clipping in FBI "Zangara" file, "Boy of 15 Suspected in Roosevelt 'Bomb,'" Associated Press, March 2, 1933.
88   "wide-spread group" . . . "Zangara must have had": C. James Todaro to Edward W. Wells, February 21, 1933, in FBI "Zangara" file.
88   "under the protection": Gallagher, 144.
88   "natural political mode of class rule": Bancroft, 155.
89   "I do not belong to any society": Key, 14–15.
89   "This is the United States": Robinson, quoted in Freidel, 171.
89   "socialistic" . . . "anarchistic" . . . "fixed idea": *New York Times*, February 17, 1933.

89 "felt it was desirable": Moley to Fred Charles of *Buffalo Times*, February 24, 1933. Moley Collection. "I interviewed Zangara after the shooting that night and in my opinion no psychiatrist would declare him insane in the legal sense of the word. I made it very clear in my statement to the newspapers after examining him that I found no political ideas. I did this not only because it was true, but because I felt it was desirable to avoid, so far as possible, any hysteria on the subject of radicalism."

90 "For even if he had remained": Davis, 2:433.

Chapter Seventeen: The Bony Hand of Death

91 "Divine Providence": Roosevelt telegram to Mrs. Cross, reprinted in the *New York Times*, February 20, 1933.

91 "To a man": *Time*, February 27, 1933.

92 "killing its elected leaders" . . . "Guarding any President": Reilly, 10–11.

92 "one of the most elaborate": February 18, 1933.

92 "Circumstances made it impossible": Moley, "Bank Crisis," 1.

92 "A most critical situation": Hoover to Roosevelt, February 17, 1933, quoted in Schlesinger, 1:476.

93 "the letter from Hoover" . . . "That the breaking point had come": Moley's notes of the reaction to Hoover's letter, Raymond Moley Collection, Hoover Institution.

93 "It would have been inconceivable": Thomas Lamont, quoted in Freidel, 175.

93 "Fundamentally, the millions": Freidel, 181.

93 "mortally stricken" . . . "steadily degenerating confidence": Moley's notes of the reaction to Hoover's letter Raymond Moley Collection, Hoover Institution.

93–94 "assumed that Roosevelt would succeed": Moley, "Bank Crisis," 13.

94 "90 percent of the so-called new deal": Hoover to Reed, February 20, 1933, quoted in Freidel, 177.

94 "cheeky" . . . "madman": Schlesinger, 1:477.

94 "It is my duty": Hoover to Roosevelt, February 28, 1933, quoted in Freidel, 188.

94 "I am equally concerned": Roosevelt to Hoover, March 1, 1933, quoted in Freidel, 189.

95 "revolution and not reform": Hoover, quoted in Alter, 182.

95 "center of the storm": Ahamed, 444.

95 "did not want": Josephson, *Money Lords*, 147.

95 "nine million dollars": Manchester, 1:88.

96 "imperturbable and betrayed": James Roosevelt and Sidney Shalett, 251.

96 "another game of chicken": Alter, 199.

96 "I decided to cut it short": Roosevelt, quoted in Freidel, 192–93. Varying accounts of this pre-inaugural exchange between Roosevelt and Hoover can also be found in Tully, 64; James Roosevelt and Sidney Shalett, 250ff.; and Moley, *First New Deal*, 148.

96 "It would be putting it mildly": James Roosevelt and Sidney Shalett, 250–51.

96 "treated like a schoolboy": Tully, 64

96 "was one of the damndest" . . . "earliest lessons": James Roosevelt and Sidney Shalett, 250–51.

96 "squabbling like children": Alter, 200.

Chapter Eighteen: Fear Itself

97 "Oh Lord": Freidel, 198.

97 "almost impenetrable": Tugwell, *Brains Trust*, 62.

98 "Here was a president": Shlaes, 146.

98 "grim as death": James Roosevelt and Sidney Shalett, 253.

98 "Protocol or no protocol": Roosevelt, quoted in Tully, 68.

99 "This" . . . "is a day of *national* consecration": For descriptions of the inauguration, see Manchester, Freidel, Leuchtenburg (*Franklin D. Roosevelt and the New Deal*), Black, Brands, and Alter. For the address itself, see Rosenman, *Public Papers*, 2:11ff.

99 "The radio networks": Manchester, 1:91.

100 "sacred ground": Martin, 12.

100 "President Roosevelt's words": Freidel, 208.

101 "FOR DICTATORSHIP": Alter, 4.

101 "A lot of us have been asking": *New York Daily News*, March 5.

101 "Nothing is so much": Cook, 1:494.

Chapter Nineteen: Bank Holiday

102 "The President outlined": Perkins, quoted in Freidel, 215.

103 "leant recklessly": Alan Brinkley, "The New Deal, Then and Now."

103 "Behind the plain desk": Clapper, *Washington Daily News*, March 6, 1933.

104 "With so many banks" . . . "eye-popping": Alter, 4.

104 "As new commander": Ibid.

104 "dictator talk": Ibid., 5. Jonathan Alter found this draft at the Franklin Delano Roosevelt Presidential Library, which "had never been referred to or quoted by historians before."

104 "all men and women": Roosevelt, quoted in Davis, 3:35.

104 "For the first time": Josephson, *Money Lords*, 154.

104 "Hoover had taken everything": Manchester, 1:92.

105 "almost a springtime mood": Schlesinger, 2:6.

105 "If he had burned down": Will Rogers, *New York Times*, March 6, 1933.

105 "persuading, leading, sacrificing": Roosevelt, quoted in Bernstein, 5.

105 "If I fail": Roosevelt, quoted in Manchester, 1:95.

105 "very, very solemn": Hickok, 103–4.

106 "One had the feeling": Eleanor Roosevelt, quoted in Alter, 222.

106 "feared the kind of desperation": Cook, 2:27.

106 "Mayor Cermak, last evening": Picchi, 133.

Chapter Twenty: I Want to Keel All Presidents

107 For the most comprehensive accounts of the legal proceedings against Zangara, the federal investigation into his political ties, his own memoir, his interrogation by police, Chapman's recollections, etc., see Picchi, which is the only full-scale exploration of the case, as well as contemporaneous press accounts. Also, see the FBI "Zangara" file.

107 "Why do you want to kill?" *Miami Herald*, February 16, 1933.

107 "When we arrived": Zangara, quoted in Picchi, 45.

108 "something of a linguist": *Miami Herald*, February 16, 1933.

108 "normal in every respect": Picchi, 49.

109 "perverse character" . . . "psychopathic personality": Donovan, 165.

109 "a sane man": Shappee, 106.

109 "They certainly mete out justice": Cermak, quoted in Brands, 281.

109 "round up" . . . "Zangara class": *Miami Herald*, February 20, 1933.

109 "The people could not understand": Zangara confession, quoted in Picchi, 253.

109 "Your Honor" . . . "You see I suffer": Zangara testimony at first arraignment. Quoted in Picchi, 116.

110 "Oh judge": Ibid. See Picchi, 121.

Chapter Twenty-one: Old Sparky

111 "Not my fault" . . . "Sure I sorry": Zangara, quoted in Picchi, 138.

111 "sea of lawn and flowers": Gottfried, 328.

112 "as a result of the bullet": Shappee, 106.

112 "These ones take care of me": Zangara, quoted in Picchi, 142.

112 "Supposed to kill the chief" . . . "I want to kill all capitalists": Zangara, quoted in Davis, "Incident in Miami," 95.

112 "Assassins roaming at will": Thompson, quoted in Davis, "Incident in Miami," 95.

113 "I want to kill the president" . . . "You is crook man too:" Zangara in second trial. Quoted in Picchi, 166.

113 "a being": Chapman, quoted in Picchi, 221.

113 "I am not making a hero": Dr. Ralph N. Green, quoted in Picchi, 190.

114 "With a courtly bow": Chapman, quoted in Picchi, 223.

114 "Viva Italia": For details of the Zangara execution, see Picchi, 190ff.

114 "The execution of a man": Chapman, quoted in Picchi, 217.

114 "Had Giuseppe Zangara": Geoffrey Ward, quoted from endorsement of Picchi.

Chapter Twenty-two: A Good Beginning

117 "confidence in the leadership" . . . "such broad powers": Davis, 3:37.

118 "well in the background": Ahamed, 453.

118 "were just a bunch of men": Moley, *After Seven Years*, 191.

118 "It won't frighten people": Moley, *First New Deal*, 172.

119 "rescue the moribund corpse": David M. Kennedy, 135.

119 "Only Roosevelt" . . . "Confusion, haste": Moley, *After Seven Years*, 191.

119 "I am told": First press conference, March 8, 1933, Alter, 253ff. Freidel, 224ff.

119 "on background" . . . "off the record": Freidel, 224–25.

119 "the most amazing": Leuchtenberg, *FDR Years*, 144.

120 "We hope" . . . "The real mark" . . . "We cannot write": Freidel, 224–25.

121 "all kinds of junk": The diary of George Harrison, quoted in Josephson, *Money Lords*, 148.

121 "the last remaining strength": Moley, *After Seven Years*, 155.

121 "Our first task": Roosevelt, quoted in Davis, 3:55.

121 "I cannot too strongly": Roosevelt, quoted in Schlesinger, 2:7.

121 "his goddamned banker friends" . . . "little county seat banks" . . . "sonofabitch" . . . "be more civil!": Williams, 626–28.

121 "The President drove the money-changers": David M. Kennedy, 136.

122 "had running through it": Davis, 3:35.

122 "superbly risen": *Wall Street Journal*. March 13, 1933.

Chapter Twenty-three: Time for Beer

124 "If the Congress chooses" . . . "been on the road" . . . "immediate action": Rosenman, *Public Papers*, 49–51.

124 "Talk of balancing": Long, quoted in Freidel, 244.

124 "to explain clearly": Davis, 3:59.

124–125 "I decided I'd try": Roosevelt, quoted in Stiles, 245. As so often happened, Raymond Moley would take credit for writing the famous and wildly successful first fireside chat—a claim Roosevelt hotly denied.

125 "the President wants to come into your home": Davis, 3:60.

125 "almost as good": Miriam Howell, quoted in Doherty, 77.

125 "I want to talk for a few minutes": Rosenman, *Public Papers*, 63–65.

126 "Our President took": "Will Rogers Claps Hands for the President's Speech," *New York Times*, March 14, 1933.

126 "People edge": Dos Passos, "The Radio Voice."

127 "Consummate politician": Smith, "How F.D.R. Made the Presidency Matter."

127 "the result of a unified plan": Moley, *After Seven Years*, 369.

127 "Future plays": Roosevelt, quoted in Hofstadter, *American Political Tradition*, 431.

127 "I think this would be a good time": Roosevelt, quoted in Freidel, 245.

127 "I recommend to the Congress": Rosenman, *Public Papers*, 66–67.

128 "the government is going to muscle in": Dialogue from the film *Gabriel Over the White House*.

128 "the amount of beer": *Newsweek*, April 15, 1933. Quoted in Winslow, 57.

128 "In the midst of the Depression": Terkel, quoted in Alter, 277.

128 "Roosevelt is the greatest leader": Wolfskill and Hudson, 143.

Chapter Twenty-four: A Gang of Common Criminals

129 "For the first time": Perkins, quoted in Schlesinger, 2:22.

129 "A bank rescue plan": Ahamed, 456.

130 "The bankers were aware": Josephson, *Money Lords*, 155.

130 "sort of a love fest": Ibid., 153.

130 "White-shoe Wall street": Fraser, *Every Man*, 431.

130 "in imposing succession": Pecora, 3–4.

131 "undesirable or worthless" . . . "Securities houses" . . . "we must break" . . . "old and young liberals" . . . "marched his staff": Schlesinger, *Congress Investigates*, 4:2555–56.

132 "less than lordly" . . . "flushed with annoyance": Davis, 3:138.

132 "preferred list" . . . "our close friends": Pecora findings, quoted in Davis, 3:139–40.

132 "It is nothing more or less": Landon, quoted in Schlesinger, 2:436.

132 "When it comes to money": Couzens, quoted in Barnard, 264.

133 "bloated masters of fortune": Long, quoted in Williams, 633.

133 "each one stolen": Long, quoted in MacPherson, 120.

Chapter Twenty-five: Traitor to His Class

134 "unscrupulous money changers": Roosevelt's first inaugural address, reprinted at http://www.bartleby.com/124/pres49.html.

134 "fewer than three dozen": Roosevelt, quoted in Fraser, *Every Man a Speculator*, 448–49.

134 "economic oligarchy": Roosevelt speech to the Commonwealth Club in

San Francisco, September 23, 1932. Hofstadter, *American Political Tradition*, 429.

135   "traitor to his class": A famous, but unattributed, quote from the era.

135   "captains of Wall Street": Pecora, 293.

135   "The testimony had brought": Ibid., 283.

136   "had brought about the transfer": Josephson, *Money Lords*, 164.

136   "a happy springtime": Ibid., 156.

136   "Your action in going off gold": Russell Leffingwell to Roosevelt, October 2, 1933, quoted in Leuchtenburg, *Franklin D. Roosevelt and the New Deal*, 51.

136   "baloney dollar": Josephson, *Money Lords*, 163.

136   "trying to cure tuberculosis": Norman Thomas, quoted in Wolfskill and Hudson, 119.

136   "Mr. Roosevelt is nothing more": William Z. Foster, quoted in Wolfskill and Hudson, 122.

137   "Although some people mistakenly": Wolfskill and Hudson, 133.

137   "the wild boys of the road": The name of the 1933 Hollywood film depicting the masses of unemployed youth menacingly roaming the land.

137   "the way I did on beer": Moley, *After Seven Years*, 173.

138   "Fascism, Hitlerism": *Time*, April 3, 1933.

138   "utter rubbish": Roosevelt, quoted in Black, 281.

138   "See that they have good food": Stiles, 264–65.

138   "to prevent a similar tragedy": Eleanor Roosevelt, quoted in Cook, 2:45.

138   "played his master card": Rollins, 387.

138   "in there and talk": Stiles, 264–65.

139   "I got out": Eleanor Roosevelt, *This I Remember*, 113.

139   "Hoover sent the army": *New York Times*, May 17, 1933.

139   "It's like selling yourself": Freidel, 265.

139   "had been anxiously": Rollins, 386.

140   "leaving no doubt": Alter, 299.

140   "At each camp": Freidel, 266.

140   "All you have to do": Rosenman, *Public Papers*, 322.

Chapter Twenty-six: A Balanced Civilization

141   "highly appropriate": Hickok, "New 'First Lady,' Made Solemn by Inaugural, Lays Plans to Simplify White House Life; To Cut Expense," Associated Press, March 5, 1933.

142   "Saturday night": Freidel, 268.

143   "Wouldn't anybody" . . . "one-man show": Manchester, 1:97.

144   "Dear Mr. President": Correspondence quoted in Manchester, 1:99.

144   "opened the New Deal floodgates" . . . "No president": Smith.

144   "Having overcome that": *New York Times*, March 26, 1933, quoted in Freidel, 288.

145 "To destroy a standing crop": Wallace, quoted in Manchester, 1:102.

146 "a supreme effort" . . . "the most important and far-reaching": Rosen-man, *Public Papers*, 246.

147 "the burden of telling the whole truth": Roosevelt, quoted in Schlesinger, 2:441.

147 "Roosevelt is an explorer": Churchill, 294.

147 "a balanced civilization" . . . "the population balance": Schlesinger, 2:319.

147 "contradictory character": Elliott Roosevelt, *F.D.R.: His Personal Letters*, 1:318.

148 "confronted with a choice": Tugwell, quoted in Schlesinger, 2:22.

148 "how close were we to collapse": Johnson, quoted in Schlesinger, 2:22.

Chapter Twenty-seven: Hankering for Superman

149 "Hankering for Superman": Lippmann, 26.

149 "the Barrymore of the capital": *Variety*, quoted in Doherty, 79.

149 "a rage for order": Ibid., 69.

149 "one of the most excitingly": *New York World Telegram*, quoted in a film advertisement in *Variety*, August 8, 1932, 24.

150 "The public has been milked": Allison, 3.

150 "The whimsical tale" . . . "sound reconstruction policies": Doherty, 69.

150 "an alternate national anthem": Fraser, *Every Man*, 411.

150 "hour of destiny": Ibid., 81.

151 "Stand by your president": *Film Daily*, March 11, 1933, 1.

151 "Just as American communists": Doherty, 70.

151–152 "Oh, don't worry" . . . "immediate and effective action" . . . "Army of Construction" . . . "one of the greatest presidents": Quoted from the film *Gabriel Over the White House*.

152 "The good news": Library of Congress, "Film Series on Religion and the Founding of the American Republic. http://www.loc.gov/exhibits/religion/films.html.

153 "I want to send you this line": Roosevelt to Hearst, April 1, 1933 at the Franklin Delano Roosevelt Presidential Library. http://www.fdrlibrary.marist.edu/archives/pdfs/dictatorship.pdf.

153 "Its reality is a dangerous item": "Gabriel Retakes," *Hollywood Reporter*, March 20, 1933, 2.

153 "Put that picture": Leff and Simmons, 39.

Chapter Twenty-eight: That Jew Cripple in the White House

154 "It is socialism": Luce, quoted in Schlesinger, 2:264–65.

154 "The excessive centralization": Lippmann, quoted in Manchester, 1:107.

155 "Nonsensical, Ridiculous": Hearst, quoted in Wolfskill and Hudson, 175.

155 "Stalin Delano" . . . "to the Mussolinis": Hearst, quoted in Nasaw, 482.

155 "rooted in suspicion" . . . "hallmark of Western culture": Manchester, 1:101.

155 "We're going at top speed": Hiram Johnson, quoted in Freidel, 447.

156 "Businessmen of 1929": Ibid., 503.

156 "The 'captains' ": William W. Ball, quoted in Freidel, 504.

156 "This is despotism" . . . "robots": Ibid., 503.

157 "In war, in the gloom": Roosevelt fireside chat, May 1933, quoted in Schlesinger, 2:114.

157 "vast army": Black, 316.

157 "Through the channels of the rich": Schlesinger, 2:567–68.

157 "the rottenest newspaper": Roosevelt paraphrased by Ickes, quoted in Schlesinger, 2:566.

157–158 "terrible" . . . "rarefied atmosphere" . . . "poison pen" . . . "I wish sometime" . . . "deliberate policy" . . . "I sometimes think" . . . "I think they": Roosevelt, quoted in Schlesinger, 2:555.

158 "a certain streak of madness": Wolfskill and Hudson, x.

158 "men who have been parasites": McCormick, quoted in Wolfskill and Hudson, 178.

158 "The republic proceeds": Mencken to Albert Jay Nock, June 1933, quoted in Wolfskill and Hudson, 173–74.

158 "What that fellow": Wolfskill and Hudson, 36.

159 "Often characterized as a blueprint": Carroll, 438.

159 "biblical capitalism": Sharlet, 123.

160 "If you were a good honest man": Letter to Roosevelt, quoted on the book jacket of Wolfskill and Hudson.

Chapter Twenty-nine: We Don't Like Her, Either

161 "We Don't Like Her, Either": Wolfskill and Hudson, 37.

161 "Peace time can be": Eleanor Roosevelt quoted in the *New York Times*, December 29, 1933.

162 "at once intimate": Douglas, 152.

162 "Fueled by power": Cook, 2:1.

162 "Dearest Babs": Roosevelt to Eleanor, March 17, 1933. Elliott Roosevelt, *F.D.R.: His Personal Letters*, 339.

162 "soldiers out if a million": Eleanor Roosevelt to Lorena Hickok, quoted in Cook, 2:44.

162 "I'm just not the sort of person": Hickok, *Reluctant First Lady*, 87.

163 "She shattered precedent": Davis, 3:173.

163 "Mrs. Roosevelt doesn't hide": Freidel, 295.

164 "That I became": Eleanor Roosevelt, quoted in Schlesinger, 2:525.

164 "For some time I have had": Carrie Chapman Carr to Eleanor Roosevelt, August 15, 1933, quoted in Freidel, 298.

165 "The only thing that reconciles me": Eleanor Roosevelt to Lorena Hickok, quoted in Alter, 259.

165 "Those who attacked the New Deal": Wolfskill and Hudson, 86.

165 "Eleanor can bite an apple": Manchester, 1:111.

165 "Despite a lithe, graceful": Halle, quoted in Cook, 1:499.

Chapter Thirty: The Shifty-Eyed Little Austrian Paperhanger

166 "The Shifty-Eyed Little Austrian Paperhanger": I. F. Stone, quoted in MacPherson, 135.

166 "During the Hundred Days": Leuchtenburg, *Franklin D. Roosevelt and the New Deal*, 197.

167 "bastards": Roosevelt, quoted by Henry Morgenthau, Morgenthau diary, May 9, 1933, quoted in Freidel, 400.

167 "I intimated as strongly as possible": Roosevelt to Cordell Hull, May 6, 1933, quoted in Freidel, 397.

167 "He began with the Jewish question" . . . "marching, uniformed columns" . . . "He once made use": Schacht, quoted in Freidel, 396.

167 "openly hostile" . . . "They represented": Black, 258–59.

168 "much-ballyhooed": Alter, 144.

168 "old fetishes": Roosevelt cable, quoted in Schlesinger, 2:222.

168 "No such message": Philip Snowden, quoted in Schlesinger, 2:224.

168 "unwilling to go to the root": Rosenman, *Public Papers*, 264ff.

168 "because they see the end": "Roosevelt Praised in German Press," *New York Times*, July 4, 1933.

168 "You have opportunities": Ramsay MacDonald to Roosevelt, quoted in Schlesinger, 2:232.

168 "As ER feared most": Cook, 2:113.

169 "Our ignorance was inexcusable": William Shirer, quoted in MacPherson, 135.

169 "Today or tomorrow" . . . "danger to Europe": Stone, quoted in MacPherson, 135.

169 "most stately Jewish pundit" . . . "Europe's problem": *Time*, quoted in MacPherson, 135.

169 "Lippmann had no illusions": Steel, 330.

169 "dictator, once he feels secure": *Time*, March 13, 1933.

170 "The universities of Germany": Dr. Lion Feuchtwanger. "Hitler's War on Culture," *New York Herald Tribune Magazine*, March 19, 1933.

170 dispatched at least two emissaries to Germany: During the interregnum Roosevelt sent Cornelius Vanderbilt (see chapter 9). In November 1933, Ambassador William Dodd in Berlin sent Roosevelt a summary of Hitler (see Black, 360).

170 "This translation is so expurgated": Roosevelt, quoted in Freidel, 122.

170 "from the moment": Tugwell, quoted in Freidel, 123–24.

170 "a strong possibility": Roosevelt, quoted in Freidel, 390.

170 "I am concerned by events": Roosevelt to Ramsay MacDonald, quoted in Schlesinger, 2:232.

Chapter Thirty-one: A Rainbow of Colored Shirts

171 "A Rainbow of Colored Shirts": Wolfskill, 84.

171 "the strongest army, navy": Smith, quoted in Dickson and Allen, 205.

172 "slapstick Waterloo" . . . "captured the entire putative army": Ferguson, 121.

172 "staged a well-publicized funeral": Dickson and Allen, 217.

172 "Amid flying chairs" . . . "smashed the bleeding head": Diggins, 585.

172 "preventive and protective Militia": Ferguson, 113.

172 "the heart of the old Indian territory" . . . "President Rosenfeld" . . . "had been planned and prophesied": Ibid., 114.

173 "idealistic or Communistic" . . . "military organization": Ibid., 122.

173 "playing soldier" . . . "various shirts and fancy breeches": Ibid., 124.

173 "The real threat": Ibid., 129.

174 "their wives insulted": Goodman, 3.

174 "shock the nation": Dickstein, quoted in Goodman, 9.

174 "to justify his increasingly large budget": Gentry, 201.

174 "did not have to look far": Ibid., 197.

174 "Despite all this burlesque and bombast" . . . "personal and political machine": Ibid., 158–59.

174 "short, fat": *Collier's*, August 9, 1933.

Chapter Thirty-two: Maverick Marine

176 "One of the really great generals": MacArthur, quoted in Cochran, 137.

176 "A splendid little war": Butler, quoted in Cochran, 138.

176–177 "vigorously brushed" . . . "first class orator" . . . "seemed stupid and unnecessary": Butler, 4–6.

177 "sunny tropic scenes": Millett, 151.

177 "If thee is determined": Cochran, 138.

178 "opera bouffee" . . . "liberate" . . . "It wasn't exactly clear" . . . "Military engagements" . . . "Butler's most bizarre exploit": Cochran, 143ff.

179 "as much for his care" . . . "I'd cross hell on a slat": McFall, 24.

179 "I do not think that anyone knows": Cochran, 155.

Chapter Thirty-three: I Was a Racketeer for Capitalism

181 "There is nothing": Stimson, quoted in Archer, 108.
181 "like an unruly schoolboy": Butler, quoted in Archer, 108.
182 "A friend of mine": Ibid., 110–11.
182 "the mad dogs who are about to break loose": "Italy's Ambassador Protests Slap at Duce by Maj. Gen. Butler," *Chicago Daily Tribune*, January 27, 1931. The story about Mussolini and the hit-and-run accident was essentially true, although Butler misquoted Cornelius Vanderbilt, who was the individual who had taken a ride with Mussolini in Italy. According to Vanderbilt, what actually happened after the child was hit by the car was that Vanderbilt yelled out and Mussolini patted his knee and said: "Never look back, Mr. Vanderbilt, always look ahead in life" (Cochran, 155).
182 "the only man that ever got": Will Rogers, quoted in Archer, 116.
182 "Handed a loaded 'pineapple'": Butler, 305–6.
183 "General": Archer, 117.
183 "Unless we are mistaken" . . . "unfortunate error": Ibid., 113–14.
183 "preparing to fight": Thomas, 308.
183 "YOU'RE A VERY BAD BOY": Archer, 115.
183 "cemented my decision": Butler, quoted in Thomas, 310.
183 "thirty-three years and four months": Butler, quoted in McFall, 24.
184 "swell racket" . . . "might have given": FBI FOIA file on Smedley Butler.
184 "the greatest bill collector": Butler, quoted in *Chicago Daily Tribune*, September 28, 1935.
184 "one of the most picturesque": Schmidt, 215.
184 "a member of the Hoover-for-Ex-President": Butler, quoted in Archer, 126.
184 "treasury raiders" . . . "millions of dollars": Butler, quoted in Schmidt, 219.
185 "Royal Family of financiers" . . . "What the hell": Schmidt, 222–23.

Chapter Thirty-four: We Want the Gold

186–188 "About five hours later" . . . "the royal family in control" . . . "We represent the plain soldiers" . . . "smelled a rat" . . . "So many queer people" . . . "make a speech" . . . "A speech about what?": U.S. Congress, *Public Hearings Report*, 2ff.
189 "bullet-shaped" . . . "close-cropped": *New York Post*, November 20, 1934.
189 "millionaire lieutenant" . . . "sort of batty": U.S. Congress, *Public Hearings Report*, 13–14.
189 "What's all this" . . . "Don't you try": Ibid., 12.
190 "a great idea" . . . "positive assurance" . . . "slip-up" . . . "If I am to be": Butler, quoted in Schmidt, 225.
190 "There is something funny": U.S. Congress, *Public Hearings Report*, 14.

190 "That speech": Ibid., 13.

191 "I have got 30 million dollars": U.S. Congress, *Public Statement*, 2.

191 "You know the President is weak" . . . "Why do you want to be stubborn?": Clark, quoted in Archer, 148.

191 "Although our group is for you": Clark, quoted in Gentry, 202.

191 "You know as well as I do": Butler testimony, quoted in Spivak, 320.

Chapter Thirty-five: Coup d'État

192 "like a bad penny": Butler, quoted in Archer, 18.

192 "Well, then, we will think": U.S. Congress, *Public Hearings Report*, 15.

193 "contemplated the desirability": Roosevelt to Kalinin, quoted in Morgan, 397.

193 "A great many people": Davis 3:340.

194 "Gentlemen" . . . "I just returned" . . . "There is a Fascist Party" . . . "Everywhere you go": U.S. Congress, *Public Statement*, 10–11.

194 "superorganization . . . an amalgamation" . . . "get the soldiers together": Archer, 23.

195 "Did it ever occur to you?" . . . "We have got the newspapers": U.S. Congress, *Public Hearings Report*, 18.

195 "man on a white horse": Ibid., 21.

195 "constitutional": Butler, quoted in Seldes, *You Can't Do That*, 175.

195 "agents of Wall Street": Weber, 201.

195–196 "The President doesn't need the support" . . . "Don't you understand": Ibid., 4.

196 "analogous to Mussolini's" . . . "was not in sympathy" . . . "forced to resign": Gentry, 202. See also U.S. Congress, *Public Hearings Report*, 21.

196 "We want to ease up" . . . "You want to put somebody in there": U.S. Congress, *Public Hearings Report*, 18.

196 "His protagonists in the present scrap": Schmidt, 225.

196 "You watch": U.S. Congress, *Public Hearings Report*, 20.

196–197 "to combat radicalism" . . . "fomenting class hatred": Archer, 30.

197 "plot to seize the White House": Ibid., 32.

Chapter Thirty-six: The Bankers Gold Group

198 "There was definitely something crazy": Gentry, 203.

198 "bankers gold group": Schmidt, 223.

198–199 "by selling them political" . . . "enraged by Roosevelt": Archer, 33. See also U.S. Congress, *Public Hearings Report*, 19.

199 "irrepressible temper and tongue": Ibid., 34.

199 "in hot water": Wolfskill, 82.

199 "Remington Arms": "U.S. Congress, *Public Hearings Report*, 21.

199–200 "We need a Fascist government" . . . "obtained enough information" . . . "unemployment situation" . . . "muffed it terrifically" . . . "solve it overnight" . . . "ideal" . . . "putting all of the unemployed": Ibid., 21–22.

200 "I have been in 752 different towns": Ibid., 19.

200 "If you get 500,000 soldiers": Ibid., 18.

200 "Hoover knew a loaded gun": Gentry, 204.

201 "with Hoover's skillful handling": Ibid., 201.

201 "a very careful and searching": Hoover memo, May 10, 1934, FBI FOIA file.

202 "Five Negroes on my place": Spivak, 295.

202 "hid the fact": Slayton, 380.

202 "The financial community": Wolfskill, 29.

202 "New Deal spokesmen": Wolfskill, ix.

Chapter Thirty-seven: The Investigation

204 Because of the controversial nature of some of the secondary texts relating to the alleged coup, I have relied on the primary and secondary sources I found to be most credible: The congressional hearings, reports, and published testimony; the initial reporting of Paul Comly French; the statements of Congressmen Dickstein and McCormack; General Butler's initial claims and later statements on the matter; and the analyses and accounts of journalists and academics, including Curt Gentry, Clayton Cramer, Arthur McFall, Hans Schmidt, Robert Cochran, Gerard Zilg, Jules Archer, Nicholas Fox Weber, George Seldes, and George Wolfskill. Journalist John L. Spivak, while researching Nazism for *New Masses* magazine, obtained permission from Dickstein to examine HUAC's public and private documents. His two-part series, titled "Wall Street's Fascist Conspiracy," while revealing and explosive, was stigmatized for its extreme left-wing slant in much the same way *Time* magazine's coverage was criticized for its right-wing slant.

204 "To be perfectly fair": Butler, quoted in Seldes, *You Can't Do That*, 175.

205 "his position on sound money": U.S. Congress, *Public Hearings Report*, 36.

205 "study securities": Ibid., 31.

205 "superorganization": Ibid., 34.

205 "hanging himself": Dickstein, quoted in Weber, 196.

205 "if the facts warrant": "Inquiry Pressed in 'Fascist Plot,'" *New York Times*, November 22, 1934.

205 "a damned lie": *New York Post*, November 20, 1934.

206 "strongly urged" . . . "American Fascist movement": *Washington Times*, November 21, 1934.

206 "I believe that Clark has cold feet" . . . "MacGuire is shielding somebody": "Watch 2 in Paris After Expose of Fascist 'Coup,'" *Chicago Daily Tribune*, November 27, 1934.

206 "immediate emphatic denials" . . . "barked" . . . "He had better" . . . "perfect moonshine" . . . "expressed amazement and amusement": "General Butler Bares 'Fascist Plot' to Seize Government by Force," *New York Times*, November 21, 1934.

207 "This committee has had no evidence": U.S. Congress, *Public Statement*, 1.

207 "still intends to get to the bottom" . . . "neither as whitewash": "Butler Plot Inquiry Not to Be Dropped," *New York Times*, November 26, 1933.

207 "The press . . . handled the Butler": Wolfskill, 97.

207 "Plot Without Plotters" . . . "his spurs clinked loudly" . . . "Such was the nightmarish": *Time*, December 3, 1934.

207 "What can we believe?": Wolfskill, 97.

208 "was able to verify": Archer, 192.

208 "Evidence was obtained" . . . "In making public": "The Fascist Plot Officially Confirmed." U.S. Congress, Report No. 153.

209 "bowing to the power": Butler, quoted in Weber, 204.

209 "you and I were cut out": Butler, quoted in Schmidt, 218.

210 "The committee found": Cochran, 156.

210 "quickly and quietly fizzled": McFall, 24.

210 "Schnozzle, Gimlet Eye" . . . "that General Butler's story": Weber, 205.

210 "Dear John": Letter from official with the Six Companies Inc. to Congressman John McCormack, November 22, 1934. The letter remained classified until released by the FBI under the Freedom of Information Act in 2010. FBI censors redacted the identity of the correspondent.

211 "the President take the people": Letter from Roosevelt supporter to the president, March 18, 1935. The identity of the author was redacted by FBI censors.

211 "No one quite knew": Schlesinger, 3:83

211 "The Fascist plot": Seldes, *You Can't Do That*, 185.

211 "little reason to doubt" . . . "working both ends": Schmidt, 227.

211 "blown the whistle": Ibid., 228.

212 "The Congressional Committee": Baldwin, quoted in Spivak, 330.

212 "cocktail putsch": Schlesinger, 3:83.

212 "History is littered": Anthony J. Principi, "Veterans as Revolutionaries," speech to the Smithsonian's Wilson Library, March 14, 2001.

212 "There was no doubt": McCormack, quoted in Weber, 205.

Chapter Thirty-eight: Are You Better Off Than You Were Last Year?

214 "I am interested in having it": Roosevelt, quoted in Archer, 186.

215 "An apparently serious": Cramer, 46.

215   "in the interest of both": Ickes, quoted in Cramer, 46.

215   "one of the most extensive": Wolfskill and Hudson, 161.

215   "save the Constitution": Elliott Roosevelt, *F.D.R.: His Personal Letters*, 1:381.

215   "Roosevelt's friends": Rosenman, quoted in Wolfskill, 163.

215   "If the First Hundred Days": Morgan, 423.

216   "hellhound of Wall Street": Perino, 287.

216   "There's finally a cop": Will Rogers, quoted in Perino, 294.

216   "Set a thief": Beschloss, 88.

216   "The private and uncontrolled": Schlesinger, *Congress Investigates*, 2743.

216   "had nudged the United States": Ibid., 2745.

216   "depended to a large extent': Ibid., 2747.

216   "The time has come": Ibid., 2754.

217   "the financial angel" . . . "brought a thunderous clap": Ibid., 2756.

217   "caricature of capitalism": Shlaes, 190.

217   "lack of appreciation": Black, 393.

217   "Are You Better Off": Roosevelt campaign slogan.

217   "There has been no such popular endorsement": Hearst, quoted in Schlesinger, 3:1.

217   "He has been all but crowned by the people": William Allen White, quoted in Schlesinger, 3:1.

Epilogue: The Paranoid Style of American Politics

219   "Smedley" . . . "call out the standing army" . . . "they would take care" . . . "I pointed out": The account of Coughlin's recruitment of Butler can be found in the FBI FOIA file on Smedley Butler.

220   "subversive activities": Hoover, quoted in Gentry, 207.

220   "apparently promised": Gentry, 206.

220   "Imagine a bloodless": *Newsmax*, October 2009.

221   "several reader complaints": Ibid.

221   "the paranoid style": Hofstadter, *Paranoid Style*.

221   "has changed as much": *Politics Daily*, October 2009.

Bibliography

Books

Ackerman, Kenneth D. *Young J. Edgar*. New York: Carroll & Graf, 2007.

Ahamed, Liaquat. *Lords of Finance: The Bankers Who Broke the World*. New York: Penguin, 2009.

Allen, Frederick Lewis. *The Lords of Creation*. New York: Harper & Brothers, 1935.

Allen, Henry. *What It Felt Like: Living in the American Century*. New York: Pantheon Books, 2000.

Alter, Jonathan. *The Defining Moment: FDR's Hundred Days and the Triumph of Hope*. New York: Simon & Schuster, 2006.

Archer, Jules. *The Plot to Seize the White House*. New York: Skyhorse Publishing, 2007.

Athans, Mary Christine. *The Coughlin-Fahey Connection: Father Charles E. Coughlin, Father Denis Fahey, C.S.Sp., and Religious Anti-Semitism in the United States, 1938–1954*. New York: Peter Lang, 1991.

Barnard, Harry. *Independent Man: The Life of Senator James Couzens*. Detroit: Wayne State University Press, 2002.

Bennett, David H. *Party of Fear: From Nativist Movements to the New Right in American History*. New York: Vintage Books, 1990.

Berlet, Chip, and Matthew N. Lyons. *Right-Wing Populism in America: Too Close for Comfort*. New York: Guilford Press, 2000.

Bernstein, Irving. *Turbulent Years: A History of the American Worker, 1933–1941*. Boston: Houghton Mifflin, 1969.

Beschloss, Michael R. *Kennedy and Roosevelt: The Uneasy Alliance*. New York: W. W. Norton, 1980.

Black, Conrad. *Franklin Delano Roosevelt: Champion of Freedom*. New York: Public Affairs, 2005.

Bornstein, Joseph. *The Politics of Murder*. New York: William Sloan Associates, 1950.

Brands, H. W. *Traitor to His Class: The Privileged Life and Radical Presidency of Franklin Delano Roosevelt*. New York: Doubleday, 2008.

Brinkley, Alan. *Voices of Protest: Huey Long, Father Coughlin, and the Great Depression*. New York: Alfred Knopf, 1982.

Bukowski, Douglas. *Big Bill Thompson, Chicago, and the Politics of Image*. Urbana: University of Illinois Press, 1998.

Burns, James MacGregor. *Roosevelt: The Lion and the Fox*. New York: Harcourt Brace, 1956.

———. *Roosevelt: The Soldier of Freedom*. New York: Harcourt Brace Jovanovich, 1970.

Butler, Smedley. *Old Gimlet Eye: The Adventures of Smedley D. Butler*. As told to Lowell Thomas. New York: Farrar & Rinehart, 1933.

Carroll, James. *Constantine's Sword: The Church and the Jews*. Boston: Houghton Mifflin, 2001.

Churchill, Winston. *The Great Republic: A History of America*. New York: Modern Library, 2001.

Clarke, James W. *American Assassins*. Princeton, NJ: Princeton University Press, 1982.

Cook, Blanche Wiesen. *Eleanor Roosevelt*. Vol. 1, *1884–1933*. New York: Viking, 1992.

———. *Eleanor Roosevelt*. Vol. 2, *1933–1938*. New York: Viking, 1997.

Coughlin, Charles E. *Eight Discourses on the Gold Standard and Other Kindred Subjects*. New York: Arno Press, 1974.

Daniels, Jonathan. *The Time Between the Wars*. Garden City, NY: Doubleday & Co., 1966.

Davis, Kenneth. *FDR*. Vol. 2, *The New York Years, 1928–1933*. New York: Random House, 1994.

———. *FDR*. Vol. 3, *The New Deal Years, 1933–1937*. New York: Random House, 1979.

Detzer, Dorothy. *Appointment on the Hill*. New York: Henry Holt, 1948.

Dickson, Paul, and Thomas B. Allen. *The Bonus Army: An American Epic*. New York: Walker & Company, 2004.

Dickstein, Morris. *A Cultural History of the Great Depression*. New York: W. W. Norton, 2009.

Doherty, Thomas. *Pre-Code Hollywood: Sex, Immorality, and Insurrection in American Cinema, 1930–1934*. New York: Columbia University Press, 1999.

Donovan, Robert J. *The Assassins*. New York: Harper & Brothers, 1952.

Douglas, Helen Gahagan. *A Full Life*. New York: Doubleday, 1982.

Downey, Kirsten. *The Woman Behind the New Deal*. New York: Nan A. Talese, 2009.

Engelbrecht, H. C., and F. C. Hanighen. *Merchants of Death*. Garden City, NY: Garden City Publishing, 1937.

Farley, James A. *Jim Farley's Story: The Roosevelt Years*. Westport, CT: Greenwood Press, 1984.

Ferguson, Charles W. *Fifty Million Brothers: A Panorama of American Lodges and Clubs*. New York: Farrar & Rinehart, 1937.

Flynn, John T. *As We Go Marching*. New York: Arno Press, 1972.

Fraser, Steven. *Every Man a Speculator: A History of Wall Street in American Life*. New York: Harper Collins, 2005.

———. *Labor Will Rule: Sidney Hillman and the Rise of American Labor*. New York: Free Press, 1991.

Freidel, Frank. *FDR: Launching the New Deal*. Boston: Little Brown, 1973.

Galbraith, John Kenneth. *The Great Crash: 1929*. Boston: Houghton Mifflin, 1961.

Gallagher, Dorothy. *All the Right Enemies: The Life and Murder of Carlo Tresca*. New Brunswick, NJ: Rutgers University Press, 1988.

Gentry, Curt. *J. Edgar Hoover: The Man and the Secrets*. New York: W. W. Norton, 1991.

Goldberg, Jonah. *Liberal Fascism: The Secret History of the American Left from Mussolini to the Politics of Change*. New York: Broadway Books, 2007.

Goodman, Walter. *The Committee*. New York: Farrar, Straus & Giroux, 1968.

Gottfried, Alex. *Boss Cermak of Chicago*. Seattle: University of Washington Press, 1962.

Grunwald, Lisa, and Stephen J. Adler. *Letters of the Century: America 1900–1999*. New York: Dial Press, 1999.

Gunther, John. *Roosevelt in Retrospective*. New York: Harper, 1950.

Gurewitsch, A. David. *Eleanor Roosevelt: Her Day*. New York: New York Times Book Company, 1974.

Handlin, Oscar. *Al Smith and His America*. Boston: Little Brown, 1958.

Hapgood, Norman. *Professional Patriots*. New York: Albert & Charles Boni, 1927.

Hatch, Alden. *Remington Arms: An American History*. Remington Arms Company, 1972.

Hickok, Lorena. *Reluctant First Lady*. New York: Dodd Mead, 1962.

Hirshson, Stanley P. *General Patton*. New York: Harper Collins, 2002.

Hofstadter, Richard. *The American Political Tradition and the Men Who Made It*. New York: Vintage, 1989.

————. *The Paranoid Style in American Politics and Other Essays*. New York: Alfred A. Knopf, 1965.

Houck, Davis W. *Rhetoric as Currency: Hoover, Roosevelt, and the Great Depression*. College Station: Texas A&M University Press, 2001.

Ickes, Harold L. *The Secret Diary of Harold L. Ickes*. 3 vols. New York: Simon & Schuster, 1953–1954.

Janeway, Michael. *The Fall of the House of Roosevelt: Brokers of Ideas and Power from FDR to LBJ*. New York: Columbia University Press, 2004.

Jeansonne, Glen. *Gerald L. K. Smith: Minister of Hate*. New Haven, CT: Yale University Press, 1988.

Johnson, Walter, ed. *Selected Letters of William Allen White*. New York: Holt, 1947.

Josephson, Matthew. *Infidel in the Temple: A Memoir of the Nineteen-Thirties*. New York: Alfred A. Knopf, 1967.

————. *The Money Lords: The Great Finance Capitalists, 1925–1950*. New York: Weybright & Talley, 1972.

Kahn, Albert E. *High Treason: The Plot Against the People*. New York: Lear, 1950.

Kennedy, David M. *Freedom from Fear: The American People in Depression and War*. Oxford: Oxford University Press, 1999.

Kennedy, Joseph P. *I'm for Roosevelt*. New York: Reynal & Hitchcock, 1936.

Kennedy, Susan Estabrook. *The Banking Crisis of 1933*. Lexington: University Press of Kentucky, 1973.

Kleeman, Rita Halle. *Gracious Lady*. New York: D. Appleton-Century, 1935.

Klehr, Harvey. *The Heyday of American Communism: The Depression Decade*. New York: Basic Books, 1984.

Lash, Joseph P. *Eleanor: The Years Alone*. New York: W. W. Norton, 1972.

Leff, Leonard J., and Jerold Simmons. *The Dame in the Kimono: Hollywood, Censorship and the Production Code*. Lexington: University Press of Kentucky, 2001.

Leuchtenburg, William E. *The FDR Years*. New York: Columbia University Press, 1995.

————. *Franklin D. Roosevelt and the New Deal*. New York: Harper, 1963.

Lewis, Sinclair. *It Can't Happen Here*. Garden City, NY: Doubleday, 1936.

Lippmann, Walter. *Interpretations, 1931–1932*. New York: MacMillan, 1932.

Lisio, Donald J. *The President and Protest: Hoover, Conspiracy, and the Bonus Riot*. Columbia: University of Missouri Press, 1974.

Long, Huey Pierce. *My First Days in the White House*. Harrisburg, PA: Telegraph Press, 1935.

MacPherson, Myra. *All Governments Lie: The Life and Times of Rebel Journalist I. F. Stone.* New York: Scribner, 2006.

Manchester, William. *The Glory and the Dream.* 2 vols. Boston: Little Brown, 1973.

Marcus, Sheldon. *Father Coughlin: The Tumultuous Life of the Priest of the Little Flower.* Boston: Little Brown, 1973.

Martin, George. *Madame Secretary: Frances Perkins.* Boston: Houghton Mifflin, 1976.

Messner, Julian. *Forerunners of American Fascism.* New York: Montauk Bookbinding, 1935.

Millett, Allan Reed. *Semper Fidelis: The History of the United States Marine Corps.* New York: Free Press, 1991.

Moley, Raymond. *After Seven Years.* Lincoln: University of Nebraska Press, 1967.

———. *The First New Deal.* New York: Harcourt Brace, 1966.

Morgan, Ted. *FDR: A Biography.* New York: Simon & Schuster, 1985.

Mugglebee, Ruth. *Father Coughlin of the Shrine of the Little Flower.* Boston: L. C. Page, 1933.

Nasaw, David. *The Chief: The Life of William Randolph Hearst.* Boston: Houghton Mifflin, 2000.

Nevins, Allan. *Herbert H. Lehman and His Era.* New York: Charles Scribner, 1963.

Noel-Baker, Philip. *The Private Manufacture of Armaments.* London: Victor Gollancz, 1936.

Pacyga, Dominic A. *Chicago: A Biography.* Chicago: University of Chicago Press, 2009.

Patterson, James T. *Congressional Conservatism and the New Deal: The Growth of the Conservative Coalition in Congress, 1933–1939.* Lexington: University of Kentucky Press, 1967.

[Pearson, Drew, and Robert S. Allen]. *More Merry-Go-Round.* New York: Liveright Publishers, 1932.

Pecora, Ferdinand. *Wall Street Under Oath: The Story of Our Modern Money Changers.* New York: Simon & Schuster, 1939.

Peel, Roy V., and Thomas C. Donnelly. *The 1932 Election: An Analysis.* New York: Farrar & Rinehart, 1935.

Perino, Michael. *The Hellhound of Wall Street: How Ferdinand Pecora's Investigation of the Great Crash Forever Changed American Finance.* New York: Penguin, 2010.

Pernicone, Nunzio. *Carlo Tresca: Portrait of a Rebel.* New York: Palgrave MacMillan, 2005.

Phillips-Fein, Kim. *Invisible Hands: The Making of the Conservative Movement from the New Deal to Reagan.* New York: W. W. Norton, 2009.

Picchi, Blaise. *The Five Weeks of Giuseppe Zangara: The Man Who Would Assassinate Roosevelt.* Chicago: Academy Chicago Publishers, 1998.

Rollins, Alfred B., Jr. *Roosevelt and Howe.* New York: Knopf, 1962.

Roosevelt, Eleanor. *This I Remember.* New York: Harper, 1949.

Roosevelt, Elliott, ed. *F.D.R.: His Personal Letters, Early Years.* 3 vols. New York: Duell, Sloan & Pearce, 1947.

Roosevelt, Elliott, and James Brough. *Mother R: Eleanor Roosevelt's Untold Story.* New York: G. P. Putnam's Sons, 1977.

Roosevelt, James, and Bill Libby. *My Parents: A Different View.* Chicago: Playboy Press, 1976.

Roosevelt, James, and Sidney Shalett. *Affectionately, F.D.R.* New York: Harcourt Brace, 1959.

Roosevelt, Sara Delano. *My Boy Franklin.* New York: R. Long & R. R. Smith, 1933.

Rosen, Elliot A. *Hoover, Roosevelt and the Brains Trust.* New York: Columbia University Press, 1977.

Rosenman, Samuel I., ed. *The Public Papers and Addresses of Franklin D. Roosevelt.* New York: Russell & Russell, 1969.

———. *Working with Roosevelt.* New York: Harper, 1952.

Ross, Alex. *The Rest Is Noise: Listening to the Twentieth Century.* New York: Picador, 2007.

Schlesinger, Arthur M. Jr. *The Age of Roosevelt.* Vol. 1, *The Crisis of the Old Order* (First Mariner Edition, 2003). Vol. 2, *The Coming of the New Deal* (1959). Vol. 3, *The Politics of Upheaval.* (1960). Boston: Houghton Mifflin.

———, ed. *Congress Investigates: A Documented History, 1792–1974.* Vol. 4. New York: Chelsea House Publishers, 1975.

Schmidt, Hans. *Maverick Marine: General Smedley D. Butler and the Contradictions of American Military History.* Lexington: University of Kentucky Press, 1987.

Schwarz, Jordan A. *The Interregnum of Despair: Hoover, Congress, and the Depression.* Urbana: University of Illinois Press, 1970.

Seldes, George. *One Thousand Americans.* New York: Bonbi & Gaer, 1947.

———. *Sawdust Caesar: The Untold History of Mussolini and Fascism.* New York: Harper & Brothers, 1935.

———. *You Can't Do That: A Survey of the Forces Attempting, in the Name of Patriotism, to Make a Desert of the Bill of Rights.* New York: Modern Age Books, 1938.

Shannon, David A. *The Great Depression*. Englewood Cliffs, NJ: Prentice Hall, 1960.

Sharlet, Jeff. *The Family: The Secret Fundamentalism at the Heart of American Power*. New York: Harper Perennial, 2008.

Shlaes, Amity. *The Forgotten Man: A New History of the Great Depression*. New York: Harper Perennial, 2007.

Slayton, Robert A. *Empire Statesman: The Rise and Redemption of Al Smith*. New York: Free Press, 2001.

Sobel, Robert. *The Great Bull Market*. New York: W. W. Norton, 1968.

Spivak, John L. *A Man in His Time*. New York: Horizon Press, 1967.

Steel, Ronald. *Walter Lippmann and the American Century*. Boston: Little Brown, 1980.

Sternsher, Bernard. *Rexford Tugwell and the New Deal*. New Brunswick, NJ: Rutgers University Press, 1964.

Stiles, Lela. *The Man Behind Roosevelt*. New York: World Publishing, 1954.

Summers, Anthony. *Official and Confidential: The Secret Life of J. Edgar Hoover*. New York: G. P. Putnam's Sons, 1993.

Swing, Raymond. *Forerunners of American Fascism*. New York: J. Messner, 1935.

Terkel, Studs. *Hard Times: An Oral History of the Great Depression*. New York: Pantheon, 1970.

Tugwell, Rexford Guy. *The Brains Trust*. New York: Viking, 1969.

———. *The Democratic Roosevelt*. Garden City, NY: Doubleday, 1957.

———. *In Search of Roosevelt*. Cambridge, MA: Harvard University Press, 1972.

Tully, Grace. *F.D.R., My Boss*. New York: Scribner, 1949.

Vanderbilt, Cornelius Jr. *Man of the World: My Life on Five Continents*. New York: Crown Publishing, 1959.

Ward, Geoffrey C. *Before the Trumpet*. New York: Harper & Row, 1985.

Ward, Louis B. *Father Charles E. Coughlin: An Authorized Biography*. Detroit: Tower Publications, 1933.

Warren, Donald. *Radio Priest: Charles Coughlin the Father of Hate Radio*. New York: Free Press, 1996.

Warren, Earl. *A Republic, If You Can Keep It*. New York: Quadrangle Books, 1972.

Warren, Frank A., III. *Liberals and Communism: The "Red Decade" Revisited*. Bloomington: Indiana University Press, 1966.

Watkins, T. H. *Righteous Pilgrim: The Life and Times of Harold L. Ickes, 1874–1952*. New York: Holt, 1990.

Weber, Nicholas Fox. *The Clarks of Cooperstown*. New York: Alfred A. Knopf, 2007.

White, William Allen, and Walter Johnson. *Selected Letters of William Allen White 1899–1943*. New York: Henry Holt, 1947.

Williams, T. Harry. *Huey Long*. New York: Vintage, 1990.

Wiltz, John E. *In Search of Peace*. Baton Rouge: Louisiana State University Press, 1963.

Winslow, Susan. *Brother, Can You Spare a Dime? America from the Wall Street Crash to Pearl Harbor: An Illustrated Documentary*. New York: Paddington Press, 1976.

Wolfskill, George. *The Revolt of the Conservatives*. Boston: Houghton Mifflin, 1962.

Wolfskill, George, and John A. Hudson. *All But the People*. New York: MacMillan, 1969.

Zangara, Giuseppe. *Memoir*. Unpublished. Reprinted in Picchi.

Zilg, Gerard Colby. *Du Pont: Behind the Nylon Curtain*. Englewood Cliffs, NJ: Prentice-Hall, 1974.

Magazines, Journals, and Newspapers

Allison, Courtney. "Cecil B. De Mille Talking." *Variety*, June 23, 1931.

Amenta, Edwin, Kathleen Dunleavy, and Mary Bernstein. "Stolen Thunder? Huey Long's 'Share Our Wealth,' Political Meditation, and the Second New Deal." *American Sociological Review* (October 1994): 678–702.

Associated Press. "Boy of 15 Suspected in Roosevelt 'Bomb.'" March 2, 1933.

Athans, Mary Christine. "A New Perspective on Father Charles E. Coughlin." *Church History* 56 (June 1987).

Atlanta Constitution. "Butler Quizzed on Fascist Plot." November 21, 1934.

———. "'Fascist Plot' Bubble Pricked by Evidence." November 26, 1934.

Bancroft, Nancy. "American Fascism: Analysis and Call for Research. *Phylon* 43, no. 2 (2nd qtr., 1982): 155–66.

Berkson, Seymour. "Di Silvestro Links Zangara in Bomb Death." *The Philadelphia Inquirer*. March 18, 1933.

Brinkley, Alan. "Comparative Biography as Political History: Huey Long and Father Coughlin." *History Teacher* 18, no. 1 (November 1984).

———. "Huey Long, the Share Our Wealth Movement, and the Limits of Depression Dissidence." *Louisiana Historical Association*, Spring 1981.

———. "The New Deal, Then and Now." Essay for the Gilder Lehrman Institute of American History, March 2009.

Chicago Daily Tribune. "Find Mystery in $46,000 of 'Coup Plotter.'" November 26, 1934.

———. "Group in House Ends Inquiry on Fascist 'Putsch.'" November, 25, 1934.

———. "Italy's Ambassador Protests Slap at Duce by Maj. Gen. Butler." January 27, 1931.

———. "Reds Claim U.S. Hushed Details of Fascist 'Plot.'" February 18, 1935.

———. September 28, 1935.

———. "Veterans' Head May Testify on 'Fascist Plot.'" November 23, 1934.

———. "Watch 2 in Paris After Expose of Fascist 'Coup.'" November 27, 1934.

———. "What! Another John Brown." November 22, 1934.

Christian Science Monitor. "Inquiry Pushed on Butler Report of 'Fascist March.'" November 21, 1934.

———. "McGuire Called Back as Witness in Fascist Inquiry." November 22, 1934.

Churchill, Winston S. "While the World Watches." *Collier's*, December 29, 1934.

Ciano, Peter G. "The Moral Imprint of Early Twentieth Century Italian-American Radical Labor." *Proteus*, 1990.

Clapper, Raymond. *Washington Daily News*, March 6, 1933.

Clark, Charles S. "An American Nazi's Rise and Fall." *American History*, February 2006.

Cochran, Robert T. "Smedley Butler: A Pint-Size Marine for All Seasons." *Smithsonian*, June 1984, 137–56.

Collier's. August 9, 1933.

Cramer, Clayton E. "An American Coup d'État?" *History Today*, November 1995.

Cremoni, Lucilla. "Antisemitism and Populism in the United States in the 1930s: The Case of Father Coughlin." *Patterns of Prejudice* 32, no. 1 (1998): 25–37.

Davis, Kenneth. "Incident in Miami." *American Heritage* 32, no. 1 (1980): 86–95.

Dickson, Paul, and Thomas B. Allen. "Marching on History." *Smithsonian*, February 2003.

Dickstein, Morris. "Steinbeck and the Great Depression." *South Atlantic Quarterly*, Winter 2004.

Diggins, John P. "The Italo-American Anti-Fascist Opposition." *Journal of American History*, December 1967.

Donovan, Robert J. "Assassins: Brothers Under the Psyche." *Los Angeles Times*, September 1, 1972.

Dos Passos, John. "The Radio Voice." *Common Sense*, February 1934.

———. "The Veterans Come Home to Roost." *New Republic*, June 29, 1932, 177.

Duffus, R. L. "Rulers of the Vast Empire of Du Pont." *New York Times*, September 30, 1934.

Egan, Timothy. "When FDR Found 'the Forgotten Man.'" *New York Times*, August 28, 2008.

Feuchtwanger, Lion. "Hitler's War on Culture." *New York Herald Tribune Magazine*, March 19, 1933.

Flynn, John T. "Other People's Money." *New Republic*, November 27, 1935.

Folliard, Edward. "When Reds Invaded Washington." *Washington Post*, December 2, 1956.

French, Paul Comly. "$3,000,000 Bid for Fascist Army Bared." *New York Post*, November 1934.

Fusco, Gian Carlo. *The Anarchist and the Mob*. Translated by Gregory Conti. Raritan 25, no. 4 (Spring 2006): 4–19.

Godine, Amy. "Notes Toward a Reappraisal of Depression Literature." *Prospects* 5 (1980): 197–239.

Gorn, Elliott J. "The Meanings of Depression-Era Culture." *Chronicle of Higher Education*, June 26, 2009.

Gowren, Clay. "Shot Aimed at FDR Took Cermak's Life." *Chicago Tribune*, November 23, 1963.

Gribble, Richard. "The Other Radio Priest: James Gillis's Opposition to Franklin Delano Roosevelt's Foreign Policy." *Journal of Church and State* 44, no. 3 (June 2002).

Haas, Edward F. "Huey Long and the Dictators." *Louisiana History: The Journal of the Louisiana Historical Association* 47, no. 2 (Spring 2006): 133–51.

Henry, Thomas R. "Health Threat to Army Grows." *Evening Star*, June 12, 1932.

Hickok, Lorena. "New 'First Lady,' Made Solemn by Inaugural, Lays Plans to Simplify Whole House Life; To Cut Expense." Associated Press, March 5, 1933.

Jeansonne, Glen. "Gerald L. K. Smith: From Wisconsin Roots to National Notoriety." *Wisconsin Magazine of History*, Winter 2002–3.

———. "Huey Long and the Historians." *History Teacher*, February 1994.

Jelliffe, Smith Ely. "What! No Pictures?" *Journals of Criminal Law and Criminology* 24, no. 6 (March–April 1934).

Kendrick, J. M. "Roosevelt Administration Holds 1933 News Spotlight." *Atlanta Constitution*, December 31, 1933.

Kennedy, David M. "The Depression: An Overview." Gilder Lehrman Institute of American History, 2009.

Key, David. "I Want to Keel All Presidents." *South Florida History Magazine* 25, no. 1–2 (Spring–Summer 1997): 10–17.

Lerner, Max. "A Hatemonger Who Failed." *Los Angeles Times*, April 21, 1976.

Los Angeles Times. "Inquiry Held on Fascism." November 22, 1934.

———. "Paris Cable Raps Butler." November 24, 1934.

Lyle, John H. "A Little Man with Burning Eyes Killed Chicago's Mayor. Was It a Mafia Plot?" *Chicago Daily Tribune*, April 14, 1957.

McFall, J. Arthur. "Personality." *Military History* 16 (February 2003): 24.

McIver, Stuart. "1926 Miami: The Blow That Broke the Boom." *Florida Sun Sentinel*, September 19, 1993.

Miami Herald. February 16, 1933.

Miller, Hope Ridings. "New Dealers and 'Economic Royalists' Will Meet This Week to Watch a DuPont Marry a Roosevelt." *Washington Post*, June 27, 1937.

Moley, Raymond. "Bank Crisis, Bullet Crisis—Same Smile. Five Years of Roosevelt and After." *Saturday Evening Post*, July 29, 1939.

Nasser, Alan. "FDR's Response to the Plot to Overthrow Him." *Counterpunch*, October 5–8, 2008.

Newsmax. October 2009.

Newsweek. April 15, 1933.

New York Daily News. March 5, 1933.

New York Post. November 20, 1934.

———. "Butler Plot Inquiry Not to Be Dropped. November 26, 1933.

———. "General Butler Bares 'Fascist Plot' to Seize Government by Force." November 21, 1934.

———. "Inquiry Pressed in Fascist Plot." November 22, 1934.

———. May 17, 1933.

New York Times. "Official Report of the Proceedings of the Democratic National Convention." June 20–July 4, 1932.

———. Roosevelt's account of assassination attempt. February 17, 1933.

———. "Roosevelt Praised in German Press." July 4, 1933.

———. "Will Rogers Claps Hands for the President's Speech." March 14, 1933.

———. "Zangara Planned Attack All Alone." February 17, 1933.

Ortiz, Stephen R. "Rethinking the Bonus March: Federal Bonus Policy, the Veterans of Foreign Wars, and the Origins of a Protest Movement." *Journal of Policy History* 18, no. 3 (2006).

Parker, Richard. "The Crisis Last Time. *New York Times*. November 9, 2008.

Politics Daily. October 2009.

Reilly, Michael F. "I Guarded FDR." As told to William J. Slocum. *Saturday Evening Post*, September 7, 14, 21, 28, and October 5, 1946.

Rogers, Will. *New York Times*, March 6, 1933.

Russell, Francis. "How I Changed My Mind About the Sacco-Vanzetti Case." *Antioch Review* 25, no. 4 (Winter 1965–66).

Shappee, Nathan D. "Zangara's Attempted Assassination of Franklin D. Roosevelt." *Florida Historical Quarterly* 37, no. 2. (October 1958): 101–10.

Sherrill, Robert. "Du Pont." *New York Times,* December 15, 1974.

———. "No More Eating Rats." *New York Times,* December 15, 1974.

Smith, Jean Edward. "How F.D.R. Made the Presidency Matter." *New York Times,* January 16, 2009.

Spivak, John. "Wall Street's Fascist Conspiracy." *New Masses,* http://coat.ncf .ca/our_magazine/links/53/spivak-NewMasses.pdf.

Stowell, Ellery C. "The General Butler Incident." *American Journal of International Law,* April 1931.

Sullivan, Mark. "Roosevelt Declared Headed Farther Left." *Los Angeles Times,* April 28, 1935.

Theoharis, Athan G. "The FBI's Stretching of Presidential Directives, 1936–1953." *Political Science Quarterly* 91, no. 4. (Winter 1976–77).

Nation. March 8, 1933.

Time. April 3, 1933.

———. "DEMOCRATS: Incredible Kingfish." October 3, 1932.

———. March 13, 1933.

———. "Plot Without Plotters." December 3, 1934.

———. "The Presidency: Wanted: A Poem." October 3, 1932.

Wall Street Journal. March 13, 1933.

Washington Post. February 18, 1935. "Probers Veiling Fascist Plot in U.S. Russian Press Charges."

Washington Times. November 21, 1934.

Winn, Marcia. "Du Ponts Give In; Decide to See Wedding." *Chicago Daily Tribune,* June 30, 1937.

Government Documents

F.B.I. files were obtained through the Freedom of Information Act on the following individuals: Smedley Darlington Butler; Charles E. Coughlin; Huey Long; and Giuseppe Zangara. The file on the assassination attempt on Franklin D. Roosevelt was also obtained.

U.S. Congress. House. Special Committee on Un-American Activities, Investigation of Nazi Propaganda Activities and Investigation of Certain Other Propaganda Activities. 74th Cong. 1st sess., Report no. 153. February 1935.

U.S. Congress. House. Special Committee on Un-American Activities, Investigation of Nazi Propaganda Activities and Investigation of Certain Other Propaganda Activities. *Public Hearings Report of HUAC.* 73rd Cong., 2nd sess., December 29, 1934.

U.S. Congress. House. Special Committee on Un-American Activities, Investigation of Nazi Propaganda Activities and Investigation of Certain Other Propaganda Activities. *Public Statement on Preliminary Findings of HUAC.* 73rd Cong., 2nd sess., November 24, 1934.

U.S. Congress. House. Committee on Ways and Means. *Payment of Adjusted-Compensation Certificates.* 72nd Congress, 2nd sess., 382–83. 73rd Cong., 2nd sess. November 1934.

Manuscript Collections and Individual Papers

America First Committee. Hoover Institution. Stanford University, California.

American Liberty League. Hoover Institution. Stanford University, California.

American Legion. Hoover Institution. Stanford University, California.

Raymond Moley Collection. Hoover Institution. Stanford University, California.

John W. McCormack. Oral History Interview. March 30, 1977. Ethel G. Phillips Collection. John F. Kennedy Presidential Library, Boston, Massachusetts.

Index

U.S. Congress (*continued*)
  the Hundred Days, 123, 144–48
  Nye Committee, 216–17
  Pecora Committee, 130, 131–33, 134–36
  Prohibition repeal, 127–28, 145, 163
  Pujo Committee, 130, 131, 132
  resistance to New Deal, 155
  Second Hundred Days, 215–17
  Special Committee Investigating the
    Munitions Industry, 216–17
  Special Committee to Investigate Nazi
    Propaganda Activities, 174
  Un-American Activities Committee, 201,
    204–9
  Ways and Means Committee, 21
  See also New Deal
U.S. Constitution, 2, 49, 156
U.S. Marines, 11, 177–80, 181
U.S. military, Butler's speeches on, 184–85

V
Vallee, Rudy, 16
Vanderbilt, Cornelius, Jr., 54–55
Van Zandt, James, 195, 212
veterans
  and government stability, 212
  reduction in pensions of, 124
  of World War I, 28
  See also Bonus Army; bonus for World
    War I veterans
Veterans Administration, 36
Veterans of Foreign Wars (VFW), 184, 192
Victor Emmanuel III, king of Italy, 83
Villard, Oswald Garrison, 18
violence in America, 91–92
Volstead Act (1919), 127–28

W
Wallace, Henry, 145
Wall Street
  and American Legion pressure for gold
    standard, 185, 188–89, 190–91, 192,
    212–13
  attempt to overthrow the government,
    186–91, 192, 194–96, 210–11, 215
  bilking by financial capitalists, 23, 62
  and Butler, 209, 214
  Coughlin's denouncement of financiers, 58
  and FDR, 135
  New Deal regulations, 155, 215–17
  and Nye Committee, 216–17
  and Pecora Committee, 130, 131–33,
    134–36

  reopening after ten day hiatus, 129
  stock market crash (1929), 16–17, 23, 62,
    130–32
Wall Street Journal, 122
Wall Street Under Oath (Pecora), 130
Walsh, Thomas, 117
war debts, 48
War Department and fear of "Reds," 52
Ward, Geoffrey C., 114
Warren, Donald, 58
Washington News, 36
Washington Star, 22–23
Waters, Walter W., 28
Ways and Means Committee, House, 21
wealthy persons' avoidance of taxes,
    132–33. *See also* disparity between rich
    and poor
Weber, Nicholas Fox, 211
welfare. *See* public welfare
White House
  Hoover in, 22–23, 30–31
  Hoover keeps FDR waiting, 27, 96
  inaugural ball, 102
  press corps and FDR, 119–20
  Roosevelt lifestyle, 141–42, 163
  See also fireside chats
White Shirts, Chattanooga, Tennessee,
    172–73
White, William Allen, 46, 217
Wild Boys of the World (film), 149–50
Williams, T. Harry, 58
Wilson, Woodrow, 10, 178, 179
Wolfskill, George, 202
Women's Democratic News, 163
women's rights and Eleanor Roosevelt,
    161–65
women's suffrage, 9, 161–62
Woodin, William, 102, 103, 118
World Monetary and Economic Confer-
    ence, London, England, 167, 168
World War I, 11, 48, 103, 179
World War I veterans, 28. *See also* Bonus
    Army; bonus for World War I veterans

Z
Zangara, Giuseppe
  arrest, trials, and sentencing, 107–10,
    112–13
  biographical info, 83–87, 89–90
  death by electric chair, 113–14
  investigation of, 78–80, 86–87, 88, 89–90
  reason for assassination attempt, 75, 76
  witnesses, 80–82

A Note on the Author

SALLY DENTON is the author of *The Pink Lady*, *Passion and Principle*, *Faith and Betrayal*, *American Massacre*, *The Bluegrass Conspiracy*, and, with Roger Morris, *The Money and the Power*. She has been the recipient of a Guggenheim Fellowship, two Western Heritage awards, a Lannan Literary Grant, and has been inducted into the Nevada Writers Hall of Fame. Her writing has appeared in the *New York Times*, the *Washington Post*, and *American Heritage*.